8 Days of Crisis
on the Hill

Political blip...or Stephen
Harper's Revolution Derailed?

8 Days of Crisis on the Hill

Political blip...or Stephen Harper's Revolution Derailed?

Thomas W. Joseph

iUniverse, Inc.
New York   Bloomington

8 Days of Crisis on the Hill; Political blip...
or Stephen Harper's Revolution Derailed?

Copyright © 2009 by Thomas W. Joseph

Library and Archives Canada Cataloguing in Publication
Joseph, Thomas, 1942 –
8 Days of crisis on the Hill, Political blip...or Stephen Harper's Revolution Derailed? /
Thomas Joseph

iUniverse books may be ordered through booksellers or by contacting:

iUniverse
1663 Liberty Drive
Bloomington, IN 47403
www.iuniverse.com
1-800-Authors (1-800-288-4677)

Because of the dynamic nature of the Internet, any Web addresses or links contained in this book may have changed since publication and may no longer be valid. The views expressed in this work are solely those of the author and do not necessarily reflect the views of the publisher, and the publisher hereby disclaims any responsibility for them.

ISBN: 978-1-4401-4135-5 (pbk)
ISBN: 978-1-4401-4136-2 (ebk)

Printed in the United States of America

iUniverse rev. date: 5/11/2009

1. Canada –politics. 2. Canada-parliamentary politics, alternative coalition government, economic crisis, political crisis, constitutional crisis, national unity crisis. 3. Canada – political parties. 4. Stephen Harper – political leadership, economic leadership, leadership style and methods. 5. Conservative Party of Canada – formation, elections, coalition of conservatives. 6. Conservative ideology. I. Title.

Cover design by Tom Joseph.

Preface

The events unleashed by the November 27th, 2008, Economic and Fiscal Statement captured Canadian's attention like few happenings on Parliament Hill have done in recent years. The drama of a Prime Minister and government teetering on the edge of defeat at the hands of an unexpected coalition of opposition parties, kept Canadians glued to their televisions and radios for eight days. Though the Conservative government survived this 'crisis', the fallout continued to unfold into 2009.

As an interested citizen, the leadership of Stephen Harper and the actions of his government infuriated me. Harper and his party demonstrated a willingness to use any tactic including lying, misrepresentation and accusations of opposition MPs being 'traitors' in order to hold on to power. They instigated the crisis and quickly turned an economic crisis into a political crisis, constitutional crisis and a national unity crisis. They were willing to sacrifice everything in order to hold onto power.

As a Canadian citizen and retired college and university professor of political studies, the Prime Minister's behaviour required examination. What began as a letter–to-the-editor of the Thunder Bay *Chronicle-Journal*, titled "Stephen Harper: Master strategist or master stumbler?", became a more serious account of the events, their importance and how they reflected his political beliefs, behaviour and methods.

Each of the 'crisis' that engulfed the Hill over those eight days had political consequences for those involved and for the parliamentary system. Stephen Harper may have survived to fight another day but in doing so he may have committed his most serious strategic error and will pay a heavy price for it over the next months and years.

It is my contention that his long term goal to make the Conservative party Canada's 'natural governing party' and to move Canadian society to the right has been derailed. Of course only time will tell if this conclusion is valid.

A special thanks to Margo, Christopher, Alexander and Aubrey for their encouragement and helpful advice.

Thomas W. Joseph
Thunder Bay, Ontario, Canada
May, 2009.

Contents

Chapter 1
And Canadians say politics is dull and boring!!

Whew!! What a week it was as we went from being the 'peaceable kingdom' talking about the need for cooperation and consultation to what many described as 'a full blown national crisis'. The Prime Minister and Conservative Government had turned an 'economic crisis' into a 'political crisis', then a 'constitutional crisis'. And if that wasn't enough of a week's work, the Prime Minister managed to also turn it into a 'crisis of national unity'.

And some say Canadian politics and politicians are boring!!!!!

On election eve October 14, 2008, and in the days that followed, our political leaders appeared to understand the need for a more cooperative approach to governing the country. Prime Minister Stephen Harper stated "we will continue to respect the principle that government is accountable to the people's representatives in Parliament assembled. ... This is a time for all of us to put aside political differences and partisan considerations and to work cooperatively for the benefit of Canada. We have shown that minority government can work, and, at this time of global economic instability, we owe it to Canadians to demonstrate this once again. We ask all members of all parties, to work together to protect the economy and weather the world financial crisis." [1]

The election produced another minority parliament as the Conservatives, New Democrats and Bloc Québécois gained seats in the House while the Liberals lost seats. All leaders and parties seemed to recognize the need for consensus-building. Parliament could not be the rambunctious, partisan and rancorous place it had become during the previous sessions. Consultation and cooperation would be the name of the game especially at this time of increasingly dire economic news. Canadians were hopeful.

What happened?

Between election evening October 14 and the delivering of the government's much anticipated economic update statement November 27, a seismic economic shift occurred in the United States that rippled out across the globe. During the election and the weeks that followed, the Conservative government claimed that Canada's economic fundamentals were sound; that Canada was in much better straights than the U.S.; that our financial system was better regulated and supervised; that our banks were not in any danger; and, that Canada was not threatened by deficits.

Almost daily, stories appeared in the media revealing the precarious state of one or another major American financial institution or corporation. Nonetheless, the Conservative's continued to assure Canadians that while these were perilous times, Canada would weather the storm better than other nations. Certain measures had been undertaken to bolster Canada's financial institutions and Canadians continuing access to credit. The Government talked of various measures it had taken to stimulate the economy and counteract the increasing number of layoffs and plant closures – stepped up infrastructure programs, reductions in individual and business taxes, and, investments in job creating infrastructure. Many economists and others, including the opposition parties and provincial premiers, called for more active and additional stimulus measures.

Underlying the debate was the question of deficit financing. What should the role of governments be in times of an economic downturn? Should governments run a deficit during a recession or should they avoid it at all costs? This is a central question in Keynesian economics. Since the 1970's and 1980's, when Canada went heavily into national debt and ran massive deficits year after year, many Canadians consider deficit financing a fate worse than death. All political parties vowed to run a surplus. It has become the mantra of society and any political leader or party that hinted at going into deficit was playing with fire and flirting with committing hari-kari. In this climate of opinion, the Conservative government was doing all it could to avoid any hint of slipping into a deficit or suggesting the need for such. The economic statement of Nov. 27 even went so far as to predict that Canada would likely run a small surplus in each of the next few years. Few observers agreed with this 'rosy' outlook.

News from the United States continued to reveal the extent of the economic crisis that confronted not only that country but every country around the world. Canada's economy had been increasingly integrated into the American economy, especially since the introduction of free trade in 1989. What happened there must of necessity flow over the border and affect Canada's economy. Therefore it was no wonder that all segments of the Canadian economy felt the effects of the monumental slowdown and collapse being experienced south of the border. New Brunswick's Christmas tree sales to the U.S., Ontario's auto manufacturing industries, the forest and mining industries of British Columbia, Quebec, Ontario and other parts of the country, and the demand for resource commodities, all were affected and experiencing sharp declines in demand and sales. Almost daily, news of industry cutbacks and plant closures were being reported in the media – such as British Columbia's mining industry poised to layoff possibly as many as 500 workers, U.S. Steel in Hamilton expected to layoff 150, Nortel 1,300 layoffs, Magna 850 layoffs, and, in Oshawa, unemployment claims had increased 96.4% over the previous year while they were up 30.4% in Windsor. Shockingly, it was reported that all forest related companies in Northwestern Ontario – pulp and paper and lumber mills – were silent that day, either closed down or on temporary shutdown. This was in a region very dependent upon its Boreal forests for employment and wealth. From day to day, Canada's stock markets experienced wild fluctuations registering their greatest gains one day only to be followed by their greatest losses the next. Canada's businesses and workers were in crisis.

In this uncertain environment, the Conservative government continued to go to great effort to downplay the extent of the economic situation and Canada's exposure. They delayed taking action waiting to see what steps would be taken by the new U.S. President. The government continued to deny the possibility of Canada going into a recession and into deficit. Finally, at the APEC meeting in Peru in mid-November, Harper acknowledged the likelihood of Canada entering into a recession, of running a deficit, and, of the need for a significant stimulus package that could be as much as $30 billion.

And so the government's November 27th economic update statement became a major indicator of how Canada was faring and how it would respond to what was clearly an increasingly foreboding economic collapse in the U.S. and around the world. When Finance Minster Flaherty delivered the government's economic statement in the House, he acknowledged there were difficulties but continued to claim that much had already been done, that more would eventually be forthcoming, and that Canada was being so well managed that there probably would be a small surplus over the next few years. There was little in the way of an economic stimulus package. There were some measures proposed that would give additional powers to the Finance Minister to aid Canada's financial institutions and the financial system; would assist seniors with their registered retirement income funds; and, would relieve pressures on workers and businesses contributions to federally regulated pension plans.

The opposition parties found this optimistic picture wholly inadequate and demanded immediate government recognition of the unfolding calamity being faced by Canadians in the auto manufacturing and forest industries and across the economy generally. They demanded an activist government with a strong stimulus package to cushion the effects of what was clearly a major recession.

The Government's portrayal of the economy in its economic

statement may not have triggered a concerted opposition uprising on its own. But when Harper and the Government indicated it would also remove the right to strike for public servants, cut financial assistance for pay equity cases taken before the courts, sell off some Crown assets as measures to reduce government costs, and cut public subsidies to political parties, the opposition parties considered these measures as a declaration of war. They rose up in rebellion. They sought an alternative to the governing Conservatives in the form of a Liberal-NDP coalition that would be supported by the Bloc Quebecois.

With this development, all hell broke loose on Parliament Hill.

How did we come to this contentious state of affairs?

How did a dangerously deteriorating economic situation ignite such a firestorm of political and constitutional controversy?

How did it resurrect the fault lines of national unity pitting Alberta and the West against Ontario, Quebec and the East and resurrect nationalist and separatist forces in Quebec?

How did it happen that such incendiary language spewed out of our political leader's mouths?

What seemed like a new consensual atmosphere of cooperation and consultation between the leaders and the parties quickly degenerated into one of the worst episodes in Canadian parliamentary history. Can we recover civility in the House and reconciliation in the country?

Endnotes

1. Conservative Party of Canada, "Canadians give Harper a strong mandate to lead", 14 October, 2008, www.conservative.ca.

Chapter 2
A week of Calamity on the Hill

"Be careful of what you wish for" and *"may you live in interesting times"*

In the weeks and months leading up to the opening of a new session of Parliament, Canadians had experienced a general election that many felt was unnecessary; that featured questionable campaign tactics; that over managed and sanitized party policy announcements; and, that failed to engage voter interest. And in the end, it produced another minority parliament. At the same time and in comparison, the unfolding election drama south of the border captured Canadian's attention and imagination. Many lamented the sterility of their own leaders, parties and election processes, bemoaning the fact that none of their leaders even attempted to inspire Canadians with a vision for the nation.

Canadians were not happy campers by the time the 40th Parliament met in mid November. Canadians wished for more excitement and drama from their political leaders and parties.

And so, unexpectedly, Canadians got their wishes in spades and experienced one of the most dramatic and unsettling turn of events in their history.

Setting the stage for the unfolding drama

On October 14, 2008, Canadians went to the polls and voted to give the Conservative Party and Stephen Harper the largest number of elected members in the House of Commons - 143. But it did not give Harper the majority he had hoped for leaving him 12 members short of a bare majority. On election eve, Harper stated that:

> *"the voters have entrusted us with a strengthened mandate to continue to lead the government and take Canada forward. ...*
>
> *Fellow Canadians, in forming another government, we will address three pressing priorities.*
>
> *First, we will continue to govern for all Canadians. ...*
>
> *Second, we will continue to respect the principle that government is accountable to the people's representatives in Parliament assembled. As you know, it is written that, 'to everything there is a season, and a time to every purpose ...' This is a time for us all to put aside political differences and partisan considerations and to work cooperatively for the benefit of Canada. We have shown that minority government can work, and, at this time of global economic instability, we owe it to Canadians to demonstrate this once again. We ask all members of all parties, to work together to protect the economy and weather the world financial crisis.*
>
> *Third, in accepting the renewed mandate to take Canada forward, we will keep our promises."* [1]

The Liberal Party, led by Stéphane Dion, began the campaign in trouble and continued to experience problems throughout the campaign. On election eve the party was reduced to 77 members and its lowest voter support in its history. Calls for a change of leadership began immediately. Dion soon indicated that he would resign the leadership but would remain until the party chose a new leader. The party executive set May 2 for a convention in Vancouver. Dominic LeBlanc, Bob Rae and Michael Ignatieff entered the race to replace Dion.

The Bloc Quebecois, under the leadership of Gilles Duceppe, staged a comeback of sorts to elect 49 members. Thanks to the musings of Harper regarding the place of the cultural arts in society and advocating a cut in cultural funding, Quebec voters swung away from the Conservatives back to the Bloc.

The New Democratic Party also improved its standing in the House by electing 37 members, a gain of 7. Leader Jack Layton was unable to replace the Liberals but was pleased with the results.

Elizabeth May, leader of the Green Party, overcame opposition from the Conservatives and the NDP and joined the other party leaders in the televised debates. Her efforts brought new credibility to the Greens. Nonetheless, the party failed to elect a member.

On November 19, 2008, members of the Senate and House of Commons gathered in the Senate Chamber for the Speech from the Throne delivered by the Governor General, Michaëlle Jean. The government again indicated that

"The people spoke once again in a general election on October 14th, and entrusted this Government with a renewed and strengthened mandate. ... At the same time, the people also chose to elect a minority Parliament. And in a parliamentary democracy, such as ours, the government must always be responsible and accountable to the people's representatives. ... Canadians have renewed their confidence in our Government. They have placed their trust in their representatives. And they have asked us to work together to meet the challenges before our country." [2]

The opposition parties responded to the government's plans for the coming parliamentary session and proceeded to vote 'confidence' in the government.

And so the stage was set for delivery of the Government's Economic and Fiscal Statement.

The Play Begins

Act 1: Scene 1 – The Government delivers its Economic and Fiscal Statement

On Thursday November 27, 2008, the government delivered its much anticipated Economic and Fiscal Statement. [3] Expectations were high as the economic news domestically and globally continued to be bad. At 4:10pm, Finance Minster Jim Flaherty rose in the House of Commons and delivered the government's assessment of the state of the Canadian economy and what lay ahead in the coming months and years.

To the applause and cheers of his fellow Conservative MPs, Flaherty stated that:

- *"I am pleased today to present the government's economic and fiscal statement and to set out our key short-term and long-term objectives as we prepare for the next federal budget."* …

- *"We have not been spared by the ensuing global economic downturn. … It has affected Canada and has resulted in decreases in economic growth."* …

- *"Last week's Speech from the Throne laid out a five-pronged plan to protect Canada's economic security – a plan that will define the choices we make."* …

- *"We were fully aware that difficult times were ahead when I presented our economic statement last fall. We planned for it. We made choices to put Canada in a stronger economic position." … Our sensible Canadian approach is paying off. Our country will come out of this economic crisis in a strong position because we are going into it in a strong position. … We will protect the future by maintaining strong, fiscal and financial management."* …

- *"Today's statement lays out a plan that keeps our budget balanced for now. … These measures will enable us to plan on a balanced budget framework, while recognizing potential downside risks."* …

- *"Canadians have a right to look to government as an example ... [and] ... to show restraint and respect for their money." ...*

- *"Today our government is eliminating the $1.75 per vote taxpayer subsidy for politicians and their parties effective April 1, 2009. There will be no free ride for political parties." ...*

- *"We are directing government ministers and deputy ministers ... to rein in their spending on travel, hospitality, conferences, exchanges and professional services." ...*

- *"Under an expanded new expenditure management system, the government will conduct a "... multi-year review of corporate assets, crown corporations, real property and other holdings. The review will take a careful approach on the sale of any asset considering market conditions and ensuring fair value can be realized for the benefit of taxpayers." ...*

- *"Our government expects to save over $15 billion over the next five fiscal years under the new expenditure management system. This system will be an invaluable tool to help us maintain balanced budgets, along with other steps announced today." ...*

- *"We will introduce legislation ... that would put in place annual public service wage restraints ... for each of the following three years. This restraint would also apply to members of Parliament, senators, cabinet ministers and senior public servants. The legislation would also temporarily suspend the right to strike through 2010-11."*

- *"Another issue we intend to address is the litigious, adversarial and complaints-based approach to pay equity. [Since the mid-1980's, over $4 billion has been paid in pay equity settlements.] These settlements were the result of pay equity complaints to the Canadian Human Rights Commission. ... We are introducing legislation to make pay equity an integral part of collective bargaining." ...*

- *"We are also bringing certainty to the growth of equalization."* ...

- *"We are also protecting the Canada health transfer and the Canada social transfer."* …

- *"We are taking steps to help Canadian seniors."* …

- *"We are also addressing the immediate consequences this financial distress has dealt to Canadian workers who contribute to federally regulated pension plans."* …

- *"While helping Canadian workers save, we will also help the businesses that employ them, with their ability to borrow."* …

Mr. Flaherty concluded by saying that "This government came into office looking years down the road. Our country is better off today thanks to exactly that approach. Short-term problems will not distract us from continuing to focus on the horizon."

Scene 2 - Opposition Parties Respond

Immediately following Mr. Flaherty's economic and fiscal update statement, the opposition parties had an opportunity to comment. As expected, each party was critical of the government's statement believing that it failed to address the concerns of Canadians and failed to address the unfolding economic crisis with a strong, active plan.

First to speak was Scott Brison for the Liberals.[4]

- *"… at a time when Canadians are concerned about their country's economic future, … when the international financial markets are in crisis, [when] the world is heading into recession, Canadian businesses are facing closures, and Canadians are worried about their jobs and savings, Canadians today deserve a government that would actually provide a real action plan to help the Canadian economy meet the challenges ahead.*

  However, instead of presenting us with a plan, the Conservatives have chosen symbolism over substance, rhetoric over real action and deception over decisions. They have given Canadians nothing but gimmickry when Canadians need a game plan." …

- *"The Conservatives do not have an economic plan: there is nothing for manufacturers, nothing for the automobile industry, nothing for forestry, and nearly nothing for seniors and workers facing layoffs."* ...

- *"Today the Prime Minister is trying to distract Canadians from his own economic incompetence. He hopes we will not notice that he bungled the economy during the good times and that he has no economic plan for Canada during these tough times. It is no wonder, today, that the Prime Minister wants to change the channel from economics to politics."* ...

- *"It is not about politics; it is about people."* ...

- *"He is failing Canadians by not telling them the truth, and the truth is, Canada is back in deficit. ... is failing to tell Canadians why we are back in deficit, the fact that his bad tax policy and his big spending policy is responsible for that deficit."* ...

- *"Earlier today the Minister of Finance said, "It is misguided to engineer a surplus just to say we have one." [But] that is exactly what the Conservative government is doing. It is pretending it has a surplus when in fact it has a deficit. ... The government is trying to hide this new Conservative deficit, first, with rosy growth numbers, as we enter a recession. In fact, it is predicting 0.3% growth while the OECD's prediction is 0.5% shrinkage in the Canadian economy."* ...

- *"To further bury the new Conservative deficit, the Conservatives are planning massive cuts. It should not surprise anybody that ... they actually are proud enough to list ... their pledge to cut pay equity for women. We should not be surprised that, as they start to cut during tough times, they choose ideological cuts, because during the good times what did they cut? They cut literacy, they cut women's equality and they cut the court challenges program."* ...

- *"Most disturbing, in order to hide the new Conservative deficit, [they] are preparing to sell off an imaginary list of government assets. They are preparing to sell in a buyer's market. ... [The government] has put itself in a position where pawning off assets*

> *is required because of not market opportunity, but because of fiscal desperation. ... The Minister of Finance is highly motivated to bury the deficit he fathered."*

- *"The previous Liberal government did not book revenue until an asset was actually sold. ... However, the Conservatives are booking revenue before they know what assets they are going to sell. Today, we asked financial officials for a list of the assets they intended to sell. The fact is there is no such list."*

- *"The Conservatives are not being honest about the deficit and are not being honest about the cause of the deficit. Last week, Kevin Page, the Parliamentary Budget Officer, was clear when he said:*

> *"The weak fiscal performance to date is largely attributable to previous policy decisions as opposed to weakened economic conditions.*

> *... It is pretty clear, and Mr. Page is very clear, that these bad policy decisions were the Conservative government's misguided tax policy and their big spending policy. ... government spending has ballooned by 25% in 3 years an annual growth rate of 8%. ... It is a big spending, bad tax policy government that has created a made in Canada, new Conservative deficit. ... Today, Canada is in deficit and for the first half of this year, we had the worst economic growth in the G8. That was long before the global financial turmoil."* ...

- *"The difference between the government's approach in Canada and the approach taken by our largest trading partner, the U.S., could not be more clear. The headlines said it all yesterday. 'Canada bides time, U.S. sets course. ... Other countries are acting too. Great Britain, Germany, France and Japan are all taking significant action at this time of crisis and there is no plan from the Canadian government whatsoever."*

- *"When Canadians need strong economic leadership, all they are getting from the Conservatives are cheap political schemes. ... This is not about politics. This is about people."*

Gilles Duceppe, leader of the Bloc Quebecois, responded next. [5] He stated that:

- *"What the Conservative government presented today was not an economic statement but an ideological statement. This ideology so blinds the government that it fails to see how urgent it is to act."*
  ...

- *"Worse yet, instead of attacking the economic crisis, the Conservative government has decided to attack democracy instead, as well as the rights of women and working people. The Prime Minister has preferred ideology to economics. He has placed partisanship above democracy."* ...

- *"All members remember that the Prime Minister chose to call an election for strictly partisan reasons. He decided to spend more than $300 million, an amount that could have been used to counter the economic crisis. Above all, the Prime Minister wasted precious time."* ...

- *"The difference between this Conservative government and other governments throughout the world is striking. The Government of China, for example, decided to take action by putting in place a $700 billion recovery plan. Europe announced a $318 million plan. Our American neighbours have voted for a plan worth almost $850 billion. ... Despite the surpluses accumulated over 10 years, the Conservative government not only refused to present its plan, to provide relief, it consciously chose to stifle the economy to advance its outdated ideology on the reduction of government."* ...

- *"The Prime Minister says he has already taken action by reducing taxes, but if the actions ... were sufficient, how can it be that, as he himself admits, Canada will be moving into a recession, ..."* ...

- *"The Prime Minister has put ideology before the economy. ... The government has decided to take advantage of the crisis to attack the rights of women and workers. ... [it] is proposing to suspend public servant's right to strike ... [and] decided to attack women's rights by submitting their right to pay equity to negotiation. Since when are rights negotiable?" ...*

- *"Instead of being concerned about the economy, the Prime Minister has once again decided to attack Quebec. The Prime Minister declared his love of Quebec throughout the last campaign. ... Once again he has repeated his desire to impose a federal securities commission, thereby ignoring the unanimous position of the National Assembly." ...*

- *"I met with the Prime Minister and all the leaders here to see if we could find ways to work together. I have done it in minority Parliament after minority Parliament. Canadians want us to work together. Did we hear the slightest indication from the Prime Minister and his representatives on the front bench that they were prepared to work together? Not in the slightest. Instead, it was abuse, insults and putting people down who serve in elected office." ...*

- *"People were hoping to see some real action to protect their pensions and ... their savings. What we hear in Canada is denial. We hear a government saying there really is no problem. It says it has done everything so well that there is no problem. How out of touch can the government be?" ...*

- *"I am here to say this evening that we are not about to play partisan games and watch the attack on democracy unfold while thousands of Canadians are being thrown into the streets because of the recession and the loss of jobs."*

Finally, Thomas Mulcair spoke for the New Democratic Party[6] stating that:

- *"I want to take a look at something very specific in terms of finances. The Conservatives boast of their excellence in management. Since their election at the start of 2006, program spending has increased by 24%, or $40 billion. That is the kind of management we have been subjected to." ...*

- *"Today, part of their almost imperceptible ideological maneuvering is to blame those who have been elected, to make a politician a figure to be hated, just as Karl Rove taught George W. Bush to do in the United States – attack and divide. ... the Conservatives want to muzzle the opposition and cut off their funding. And they will do all this without taking any action during the worst economic crisis Canada has seen in generations." ...*

"For the Conservatives to be able to propose any concrete change or bring any structural ideas, something that would build the economy, something that would help create and maintain jobs, they would need to admit there was a problem or that they had ever done anything wrong. ... that would require a modicum of modesty. Now that they are back in here with a minority situation, they will not even recognize that they have done anything wrong or that the public does not trust them enough to give them a majority." ...

- *"... the Conservatives do not believe the state or the government has a role in the economy. They therefore have held back." ...*

- *"What a colossal fraud. ... Last week, Kevin Page said that we were headed for a $6 billion deficit because of [the Conservative's] poor choices. And what do they have to say in today's statement? One has to read it to believe it; ...*

- *The government is planning on balanced budgets for the current and next five years, although given the downside risks, balanced budgets cannot be guaranteed."*

- *"... as [for] the proposed sale of public assets ... They want to sell off major assets that took years to acquire just to have a balanced budget. Take all the institutions we have built and created in Canada over generations: social rights, the right to collective bargaining, which was recognized by the Supreme Court of Canada. ... they want to abolish these rights ... by eliminating the right to strike. They want to take away women's right to equal pay for equal work."*

Commentary - Brief summary of what was said

The government sought to assure Canadians that while there were troubling economic developments, it had been fully aware of them and had taken measures to protect Canadians and the Canadian economy. It outlined a number of measures already taken and others it would take to ease the difficulties being faced by Canadian workers, businesses, financial institutions and seniors. It projected balanced budgets and even a small surplus. The government claimed that it had managed the economy well since its election in 2006 and could be relied upon to continue to do so through these troubled times.

The opposition parties questioned this rosy assessment. For them, they saw neither a plan nor an honest assessment of the economic crisis that was unfolding within Canada and the world. Instead, they saw a government that appeared to be in denial. Every economic indicator pointed to a worsening economic situation and definitely the economy going into a recession if not already there. They charged that the government's positive spin ignored the unequivocal conclusions drawn by Kevin Page, Parliamentary Budget Officer, that the weak fiscal performance of the Canadian economy was largely attributable to previous policy decisions rather than weakened economic conditions. The opposition parties saw the Conservative government attempting to take advantage of the economic turmoil to promote their partisan and ideological agenda. For them, this was an effort by the Conservative government to undermine worker's rights, women's rights, the rights of other political parties, and, reduce the role of government. For the opposition parties, this was an attack on democracy.

Scene 3 - The Media's take on the Economic Statement

How did the media and its political commentators react to the Conservative government's Economic and Fiscal Statement, and the comments of the opposition parties? As to be expected, there was a wide variety of commentary supporting or condemning one or both sides.

Some commentators praised the Prime Minister for his attempts to work cooperatively with the opposition. Barbara Yaffe wrote in an article (probably written prior to the actual delivery of the statement but printed on Nov. 27) in the **Vancouver Sun** that "The economic crisis has helped the PM shed his image as a petty, partisan leader, giving him more of a statesmanlike air as he tries to reassure Canadians about the future." [7] Carol Goar's comments in the **Toronto Star** gave both praise and condemnation when she wrote "To his credit, Stephen Harper has moved swiftly to shelve ideology and face facts since his re-election [re: reluctance to accept deficits]. But there is one piece of baggage Harper has yet to jettison. He can't resist the urge to point fingers. ... By finding fault with others, Harper invites scrutiny of his own record. ... If he wants Canadians to overlook his lapses, he owes the same courtesy to others. By taking cheap shots, Harper is undermining his message that Canadians need to work together to minimize the nation's economic hardship." [8]

The **Globe and Mail** took a pretty neutral stance merely noting that the government was projecting balanced budgets and small surpluses through 2012 and that "Flaherty promised a few measures to rein in government spending and small measures to help investors and make credit available to businesses." [9] It also noted that there was no stimulus.

Other commentators zeroed in on the proposed cuts to the subsidy funding of political parties. Nigel Hannaford's column in the **Calgary Herald** labeled the vote subsidy as a 'racket' whereby Canadians were subsidizing separatism. He went on to say that "if you can overlook the gamesmanship that's going on here for a moment, the Conservative government's proposal ... is not merely common sense but something akin to political virtue." [10] In a **Winnipeg Free Press** article, Duff Conacher, co-ordinator of Democracy Watch, proposed that the subsidy should be reduced but that it was democratic because "it is based on votes received and therefore balances the fact that the electoral system does not dole out seats on a proportional basis." [11]

Most commentators took a more critical view of the government's economic statement. Chantal Hebert wrote in the **Toronto Star** that the statement and proposed fiscal measures were "a triumph of cutthroat politics over meaningful policy." [12] Lorne Gunter wrote in the **National Post** that "The Conservatives were too clever by half and the opposition parties were too disingenuous by a factor of six. ... No doubt it seemed like a good idea at the time: Deal a crippling financial blow to your opponents, but tart it up as part of a larger effort to keep Ottawa from running a deficit." [13] The ***Toronto Star*** concluded that the economic update "was devoid of any stimulus for the flagging economy. Instead there were politically motivated spending cutbacks and rosy forecasts that Canada would experience a short 'technical' recession and that the federal budget would remain balanced. There is a deep flaw in this logic." [14] Andrew Coyne in ***Maclean's*** magazine wrote that "Stephen Harper has gone from denying any possibility of a deficit during the election, to conceding, post-election, that it was indeed possible, to warning it was probable, to shrugging it off as unavoidable in the circumstances. ... Harper went one step further at last week's APEC summit in Peru and now says 'No longer was the deficit an unpleasant consequence of an economic downturn. Rather it was an 'essential' instrument in fighting it.' What was once a bug is now a feature. So, to add to his ever-lengthening list of jaw-dropping about faces, the former deficit hawk has become a believer in fiscal stimulus. How convenient." [15]

Similar criticisms came from others. Many focused on the Prime Minister and his character. They spoke of Harper's 'truculence', 'miscalculations', his 'succumb[ing] to base political instincts, his 'bare-knuckle partisanship', his 'mad scramble to keep power', his 'tin ear', and, his 'insistence that politics should drive decisions'.

Act 2: Improvisation Takes Over – And all hell breaks loose

Thursday evening, Nov. 27:

1. Liberal MPs caucused in an evening meeting to determine their party's strategy.

Friday Nov. 28:

1. Former NDP leader Ed Broadbent and former Liberal PM Jean Chretien met to discuss the possibility of a Liberal-NDP coalition. This proposal was a direct result of the Conservative's stated intention to remove the public subsidies to political parties, remove the public service's right to strike, remove the right of women to seek pay

equity through the courts, and, the intention to sell off government assets.

2. During Question Period in the House, neither Prime Minister Harper nor Opposition Leader Dion were present. Aside from each side challenging each other in strong language, the debate was not much different than on other days. The opposition repeated many of the same themes each party had stated in their response to Mr. Flaherty on Thursday. The government defended itself indicating that it had already brought in stimulus measures in the previous budget, that they were setting a frugal model, and, that they were showing leadership. They accused the opposition of being uncooperative and only seeking to protect their benefits.

3. The Liberals served notice of a motion of no-confidence in the government and declared a 'viable alternative' coalition to be led by Stéphane Dion.

4. Later in the afternoon, PM Stephen Harper publicly condemned the talk of a coalition accusing it of trying to 'overturn' the results of October's election and 'installing' Stéphane Dion as prime minister.

   Harper also challenged the legitimacy of Stéphane Dion leading the coalition since he was soundly rejected by voters in the October election and had indicated his intention to step down as Liberal leader in May. Harper stated that "The opposition has every right to defeat the government, but Stéphane Dion does not have the right to take power without an election. Canada's government should be decided by Canadians, not a backroom deal. It should be your choice – not theirs." [16]

5. Late in the day, Harper used the government's parliamentary prerogative to delay the two confidence votes scheduled for Monday Dec. 1 to a week later on Monday Dec. 8.

Saturday Nov. 29:

1. Now having recognized the possibility of being defeated in the House on a no-confidence vote, the Conservatives backpedaled on their controversial proposals in an effort to diffuse the impending crisis. Transport Minister John Baird announced in the morning that the government was withdrawing the plan to cancel political party subsidies.

2. In a CBC morning interview, Baird declared that "the Conservatives will go over Parliament, over the Governor General and go to the people".

3. The NDP met in a secret strategy session to plan their strategy. Unbeknownst to them, their discussions were overheard and recorded by the Conservatives. A Conservative MP had mistakenly received notice of the meeting.

4. Conservatives issued an email to its MPs and supporters stating the 'talking points' that they should use when being interviewed by the media. They are encouraged to 'hit the pavement and airwaves' to get the government's message out.

Sunday Nov. 30:

1. Conservatives released an audio recording of the NDP's Saturday strategy session. They accused Jack Layton and the NDP of plotting weeks earlier to 'bring down the government'. Layton is heard telling his caucus members that he had had discussions with the Bloc about defeating the government. Layton was furious that the Conservatives have stooped to this kind of behaviour and had violated political protocol. He threatened to sue.

2. Flaherty announced a new budget date had been set for Jan. 27 declaring that it would be "the earliest budget date in modern times". Normally the budget is delivered in late February.

3. The Conservatives also announced the withdrawal of their plan to temporarily ban strikes by public-sector workers.

4. Word circulated late in the day that the Liberals and NDP had reached an agreement to form a coalition and that the Bloc Quebecois would support it for a minimum of 18 months.

Monday Dec. 1:

1. Question Period in the House began with 'electricity in the air'. Both the Prime Minister and the Leader of the Opposition were present. From the very first question posed by Dion and Harper's response, the charges and counter-charges escalated. So did the accusations thrown across the aisle – 'deal with the devil', 'traitor', 'secret Bloc-Liberal-NDP cabal ... plotting behind closed doors', 'illegitimate', 'undemocratic' were some accusations thrown at the opposition by the Conservatives. The opposition parties accused the government of 'playing politics', of having lost the House's 'trust and confidence', of 'double talk' and 'cook[ing] the books'.

2. Jack Layton, leader of the NDP indicated that the NDP would ask the police to investigate whether the Conservatives had broken the law by listening in and recording the NDP's Saturday strategy meeting.

3. Later in the afternoon, Dion, Layton and Duceppe formally signed an agreement to form a Liberal-NDP coalition to be supported in the House by the Bloc for a minimum of 18 months.

4. Dion wrote a letter to the Governor General outlining the serious intent of the opposition parties and encouraged her to consider allowing the coalition to form a new government when the Conservatives were defeated on a confidence vote Dec. 8.

5. Dion announced establishment of an advisory group that would include former deputy prime minister John Manly, and, former New Brunswick premier Frank McKenna.

Tuesday Dec. 2:

1. Manly and McKenna indicated they hadn't agreed to be advisors to Dion and the coalition.

2. In the House during Question Period, PM Harper vigorously defended his government and accused the opposition parties of plotting a coup and the coalition being beholden to the separatist Bloc. The heated exchanges in the House raised the spectre of a new national unity crisis. The Conservatives charged that making a 'deal … with the separatists is a betrayal of the voters of this country'. As well, they characterized the coalition as a 'Bloc coup', as '[il]legitimate and undemocratic', as 'an attack on Canada, and attack on democracy', and, 'the secret Liberal-Bloc-NDP coalition [was] seizing power in a coup d'état'. Conservatives frequently labeled all Bloc MPs as 'separatists'. The opposition parties pressed Harper and the Conservatives to abide by 'the fundamental constitutional principles of our democracy [and] face the House'. They accused the Conservatives of being more concerned with saving their jobs rather than the jobs of ordinary Canadians. As well reference was made to problems with EI, pay equity, regional development and culture.

3. Governor General Michaëlle Jean announced that she would cut short her European tour and return to Canada. What began as an economic crisis had been turned into a political crisis that threatened to become a constitutional crisis as well.

4. Conservative MPs began working the phones and appearing on media outlets in an effort to shape public opinion against the coalition.

Wednesday Dec. 3:

1. Another day of rancorous debate occurred in the House during Question Period. Many of the same arguments were repeated by both sides but now the language being used was becoming 'unparliamentary'. Conservatives called

the opposition 'socialists', 'separatists', 'socialist coalition', 'separatist coalition' and one Conservative backbencher even accused the leader of the NDP of being a 'traitor'. Opposition members referred to the Conservatives as 'putting spin' on their answers and trying to 'pull a fast one'. The Prime Minster was accused of a 'pathological inability to put aside politics'. Members of the NDP asked the Speaker to take a more proactive stand on the use of unparliamentary language. The emotional and heated exchanges between the government and the opposition added a whole new dimension to the string of 'crises' that the Economic Statement had begun. A 'national unity crisis' was now no longer lurking in the shadows. The West was now pitted against Ontario and the East, and Quebecers were being categorized as 'separatists'.

2. Speculation that the Prime Minister would cut short the current session of Parliament and ask the Governor General to prorogue Parliament increased throughout the day.

3. Harper appeared on early evening national television vowing to 'use all legal means necessary' to prevent the coalition from assuming power. He attacked the coalition for its dependence on Bloc support accusing the separatists of being out to destroy Canada. His attack was meant to undermine the legitimacy of the coalition.

4. Both Dion and Layton followed Harper with statements of their own. The arrival of Dion's tape to the television studio was delayed and, when it did finally arrive, it was badly out of focus and appeared amateurish. In his statement, Dion accused Harper and the Conservatives of failing to make the economy the priority. Instead they had acted in a very partisan way and sought to settle ideological scores. His message got lost as observers focused on the poorly produced video and the questions it raised about Dion and the Liberal's ability to lead a government when they couldn't even get a short television presentation done correctly.

Unlike Dion who tried to imitate Harper by making his comments from a prime ministerial looking desk and back drop, Layton made his comments from the hallway in front of the closed doors leading into the House of Commons. With this symbolic backdrop, he vigorously denounced Harper for 'shutting down Parliament'. In addition, he appeared to speak spontaneously without notes.

5. Late in the evening, the Governor General's plane arrived back in Ottawa. She was scheduled to receive the Prime Minister the following morning at 9:30 am.

Thursday Dec. 4:

1. Many Canadians watched on television as Prime Minister Harper arrived promptly at 9:30am at the Governor General's Rideau Hall residence. No one knew for certain what he would ask the Governor General to do but most observers believed he would ask her to prorogue Parliament. Many wondered whether the Governor General would agree to his request; whether she had other constitutional options; and, whether she would ask the coalition to form a government if the Conservatives were defeated on a confidence vote. While the media hovered outside, they commented on the unexpectedly long discussions that must be taking place between the Prime Minister and the Governor General and speculated on what it might all mean. The media and Canadians waited with anticipation. Whichever decision Michaëlle Jean gave, it would be historic. The meeting went on for about 2 ½ hours, much longer than expected, raising speculation that the Governor General was not easily going to agree to prorogation. When the Prime Minister did appear, he made a brief statement indicating that Parliament was prorogued and would reconvene Jan. 26, 2009.

2. Shortly afterwards, in a CBC interview, Liberal Bob Rae, responded with incredulity to a reporter's question as to whether the Liberals would continue to oppose the Conservatives if the government included a stimulus

package in its January budget statement. He pointedly asked "Just what don't you get?" His point was that the government had lost the confidence of the House and that trust and confidence in the Prime Minister no longer existed. It was no longer an issue of an adequate economic stimulus but had become more fundamental, that of essential trust in the honesty and integrity of the Prime Minister. In his view, Stephen Harper had conducted himself and his government in such abusive ways that opposition members no longer trusted his word or his intentions. He had thrown down the gauntlet and the opposition was determined to take up the challenge and remove him and his party from government.

Commentary – Taking a time-out to reassess and reassemble

"Now that a sudden and violent storm has passed through Canadian politics, people of all persuasions are trying to sort out what precisely happened, why the convulsion came, what damage was done and what lies ahead." [17]

The eight days between the delivery of the government's economic statement and the prorogation of Parliament captured the attention of Canadians coast to coast to coast. Many followed events with rapt attention. Many reacted strongly to each day's turn of events. Many lined up on one side or the other. Many passionately shared their views and feelings with family, friends and fellow citizens. Canadians were unquestionably engaged in the politics of their country in ways not seen or felt for some time. "Canadians were thoroughly engaged: Talk-show hosts spoke of unprecedented calls, an estimated 4.3 million Canadians watched Harper's address to the nation – a larger audience than a Grey Cup game, not seen since 9/11…" [18]

With the proroguing of Parliament, things quieted down on the Hill. MPs got back to their daily tasks and contemplated returning to their constituencies for the Christmas holidays. Each would take stock of what they and their party had said and done over the preceding eight days. Each would be in conversation with their constituents and trying to assess the public's take on the 'drama on the Hill'.

The question facing MPs and Canadians remained. Would the reconvening of the House in January see a new tone of civility and reasoned debate take place between members and their parties, or, would the previous combative and destructive level of debate resume? Could the parties and their leaders overcome their differences and animosities towards each other and work together for the betterment of Canadians and the country?

Act 3: What did the nation's journalists have to say about this week of turmoil on the Hill?

The nation's press and various political journalists gave their considered assessment of the events, the comments and the consequences of the 'violent storm' that passed through Ottawa following the government's Economic and Fiscal Statement. Many Canadians were shocked and dismayed by the tone and tenor of the comments and accusations hurled back and forth between the leaders and their parties. Canada's journalists were equally disturbed at either the actions or statements by the Prime Minister and Conservative MPs or by the opposition leaders and their MPs.

On balance though, most thought Prime Minister Harper and the Conservatives had created the crisis and handled it poorly. A review of journalist's comments focussed in on 1) who should be blamed for starting the crisis; 2) comments about the coalition; 3) comments arising from the television statements made by each leader; and finally, 4) the request and granting of prorogation.

1) Who started it all? Barbara Yaffe in the *Vancouver Sun* laid blame for the unfolding parliamentary crisis squarely on "Stephen Harper's political miscalculations [which] have put his own government, and Canada's stability, in jeopardy at a time of economic crisis." [19] In an editorial two days later, the Sun agreed stating that "Harper seems to have let his partisan instincts out of the closet at a time when we needed him to act like a statesman ... Harper made a strategic error." [20] Michael Valpy and Daniel Leblanc wrote in the *Globe and Mail* that "The game plan was good: Force an early election on the economy that the Conservatives would easily win, or take public subsidy money away from the opposition parties, especially the bankrupt Liberals, ... It was a perfect fit with Stephen Harper's war of attrition. The Prime

Minister is a man who gets up in the morning with a determination to destroy his political opponents. … There are two theories as to why he did not foresee this outcome. The first is that he believed the Official Opposition Liberals … could never agree on entering coalition talks with the other opposition parties. … The second theory is that Mr. Harper's determination to destroy Liberals borders on the pathological." [21] Other papers and journalists shared these assessments.

Marilla Stephenson writing in the **Halifax Chronicle-Herald** placed the blame on Harper's shoulders. "Prime Minister Harper, who has always chafed against the inconvenient restrictions of minority government, who has consistently played partisan politics to the hilt, finds himself embroiled in a political crisis of his own making." [22] William Neville writing in the **Winnipeg Free Press** was similarly critical of the Prime Minister. He said that "…with the electoral wars over, Prime Minister Harper indicated a willingness to abandon the confrontational approach that had been the hallmark of his first stint as prime minister. … Regrettably, Harper's conciliatory tone proved an aberration at best and, at worst and most likely, a sham and a crass political ploy. Neither in this nor any future Parliament is the opposition ever likely to trust him again. … The fury of his current attacks, media blitz and wholesale distribution of various forms of propaganda can only inflame the situation further." [23]

Carol Goar wrote in the **Toronto Star** that "For political junkies, the past week's spectacle in Ottawa may have provided riveting entertainment, but for most Canadians it was an appalling display of partisan blood sport. … The Prime Minister whom voters re-elected seven weeks ago to provide a 'firm hand on the wheel', seized the first opportunity to veer wildly into the oncoming lane, gambling that he could damage his adversaries more than he hurt himself. … he miscalculated. He is now struggling to save his discredited government." [24]

Finally, Andrew Cohen, writing in the **Ottawa Citizen**, suggested Canada suffered its own failure of intelligence beginning "with Stephen Harper, who set this train wreck in motion. … If this was the dour Mr. Harper's way of making friends and influencing people [in reference to the Economic statement's political zingers], it was novel. Hit your opponent repeatedly and he will hit back." [25]

Taking a more neutral approach, Nicholas Hirst wrote in

the **Winnipeg Free Press** that the events in parliament are "silly, mendacious, of dubious motivation and, at the same time, quite magnificent. Depending upon your political stripe you can criticize either Prime Minister Harper, Stéphane Dion and the Liberals or the power-grasping NDP and Bloc Quebecois for causing the crisis and in truth each can take a share of the blame." [26] David Frum, writing in the **National Post** considered both sides to be losers in "this parliamentary power play ... if they win, the Liberals will have an unstable coalition, zero democratic legitimacy, a savage recession and treachery in its own ranks. Sooner or later, the coalition will collapse. If the Conservatives are successfully able to prorogue Parliament, sooner or later it will have to meet and when it does the government will face a wall of mistrust, resentment and non-co-operation. Nothing will pass. No legislation will get through. Question Period will be pandemonium. If there is a second-term agenda, it is now utterly dead." [27]

None of these assessments of why the 'crisis' burst upon the Hill reflects well upon the Prime Minister and the Conservatives. But the opposition parties do not fair well either in their forming of an unlikely alternative coalition government.

2) Regarding the coalition, many questioned its validity, some quite critically. An editorial in the **Vancouver Sun** roundly roasted the Liberals. "The Liberal party, ... needs to give its collective head a shake and back off from its arrogant attempt to grasp power from the dully elected Conservative government. ... To have the temerity to try to foist himself [Dion], on Canadians after getting clobbered at the polls is not just hubris; it`s a slap on the face of voters who gave the Conservatives a stronger mandate than they received in 2006." [28] Nigel Hannaford in the **Calgary Herald** questioned the validity of Dion and the coalition partners claim to legitimacy. He stated that "How bizarre ... to see Dion and NDP leader Jack Layton, ... with Bloc Quebecois leader Gilles Duceppe ... inking an agreement to unseat the 143-seat Tories. ... To govern it would rely on the 50 seats of the Bloc. To put it mildly, that is not what Canadians voted for." [29] An editorial in the **Montreal Gazette** challenged the argument put forward by the coalition that more voters voted for the coalition parties than the Conservatives. "Nobody voted for this. Before Canadians are saddled with it, they should be able to vote for it – or against it." [30]

Terrence Corcoran, writing in the *National Post* urged Conservatives to 'seize the moment' and go for a Tory majority government. He refuted the coalition's charge that the Tories mismanaged the economy, that there is no economic plan, that there is a looming economic crisis, and, that job loses are due to Conservative policy. Interestingly, he rejected the media's portrayal of Harper – "Nor is there much truth in the media's caricature of Stephen Harper as an arrogant strategic dolt whose monumental economic and political blunder has plunged his government, the country and the economy into crisis." [31]

Other commentators questioned Harper and the Conservative's claim that the coalition was 'illegitimate and undemocratic'. A *Calgary Herald* editorial wrote that, while the coalition was legitimate, "… a government reliant upon the support of a party conceived for no other purpose than to facilitate Quebec's exit from Confederation has the legitimacy of a police force maintaining public order with the assistance of a biker gang under contract. For this reason alone, the Governor General should reject the coalition proposal." [32]

A contrary position in support of the coalition was taken in a *Toronto Star* editorial. "The [Conservative] suggestion was that the coalition deal was illegitimate and undemocratic, a coup d'état. It is nothing of the sort. It is the way our parliamentary system works, especially in the immediate aftermath of the election of a minority Parliament." [33] It went on to advocate that "… a coalition government of Liberals and New Democrats is preferable at this time to a Conservative regime led by Harper, who has demonstrated that ideology and partisanship are more important to him than providing good government."

Andrew Cohen, professor of journalism and international affairs at Carleton University, wrote in the *Ottawa Citizen* that the Liberals should learn from history. He wrote "History's counsel to the Liberals? Avoid this cashew coalition. Let a wounded Mr. Harper govern. Gloat over his reversal. Let him wear the recession. Choose a new leader, renew yourselves, raise money, and wait your chance." [34]

3) Comments on the leader's 'addresses to the nation' Wednesday evening Dec. 3, 2008 often focused on Stephen Harper's statement. Don Martin, writing in the *National Post* stated that "Prime Minister Harper had a final chance to offer an olive branch to what his MPs deride as the 'separation coalition' in his first national television address

… All Canadians witnessed was a five-minute, tense-grinned version of Mr. Harper repeating the angry themes he's been blasting in Question Period all week, just in a less confrontational fashion." [35] A similar assessment was given in a *Halifax Chronicle Herald* editorial. It said "…in a curt televised address last night, Mr. Harper said nothing about prorogation, showed no contrition for political mistakes and offered little insight on his economic plans. A prudent leader would have come with olive branches. He had sharp-edged platitudes about 'Canada's government' fighting 'backroom deals with separatists.' It was an uninspired reprise of his earlier attacks on a Liberal-NDP coalition, supported by the Bloc Quebecois, as a 'betrayal' of the public interest, undemocratic and 'unCanadian'. These are all specious arguments, but the 'unCanadian' dig is truly offensive." [36]

An editorial in the *Toronto Star* also referred to the lack of contrition on Harper's part and his attacks upon the opposition parties forming a coalition. The *Star* summed up by stating that "The speech was breathtakingly audacious, both in its twisting of the facts and its misinterpretation of our parliamentary traditions." [37]

Few commentators commented upon Dion's, Layton's and Duceppe's statements. Those that did noted that Dion and the Liberals had amply demonstrated that they were not ready to govern Canada. Barbara Yaffe wrote in the *Vancouver Sun* that "Dion's taped remarks … suffered from amateurish visuals. The outgoing leader had problems articulating in English." [38] As well she wrote that "Bloc leader Gilles Duceppe slammed Harper's address in televised comments immediately afterward, saying it 'confirmed the worst fears of Quebecer's' about the Conservative government'."

4) Comments on the proroguing of Parliament tended to note the historic nature of the decision given that parliament had only begun its first session and that prorogation was being used to circumvent meeting the House. An editorial in the *Halifax Chronicle Herald*, stated that "Stephen Harper is a lucky man. Not every minority government leader who alienates every other political party … gets a seven-week time-out to show the country he has wised up." [39] In a *National Post* article, Don Martin wrote "Stephen Harper has made dubious history as the first parliamentary runaway prime minister." [40]

Questions of just what constitutional significance the granting of prorogation would have in the future concerned many commentators. Did it open the door for a future prime minister to be able to avoid meeting the House or not? As with most such cases, only time would tell how it would be interpreted and in what circumstances it might be applied.

Act 4: Political Changes as the Dust Settled after prorogation

Scene 1 – Rallies for public opinion

Early on in the emerging confrontation, the battle to shape public opinion was set in motion. On Friday, Nov. 28, Guy Giorno, Harper's Chief of Staff, sent Conservative MPs "marching orders … for a weekend blitz to shift public opinion. [The email] include[d] very detailed scripts MPs [were] expected to follow while delivering radio interviews." [41] That effort continued through the following week.

Following prorogation, both the Conservatives and the Coalition encouraged their supporters to hold weekend rallies to express and influence public opinion. The Conservatives organized twenty-one rallies around the country. Dion and Layton spoke to a Saturday gathering of about 3,000 supporters at a Toronto city hall rally and promised to "fight the economic crisis that is unfolding together." A few blocks north, in front of the provincial legislative buildings, another rally of about 500 people gathered to 'support democracy and the Conservatives'. In Montreal, Duceppe spoke in favour of the coalition to a crowd of about 1,000. Similar rallies were held across the country.

Scene 2 - Liberals move to replace Dion

On Saturday, Dec. 6, rumblings were heard from within the Liberal party that many wanted Dion to quit. The fumbled television presentation of Thursday evening was the last straw. Whether the government fell and either the coalition formed a government or a new election was called, many Liberals could not see Dion as the leader. In a CBC interview that evening, Liberal MP Jim Kariganis called for Dion to go. Dion pondered his future over the weekend and on Monday announced he would "step aside as Leader of the Liberal Party effective as soon as [his] successor is duly chosen." [42]

Dominic LeBlanc then announced his intention to withdraw from the leadership race and indicated his support for Michael Ignatieff. While Bob Rae had been a strong voice defending Dion and the Liberal's through the week, he recognized that the process opted for selecting an interim leader would leave him little chance, he withdrew his leadership bid the next day. This left Ignatieff as the 'heir apparent'. Ignatieff was confirmed as interim leader by the Liberal caucus Wednesday morning. In a statement following the caucus meeting, Ignatieff said 'he was ready to lead a new coalition government unless Stephen Harper's Conservatives scrap their attack ads, drop their partisan edge and present a budget that addresses the needs of Canada's struggling economy.' It would all depend upon what would be in the budget.

Scene 3 – Harper extends an invitation to 'meet and cooperate'

Harper extended an invitation to Ignatieff to meet and find ways for the Conservatives and Liberals to work together on the economy. But, at the same time, Conservative campaign manager Doug Finley was sending out 'emergency' fundraising letters saying Ignatieff's acclamation as Liberal Leader was a 'stunning and unprecedented demonstration of Liberal contempt for our democratic rights.'

Harper and Ignatieff met the following day. It was described as 'cordial and businesslike'.

Scene 4 – Other developments before the Christmas break

Over the next 2 weeks, financial aid to the ailing auto industry preoccupied the government's attention. After much hesitation and wanting to see what the Americans were going to do, the Conservative's announced a $4 billion package.

Liberals John McCallum and Scott Brison met with Finance Minister Flaherty to discuss proposals for the January budget.

Surprisingly since Harper had for months vigorously rejected Ontario's claim for fair and equal treatment in the redistribution of seats in the House of Commons, he reversed the government's position and announced Ontario would receive 21 new seats instead of the 11 originally given it. Harper had previously rejected Ontario's arguments that it was being discriminated against.

Flaherty announced the establishment of a 'blue ribbon panel' to advise the government on the economy. This was a reversal of the Conservative's ridiculing Dion and the Liberals promise to establish a similar panel during the recent election.

Three days before Christmas, Harper announced the appointment of 18 new senators and 1 Supreme Court Judge. The process employed in making these appointments ignored the government's own new process and reverted back to the process Harper had vigorously criticized while in opposition.

Act 5: Where does all this leave us?

Scene 1 – Constructing a Throne Speech and Budget for survival or campaigning

With prorogation, Harper and the Conservatives bought 58 days to construct a new throne speech outlining the government's legislative plans and a budget for the second session of the 40th Parliament. The first session of this Parliament sat for only 16 days before being prematurely adjourned under the opposition's threat to defeat the government on a confidence vote scheduled for Monday Dec. 8. The throne speech for the second session was scheduled for January 26 with the budget to be delivered on January 27. Both presentations involve the House voting confidence in the government's legislative and budgetary plans.

Could the government manage this over the Christmas holidays and first weeks of January? Would the throne speech and budget include measures that would satisfy enough of the opposition's demands to pass the two confidence motions that would follow? Would the coalition partners respond as individual parties or act together with one voice?

Scene 2 – Who should be blamed for the 'crisis on the Hill'?

When the passions of the moment had passed and observers had the opportunity to assess the events and their longer term consequences, most of the media placed the blame for this explosive week in Parliament squarely on the shoulders of the Prime Minister. There were supporters of Stephen Harper and the Conservatives but they were distinctly in the minority.

Most considered the economic statement to be:

1. not much more than a rehash of previously stated government claims that it had been on top of the situation for over a year and that they would continue to monitor developments and act accordingly.

2. oblivious to the extent of the economic crisis and the major stimulus announcements being made by other governments such as the U.S. - $1.5 trillion; China - $600 billion; Britain – $418 billion; Japan – $275 billion; Germany - $213 billion. As one commentary put it, "Canada's government has looked in the mirror and decided to do away with the subsidy that sees political parties receive a couple of dollars for each vote it receives. By our government's count, doing away with this subsidy will save the national treasury approximately $30 million." [43]

3. completely out of touch with reality by ignoring all the evidence, including that presented by Parliament's own budget officer the week before, and painting a 'rosy' picture of the economy maintaining surpluses and avoiding deficits.

3. more about partisan political attacks upon the government's political opponents – the opposition parties, especially the Liberals.

4. more about taking an ideological swipe at some groups that it strongly disagreed with – these being the public service unions and women's claims for pay equity - and, the size of the federal government.

In other words, most observers considered the Prime Minister and the Conservative government to have failed the test of leadership. "*At the beginning of the very grim news, Prime Minister Harper did not seem capable of responding with coherence and conviction. Buy stocks because they have fallen in value, he advised late in the election campaign, a suggestion that will rank as one of the most disconnected comments in Canadian politics. Ever since, he and his Sancho Panza of a finance minister, Jim Flaherty, have been wobbling about, looking for the obvious recognized by everyone else: that Canada is in recession, that Canada will have a deficit next year and the year after, and that a sizable stimulus will be required to attenuate at least a few of the effects of this recession.*" [44]

Scene 3 – The opposition's response

The opposition parties reacted to the fanciful claims of the economic statement and to the government's inclusion of politically motivated 'poison pills' in the form of cuts to public subsidies for political parties, restrictions on public servant's right to strike and women's rights to use the courts for pay equity claims. They also reacted to the government's stated intention to sell off crown assets even though there was no clear plan in place and nonetheless include the hoped for amount it would receive in its financial calculations.

After having been abused and battered in the previous 2 ½ years of the first Harper minority government, the opposition parties, especially the Liberals, were not prepared to buckle under again. They saw the government's proposals for what they were, a frontal attack intended to cripple the opposition parties and their ability to effectively compete against the Conservatives. Public opinion polls initially showed a divided public but later generally showed support for the Conservatives. Therefore a majority Conservative government would likely result in the next election. Harper would have gained his cherished majority, but at what cost?

Rather than being a planned 'coup d'état' as Harper, Baird and other Conservatives claimed, the opposition parties united for their very survival. The alternative would have been to put up token resistance and protest government actions but in the end allow Conservative measures to pass. They felt betrayed by the Prime Minister who frequently talked of cooperation and consultation and working together but had clearly chosen to confront them with proposals that struck to their core values and their very existence. They chose to stand and declare 'enough, no more'.

And so the gauntlet was thrown down. The coalition was not a pretty one given the need for all three opposition parties to work together in order to claim a majority of members in the House. But in times of necessity, when 'facing the firing squad at dawn', accommodations among rivals can be agreed to.

While not something that has happened often in Canadian politics, coalitions are not unknown. In this particular case, the threat was deemed so strong that each party to the coalition was willing to make a commitment to cooperate.

Commentary – An uneasy peace settles in on Parliament Hill

Over the three weeks leading up to Christmas, the Conservatives publicly acknowledge the likelihood of Canada going into a recession; the necessity to run sizable deficits for the next few years; the appointment of a 'blue ribbon' panel to advise the government on the economy; and, announced their intention to appoint 18 new Senators.

As Christmas approached, Parliament Hill went on holiday.

The drama on the Hill that began November 27, 2008, had yet to play itself out. The initial head-on battles had been fought, changes by both sides were made, both sides suffered wounds, both sides made gains, both sides reassessed their positions in preparation for the next engagement, that is the reconvening of Parliament and the presentation of the Conservative budget.

Would Stephen Harper's Conservatives deliver enough of the goods that the opposition was demanding? Or would the government plough ahead with its own agenda feeling that public opinion was swinging to its side and that an election would likely give it a majority? [45]

The answers would have to wait until January 27 and the presentation of the budget, the opposition's reaction to it, and, the ensuing political jockeying that all would be involved in as each prepared for the next federal election.

Dénouement

These eight days of turmoil raised a number of important political issues that Canadians and their political leaders must confront. Many have roots in the social, economic, geographic and political make-up of the country. These 'cleavages' or 'fault lines' have not been easily managed in the past but Canada's political leaders have been able to contain their volatility and find workable accommodations. In this time of 'crisis', these contentious divisions have been resurrected in the heat of political battle and may not easily be put back in the genie's bottle.

Harper has always been a 'focused' individual intent upon bringing his 'vision' of a conservative society to Canadians and Canada. His formative years in Alberta and at the University of Calgary, the mentors that have shaped his thinking, and his experiences as a Reform MP in

Ottawa and as President of the National Citizens Coalition have all contributed to make him a person who is determined to advance his 'ideological vision' no matter what the costs.

As a result of Harper's leadership, Canadians face the following very real challenges. Each in turn will be examined in the following chapters.

1. Economic crisis and leadership: Is there a crisis? How should government respond? What role should government play in the economy and society? (Chapter 3)

2. Political crisis and leadership: what qualities are needed to successfully gain and hold political leadership? Has Harper demonstrated those qualities and provided the kind of leadership that Canada needs and Canadians want? What role does ideology play in this crisis? (Chapter 4)

3. Canada's Constitutional crisis: How did it come to this? What is the problem? (Chapter 5)

4. A National Unity crisis: How did it escalate into a revival of regional and ethnic tensions? Has serious damage been done? (Chapter 6)

5. The Democratic deficit: How and why are there concerns about the democratic process and damage done to it? Why are Canadians so ill-informed about their government and politics generally? (Chapter 7)

6. Stephen Harper's Political Beliefs (Chapter 8)

7. Stephen Harper's Political 'modus operandi') Chapter 9)

8. Stephen Harper: Master Strategist ... or Master Stumbler? (Chapter 10)

9. Where does all this leave us? (Chapter 11)

Endnotes

[1]   Conservative Party of Canada, "Canadians give Harper strong mandate to lead", 14 October, 2008, www.conservative.ca.

[2]   Government of Canada, "Protecting Canada's Future – Text of Speech from the Throne", 19 Nov., 2008.

[3]   Government of Canada, "Economic and Fiscal Statement", *Debates*, House of Commons, 27 Nov., 2008: 374.

[4]   Scott Brison, *Debates*, House of Commons, 27 Nov., 2008: 378.

[5]   Gilles Duceppe, *Debates*, House of Commons, 27 Nov., 2008: 381.

[6]   Thomas Mulcair, *Debates*, House of Commons, 27 Nov., 2008: 383.

[7]   Barbara Yaffe, "Stephen Harper hits his stride", *Vancouver Sun*, 27 Nov., 2008.

[8]   Carol Goar, "Less lecturing and more listening", *Toronto Star*, 28 Nov., 2008.

[9]   Editorial, "No confidence gesture", *Globe and Mail*, 27 Nov., 2008.

[10]   Nigel Hannaford, "Vote subsidy was a racket to begin with: let it go. Canada had funded separatism to tune of $5,970,311", *Calgary Herald*, 29 Nov., 2008.

[11]   Duff Conacher, "Parties entitled to half rations", *Winnipeg Free Press*, 29 Nov., 2008.

[12]   Chantal Hebert, "Tory partisanship creates toxic mood", *Toronto Star*, 28 Nov., 2008.

[13]   Lorne Gunter, "What do the Liberals want?", *National Post*, 1 Dec., 2008.

[14]   Editorial, "PM needs to fix the economy", *Toronto Star*, 29 Nov., 2008.

[15] Andrew Coyne, "Those who don't learn from Bob Rae's mistakes…", *Maclean's*, 27 Nov., 2008.

[16] Brian Laghi, et al, "Harper buys time, coalition firms up", *Globe and Mail*, 29 Nov., 2008.

[17] Jeffery Simpson, "After the storm", *Globe and Mail*, 6 Dec., 2008.

[18] Editorial, "All quiet on the eastern front – for now", *Calgary Herald*, 5 Dec., 2008.

[19] Barbara Yaffe, "Harper's partisan ploy backfires", *Vancouver Sun*, 29 Nov., 2008.

[20] Editorial, "It's the economy, stupid. Cooler heads must prevail in Ottawa for everyone's sake", *Vancouver Sun*, 29 Nov., 2008.

[21] Michael Valpe and Daniel LeBlanc, "Harper blind to blood lust in opposition ranks", *Globe and Mail*, 29 Nov., 2008.

[22] Marilla Stephenson, "Who's laughing now Mr. Harper?", *Halifax Chronicle*, 4 Dec., 2008.

[23] William Neville, "Harper finally gets his comeuppance", *Winnipeg Free Press*, 5 Dec., 2008.

[24] Carol Goar, "No one voted for a mess like this", *Toronto Star*, 5 Dec., 2008.

[25] Andrew Cohen, "A giant political gamble", *Ottawa Citizen*, 2 Dec., 2008.

[26] Nicholas Hirst, "Mendacious and magnificent", *Winnipeg Free Press*, 4 Dec., 2008.

[27] David Frum, "The poisoned chalice", *National Post*, 2 Dec., 2008.

[28] Editorial, "It's the economy stupid. Cooler heads must prevail in Ottawa for everyone's sake", *Vancouver Sun*, 29 Nov., 2008.

[29] Nigel Hannaford, "Federalist souls sold for a shot at supreme power", *Calgary Herald*, 2 Dec., 2008.

30 Editorial, "Ottawa coalition short on principles", *Montreal Gazette*, 3 Dec., 2008.

31 Terrence Corcoran, "Why the PM must persist", *National Post*, 4 Dec., 2008.

32 Editorial, "Monstrous result of ill-conceived political coupling", *Calgary Herald*, 2 Dec., 2008.

33 Editorial, "Coalition deserves chance", *Toronto Star*, 2 Dec., 2008.

34 Andrew Cohen.

35 Don Martin, "Harper ditches the olive branch", *National Post*, 4 Dec., 2008.

36 Editorial, "Harper seeking re-take on economic policies", *Halifax Chronicle Journal*, 4 Dec., 2008.

37 Editorial, "Harper adds fuel to fire", *Toronto Star*, 4 Dec., 2008.

38 Barbara Yaffe, "Leaders stand their ground with no clear solution in sight", *Vancouver Sun*, 4 Dec., 2008.

39 Editorial, "Harper buys time to wise up", *Halifax Chronicle Journal*, 5 Dec., 2008.

40 Don Martin, "No winners in political drama", *Calgary Herald*, 6 Dec., 2008.

41 "Tories reverse decision on political subsidies", *Globe and Mail*, 29 Nov., 2008.

42 Stéphane Dion, "Statement by the Honourable Stéphane Dion", 8 Dec., 2008.

43 Arron Wherry, "The Commons: Gaming the system", Maclean's.ca, 27 Nov., 2008.

44 Jeffery Simpson, "Mr. Harper's shaky aim", *Globe and Mail*, 19 Dec., 2008.

[45] Rod Breakenridge, "Bad week for Harper? Not according to the polls", *Calgary Herald*, 9 Dec., 2008.

Chapter 3
The Economic Crisis and Leadership

The economic crisis that descended upon Canada and the world should not have been a surprise. Many were uneasy about the boom that had been continuing year after year. Some financial analysts expressed their concerns and predictions that all was not well in the credit and stock markets but few wanted to hear such pessimistic forecasts. Sometime it would have to end, but no one expected the meltdown to be so sudden and so severe.

At the beginning of 2008, "there was a consensus that it would be a bumpy year" [1] but no one was forecasting precisely such a monstrous year. On the campaign trail, Prime Minister Harper stated "My own belief is that if we were going to have some sort of big crash or recession, we probably would have had it by now." [2] The hope was that maybe the worst had already passed.

The Economic Bubble Bursts

Early indications of trouble had begun in mid-summer of 2007. The subprime mortgage bubble burst putting some major U.S. mortgage lenders and insurers into serious difficulty. "The market for asset-backed commercial paper – short-term loans made up of bundled assets, including mortgages and car loans - ... had been frozen, starving banks and spawning a credit crisis. The Dow Jones industrial average went haywire, ..." [3] Later in the fall, some major Wall Street financial institutions dropped to record lows on the stock market due to huge losses – Merrill Lynch lost $8.4 billion and Morgan Stanley lost $5.7 billion. These were related to the subprime mortgage collapse. Interestingly, the public and many financial leaders did not take these developments seriously. They thought the markets would be able to handle the situation well enough.

By mid-August of 2007, major efforts were underway by central bankers in the U.S. to aggressively shore up the tightening credit markets. This didn't ease the feelings among some that this was just the beginnings of the financial storm. But as 2008 approached, hopes remained high that the storm could be weathered.

Confidence and hope were soon dashed as things got worse. "The moment of truth ... dubbed the 'midnight massacre' arrived on the evening of Sunday, July 13." [4] In response to the collapse of major lender IndyMac Federal Bank and the danger of the U.S.'s two main mortgage security companies, Fannie Mae (Federal National Mortgage Association) and Freddie Mac (Federal Home Loan Mortgage Corporation) going bankrupt, the U.S. Federal Reserve Board Chairman and the U.S. Treasury Secretary announced plans to prop them up. This signaled just how serious the unfolding financial crisis was and could be.

By mid-September, Wall Street was in a panic. On Monday, September 15, Lehman Brothers filed for bankruptcy. On the same day, Merrill Lynch avoided the same fate by selling itself to Bank of America. The next day saw insurance giant AIG rescued by an $85 billion federal government bailout. Three days later, the federal government announced a massive $700 billion bailout for the banks. While the bailout package received a bumpy ride through Congress, it did eventually pass. The Dow and Toronto Stock Exchanges recorded their largest one-day point drop in history. Not unexpectedly, these developments caused markets around the world to tumble.

Conservative Government's Response

As this economic 'crisis' developed, the Conservative government of Stephen Harper appeared confident that it was prepared to weather the impending storm. During the election, the Conservatives declared that "Prime Minister Stephen Harper understands the global financial crisis. His **plan** for the way forward has been clear and consistent: balanced budgets, lower taxes, investments to create jobs and keeping inflation low. … For the past year and a half, the Harper Government has been implementing a real plan to protect our economy." [5]

As the carnage of mid-September unfolded and during the election, Prime Minister Harper requested that a special emphasis be placed on the economy during the televised leader's debate. Strangely enough, he failed to offer anything new or even say much about the economy. This left observers wondering what had been his intentions. If this registered with voters, it didn't show in the results which for a number of reasons, not the least of which was the poor campaign run by Dion and the Liberals, the Conservatives increased their number of elected MPs.

As Harper prepared for the opening of the 40th Parliament Nov. 18, he and his finance minister Jim Flaherty frequently assured Canadians that the government was monitoring developments; that Canada was faring better than the U.S. and other countries due to its stronger regulatory systems and banking institutions; that measures already taken by the government in the previous budget were working; and, that Canada's strong commodity-based economy would help cushion the country from the worst of the economic storm.

In addition to this, the Conservatives frequently reminded Canadians that the Prime Minister was an economist by training. He was able to guide us through these economic upheavals with a "steady hand". Canadians should have confidence.

It would appear that Harper and Flaherty were in a holding pattern waiting to see where and when the dust would settle. Events were moving very fast and pressures to act were mounting daily. But what could be done? And should it be done before it was clear what the U.S.

was going to do? How could a government that fervently believed in the free market, in balanced budgets and avoiding deficits suddenly reverse itself and massively intervene in the market?

But some have wondered if Harper and the Conservatives were just holding off to see what the U.S. would do. Yes, Canada's economy was intricately linked to that of its neighbour, and yes, the U.S. was between Presidents with fellow conservative George Bush about to be replaced by Barack Obama. Bush's bailout proposals were not easily being approved by the U.S. Congress, especially by some right-wing conservative Republicans. They were eventually passed with modifications.

In such times of rapid change, can a government be expected to do much more than claim that things aren't as bad as some portray them; that they have and are taking the needed actions to alleviate and correct the problems; and, that Canadians should not be alarmed. If a government was to put too much emphasis on the negative, using such terminology as 'economic collapse', 'sudden frightful plunge', 'monstrous bust', 'a market crash and burn', 'the economy bucked and shuddered until it imploded catastrophically', it could very well cause greater trouble, perhaps a panic and financial run on the banks and cash-out on the market. Governments must maintain a public front of confidence and competence. In part, this may explain the Conservative's 2008 repeated denial of there being an economic crisis; the releasing of moderately positive forecasts; and, assurances that Canada's economic fundamentals were sound, particularly in comparison to other countries.

In the government's Throne Speech, Nov. 19, the Conservatives stated that "*This is a time of extraordinary global economic challenge and uncertainty. The world's financial system faces pressures not seen for many generations. Governments around the world have taken unprecedented steps to restore confidence in the face of a global economic slowdown.*

... we can be assured that the hard work of millions of Canadians has laid a solid foundation for our country. We have pursued policies different from those of many of our trading partners. We have paid down debt and kept spending under control. We have set public pensions on a sound footing and refinanced important programs such as health care and post-secondary education. Our banks are among the strongest and the best regulated in

the world. Canadian households and businesses have been prudent and avoided taking on the excessive debt witnessed elsewhere. … Embarking on its renewed mandate, our Government is committed to providing the strong leadership that Canadians expect. It will protect Canadians in difficult times. …Our Government has a clear approach to Canada's economic security." [6]

Conservative Government's Economic Competence Questioned

On the other hand, Jeffery Simpson, writing in the **Globe and Mail**, put forward the view that "So many different, even contradictory, messages have emanated from the government that it would appear the blinkers of ideology, rapidly deteriorating economic circumstances and inexperience combined to produce confusion." [7] Though to be fair, few financial observers and political leaders have had any better grip on the unfolding economic meltdown and how best to respond to it.

What has been evident is that the opposition parties and Canadians generally, have responded to the cascading bad news by looking to the government for action. By taking a 'steady as she goes', 'we are keeping an eye on it', and, 'trust us approach', Harper and the Conservatives have left Canadians wondering if they in fact are managing the economy well. Harper's comment in a CBC National News interview when the markets were experiencing record losses – 'buy stocks because they have fallen in value' - suggested to many that he was out of touch.

The Conservatives frequently remind Canadians that Stephen Harper is a trained economist and therefore is well suited to manage the economy and guide it through these troubled times. In Harper's first minority government, a number of measures were taken to 'improve the economy'. These included a series of tax cuts designed to leave more money in the hands of individual taxpayers and help businesses; an immediate cut of 1% in the GST with another to follow; and, doubling the level of federal funding for infrastructure projects. Further measures were taken in 2008 to better cushion the Canadian economy from the developing economic crisis in the U.S. and globally.

The Government's Economic and Fiscal Statement delivered Nov. 27, 2008, painted a positive picture of the Canadian economy, projected balanced budgets and small surpluses in the next few years, and, spending restraint. But within days of delivering its economic statement, the government withdrew many of its proposed measures and began acknowledging that Canada was not in a 'technical recession' but likely in a recession and would be for some time. As well, Harper and Flaherty reversed themselves on their projections of balanced budgets and small surpluses in the next few years. Whereas Harper and Flaherty had consistently rejected the idea of running a deficit, they now spoke of the need for a massive stimulus that would plunge Canada into deficits for a number of years. Confusion appeared rampant when two days after Flaherty released estimates that there would be deficit spending in the range of $5 billion in 2009-10 and $6 billion in the following year, Harper stated the stimulus might be as high as $30 billion.[8]

Prior to prorogation of Parliament, Harper and Flaherty repeatedly told the opposition to wait until it delivered its February budget. They said it would contain a more comprehensive response to the current economic needs of the country. But soon after proroguing Parliament, the government announced with much fanfare that it was moving up the budget to January 27, one day after Parliament resumed sitting.

With all these reversals involving important economic projections and policy initiatives, Canadians could only wonder how competent their government was. "The prime minister's standing, ... [has] been severely damaged. The government's decision to so blatantly and rapidly reverse itself on a policy it announced with such conviction just days before is unprecedented in recent history." [9]

Harper has definitely put a fiscally conservative stamp on the federal government's management of the economy in the three years he has been Prime Minister. Of particular note is the emphasis on tax cuts for businesses and other measures intended to ease the burden on business. Other cuts, such as the 2% cut to the GST, were intended to 'put more money back in the hands of taxpayers' believing that they would know best where to spend it to meet their needs. These measures fit with their fiscally conservative philosophy but at the same time were strategically targeted to certain political groups to win their support at the polls. In this they have been relatively successful. It has made little difference that some of their measures, such as the cuts to the GST, were criticized by most economists as being a poor method of tax relief and would cut into federal revenues in a major way. They were politically catchy and popular and won the Conservatives votes.

Harper and other fiscal conservatives regularly speak of the need to contain government expenditures and to reduce them through repeated reviews of departmental spending and programs. They are doing this and undoubtedly are finding savings. At the same time they are re-directing funds and expanding expenditures in other areas such as the military. But in the first 2 ½ years as the government, federal spending rose by about 25%, at an annual growth rate of 8%! This contrasts sharply with an average of 2.5% per year in line with inflation under the previous Liberal government. When this large expenditure increase is combined with the fact that the Conservatives inherited a $13.2 billion surplus and 2 ½ years later have managed to reduce it to near zero raises important questions about the Conservative government's motives and management capabilities.

What is Stephen Harper's economic philosophy?

As a university student at the U. of Calgary, Stephen Harper became an avid fan of American intellectual conservative William F. Buckley, Jr. and his weekly television show 'Firing Line'. Later he immersed himself in the works and thinking of Adam Smith, the father of capitalism, and Friedrich Hayek. At the same time he embraced the neo-conservative ideology of the Republican Party under Reagan in the U.S. and the Conservative party under Margaret Thatcher in Britain. He "wondered why Canada was stuck with statist policies that were leading to ruin." [10]

When Harper became active in politics it was with the Progressive Conservative party. Soon after he left the party having become disillusioned with the Mulroney Conservative government and Ottawa politics. For him the Progressive Conservative party was too centrist in its ideology and too short of principles. In 1987 he was invited by Preston Manning to deliver a speech at the founding convention of the Reform Party of Canada in Winnipeg. He became their chief policy officer and held that position until he was elected to parliament in the 1993 federal election. By early 1997, he had again become disillusioned with Ottawa politics and was in disagreement with Manning's handling of the national unity debate. He resigned his seat in early 1997 and joined the National Citizens Coalition (NCC) as its vice-president. He soon moved up to become its president. The NCC is an organization promoting 'more freedom with less government'. It is clearly a right-of-centre, conservative organization. There he vigorously defended taxpayer's rights, questioned official bilingualism, accused federal politicians of 'appeasement' of Quebec separatists, and, fought against any limits on third-party election campaign spending.

Early in 2002, Harper successfully ran for the leadership of the transformed Reform Party now the Canadian Alliance. He returned to Parliament in June of 2002 being elected from the constituency of Calgary Southwest. He soon set about to 'unite the right' and, in October 2003, succeeded in concluding a merger of the Progressive Conservative Party and the Canadian Alliance under the banner of the Conservative Party Canada (CPC). He became leader of this new conservative party.

All of the above highlights the fact that Stephen Harper has been a committed conservative motivated to establish a truly principled, right-of-centre conservative party in Canada. He has not been shy in stating this aim. He envisions not only the long-term viability of the CPC but intends to move the Canadian people and society to the right. To achieve this longer term goal, he has recognized the need to moderate conservative policies and principles in order to gain public support at the polls. Some observers see his 'moderation' resulting from his leadership experience as party leader and prime minister. Many observers characterize this as exhibiting the necessary pragmatism that all leaders must be willing to apply and indeed successful politics requires. Undoubtedly there is some merit in this interpretation.

On the other hand, it might just as well be said that it stems from a cleverly designed strategic plan whereby his moderation reflects a well-thought out plan to shift the Canadian political culture away from the centrist left of the Liberals and NDP. The longer term plan may very well be to make the Conservative Party the 'naturally governing party' supplanting the Liberals who have held power throughout much of the past 100 years and have set the tone for Canadian politics in the process. The Liberals and the NDP regard government intervention in society as a needed actor able to ameliorate the inequalities and injustices that arise from free-enterprise capitalism.

For Harper and the Conservative Party he is leading, interventionist governments are at the root of much of today's problems. "Rather than seeing the state as a motor for economic growth," monetarists and other economic schools "insisted the large, postwar, big-spending state was the problem. Mr. Harper accepted that analysis, and carries it with him to this day." [11] Neither has he abandoned his earlier views prepared in a paper for but not delivered to an early Reform gathering in Vancouver (May 1987). In it he denounced the "liberal-socialist philosophy" as "an economic disaster for Canada" and called for "a genuine conservative option, a Taxpayer's Party," which would represent "the public interest of the taxpayer" against "expenditure demands of special interest groups." Who were these 'special interest groups'? Well, they were women's rights groups, various social issue groups, environmental groups, worker's rights groups especially the unions, French language rights and special status for Quebec, ethnic groups, aboriginal rights groups, and various other groups within society seeking to improve their situation. In all of these cases, the active participation of the government/state meant that government was increasingly interfering in individual citizen's and business's affairs and needing to maintain a high tax regime to pay for it all. This violated the fiscal conservative belief in small government, lower taxes and greater freedom for individual citizens to control their own lives free from government interference.

Many have noted Harper's commitment to conservatism. Descriptions refer to him being a 'conservative Conservative', an 'ideological conservative', 'more of a politician of conviction than a politician of consensus', 'a strong ideologue focused on a specific set of principles', and, a 'libertarian conservative'. On this later description, Harper himself has denied such saying "I tend to come from the small government end of conservatism. I would not describe myself as a libertarian, by any means. But the kind of conservatism I stand for is one that I view as completely consistent with the Reform agenda of significant democratic change." [12] Earlier in 1997, Harper described "economic conservatism… as libertarian in nature, emphasizing markets and choice. Libertarian conservatives work to dismantle the remaining elements of the interventionist state and move towards a 'market society for the 21st century." [13]

Shortly after becoming prime minister 2006, he stated that "I don't think my fundamental beliefs have changed in a decade. But certainly my views on individual issues have evolved, and I deal with the situation as I find it." [14] What are those economic 'fundamental beliefs' that Harper believes in?

Consistently through his years as Reform's chief policy officer, Member of Parliament, president of the National Citizens Coalition, and, leader of the Canadian Alliance and then Conservative parties, Harper has advocated for

1) A decentralized confederation that respects the responsibilities assigned to each level of government. This reflects a 'conservative' view that an activist central government intervenes too much in society's affairs and imposes policies and programs that interfere in an individual's rights and freedoms. Examples of such policies and programs would be public medicare, affirmative action programs, and bilingualism. It also encourages a higher tax burden on individuals and a growth in the federal bureaucracy.

2) A re-structured equalization program which would make major changes in the way funds are re-distributed among the provinces, especially the amounts going to Quebec. This reflects a Western Canada and Alberta view that it is unfairly treated while Quebec gains considerably more than it contributes. The belief that Alberta was especially paying a high price in confederation led Harper to co-sign the 'Alberta Agenda' document that quickly became known as the 'firewall letter'.

3) Governments must manage their finances so as to run balanced budgets and avoid running deficits. If government revenues decline or if expenditures increase, governments should cut back on programs and costs. This would apply when faced with a recession.

4) Taxes should be reduced to their lowest level leaving as much money in the hands of individual citizens as possible. Tax cuts are appealing to voters but set in motion the reduction of government revenues requiring further cuts

in programs and services. Various social programs and infrastructure programs should be financed voluntarily rather than through higher taxes.

5) Privatization and de-regulation as means to ease the burdens on businesses and reduce the role of the federal government and the attendant costs. The belief here is that businesses can better manage their affairs and are responsible and capable of monitoring their activities without government oversight.

One last observation, as for Finance Minister Flaherty, how he has managed to remain the minister has many Canadians shaking their heads. As one journalist phrased it "… here's a guy, … who has just completely botched a major economic policy statement at a time of global financial turmoil. It was so wrongheaded that much of it had to be recanted, humiliatingly withdrawn in the ensuing two days. And yet most everyone is giving the guy who did the deed, … the big green light. Bay Street isn't complaining. The media aren't calling for his sacking. When other finance ministers have blown it, … they were thrown under the bus. … The answer to the survival question is hardly shrouded in mystery. Jim Flaherty stays because Jim Flaherty isn't really the Finance Minister." [15] Flaherty delivered the policies and directives given to him by the prime minister. How then could Harper fire Flaherty? To do so would be to admit that he himself had grossly erred. As witnessed in the Dec. 3 Wednesday evening television address to the nation, Harper does not admit to making errors.

And so Harper and Flaherty continue to formulate the policies that affect the Canadian economy and the economic wellbeing of Canadians. All attention now shifted to what would be included in the Jan. 27 budget. Would there be a 'significant' stimulus? What would it be directed towards – infrastructure projects? employment insurance improvements? What other measures would be taken? Would there be tax cuts, and if so, what form would they take? There are many competing interests claiming the need for assistance. As well, there are many organizations and professionals recommending one form of stimulus or another. Harper and Flaherty will have no shortage of demands and suggestions. Their task would be to sort them out and come forth with a reasonable and effective package of proposals that will not only meet the demands of the opposition parties, but also be effective in aiding the economy. To fail would condemn their government to defeat.

Overview from the Past

The health of a nation's economy is naturally of prime concern to its citizens. Voters pay particular attention to the economic credentials of party leaders, proposed policies and the economic record of their parties.[16]

Harper and the Conservatives claim to be sound managers of Canada's economy and much is made of the fact that Harper is an economist and a committed fiscal conservative. But while the Conservatives today claim to be different from previous conservative parties – Progressive Conservative , Reform and Canadian Alliance, the conservative record from the past continues to linger with older Canadians. The Conservative Party was in power during the worst years of the Great Depression in the 1930's. PM R.B. Bennett and the Conservative party were vilified for the hardships Canadians encountered. 'Bennett burgs' and 'Bennett buggies' were derogatory names given to tar paper shacks and horse pulled cars. When John Diefenbaker's Progressive Conservative party (PC's) was in power from 1957-1963, Canada experienced the devaluation of the dollar and a recession. When Joe Clark led the Progressive Conservative's to a minority government in 1979-1980, he soon lost a confidence motion on a tax bill. When Brian Mulroney led the PC's from 1984-1993, his government ran yearly deficits and greatly expanded the national debt. As a result of these experiences, Canadians have come to associate the Conservative Party in its various forms as a party of questionable economic management. For older Canadians, 'Conservative governments mean hard times for the working man'.

Turning now to the Liberal Party, it continues to boast of its success in removing the deficit and running surpluses under Finance Minister Paul Martin in the 1990's into 2006. It misses no opportunity to remind the Conservatives and Canadians that when it left office early in 2006, it had left a $13 billion surplus for the incoming Harper government and that, due to Conservative tax and spending policies, it no longer existed.

Generally, the Liberal party has had a more successful record developed over the years since the Great Depression. The Liberals missed the worst years and returned to power in 1935 when things were beginning to improve. World War II helped pull Canada out of the Depression and the economic boom that followed the war gave the Liberals a reputation as good economic managers. It helped that they were defeated by the Conservatives in 1957 when the economy was about to go into recession. Liberal governments under Pierre Trudeau (1968-1979; 1980-1984) encountered economic difficulties and ran deficits. When the Liberals again came to power in 1993, they performed an economic miracle by eliminating the deficit and running surpluses year after year.

Interim leader Michael Ignatieff (to be confirmed at the Liberal convention, Vancouver, May, 2009) doesn't have an economic public record to examine having entered active politics in the 2006 federal election. Prior to this, he taught at Cambridge and Oxford universities in Britain, Harvard in the U.S. and the University of Toronto, specializing in human rights and international affairs. Canadians will have to wait and see what economic approach he brings to the Liberal party.

The New Democratic Party (NDP) and its predecessor the Cooperative Commonwealth Federation (CCF) have usually been branded poor managers of the economy because they are committed to an interventionist approach to government as they try to provide social programs for the disadvantaged in society and protect society and workers from the excesses of the free market. They have always faced a hostile business community and media that characterized them as a threat to growth in the economy due to higher taxes on businesses, higher spending on social programs, and expanded benefits for labour. For many in business, they are regarded as 'socialists' bordering on communists. They have been portrayed as 'ideological pariahs' by the economic, social and political elites in Canada. Their record in government has been limited to that of being successful at the provincial level having formed a government at various times in British Columbia, Saskatchewan, Manitoba, and Ontario. Their record is not much different than that of the Conservatives and Liberals each of which has enjoyed successes and failures at various times.

Current leader Jack Layton is a former councilor on Toronto and Metro Toronto city councils (1982-2003). There he became an outspoken leader advocating for left-wing social and economic causes. He also served as *de facto* head of a reformist coalition that gained control of Toronto's council in 1988. As well he served on the board of the Toronto Harbour Commission and headed the Federation of Canadian Municipalities. He holds bachelors (McGill) and Ph.D. (York) degrees in political science. Layton has lead the NDP since 2003.

The Bloc Quebecois (BQ) has not formed a government nor been part of a government. It began in 1990 when Lucien Bouchard left the Mulroney cabinet and Progressive Conservative party in a disagreement over constitutional reform and Quebec. He proceeded to form the BQ to represent Quebecers in Parliament. He was joined by some other dissatisfied Conservatives and Liberals. The BQ has had representation in Parliament since 1990 but first ran as a party in the 1993 federal election where it gained 54 seats and became the official opposition. In 1997, Gilles Duceppe became leader. The Bloc is considered a social democratic party. Initially, it was to be a 'temporary coalition' to promote Quebec sovereignty. When the 1995 referendum failed, the Bloc shifted its focus to the protection of Quebec's interests (provincial rights) and the representation of Quebecers. It has drawn support from organized labour and more conservative rural voters.

Current leader Gilles Duceppe is a former trade union organizer and negotiator. His early experiences with social injustices led him towards membership in the Worker's Communist Party of Canada, militant Maoism and a deep suspicion of capitalism. He also was drawn towards the sovereignty option when Rene Levesque formed the Mouvement Souverainete-Association in the late 1960's. He has been leader since 1997.

Conclusions

Unquestionably, there was an economic crisis challenging governments, businesses and individuals to find ways to 'buffer' the effects of banking and lending credit restrictions, corporate bankruptcies and down-sizing, and individual over-extended credit debts. Every country and government was scrambling to implement measures that would contribute to the unprecedented global effort to restore consumer and business confidence and help ease the needed economic adjustments that must be made. Political, economic and financial leaders conveyed qualified optimism that these measures would succeed and that a return to more stable times would come by the end of 2009. But what else could be expected of them. Anything less would further fuel the widespread unease and fear that already permeated the economy and market. Canadians could only wait and hope.

Prime Minister Harper and the Conservative government had shown great flexibility through this unfolding drama. From denial and 'look on the rosy side' to 'a budget in due time', they then found themselves in a situation whereby a failure to not act and act in a major way may very well bring down the government. They no longer were able to control the agenda of economic policy and management because their Economic and Fiscal Statement Nov. 27, 2008, dismally failed. Their fate now depended upon the opposition parties and the public's assessment of whether they were doing enough and enough of the right kinds of measures. Would Stephen Harper and the Conservative government hold to their fiscal conservative values or would they 'hold their nose' and implement a stimulus package that contravened their cherished economic beliefs?

Canadians got the answer when the budget was delivered in Parliament, Jan. 27, 2009. The Conservative's delivered the largest deficit budget in Canadian history.

Endnotes

[1] Ira Gluken, "a dean of wealth management in Canada", cited in Jessica Leader, "How '08 went Bust", *Globe and Mail*, 26 Dec., 2008.

[2] Paul Wells, "Harper's new tack: change you can't believe", *Maclean's*, 8 Dec., 2008.

[3] Leader.

[4] Leader.

[5] Conservative Party of Canada, "A plan for the economy vs proposals for financial disaster", 7 Oct., 2008, www.conservative.ca.

[6] Government of Canada, "Speech from the Throne – Protecting Canada's Future", 19 Nov., 2008.

[7] Jeffery Simpson, "Mr. Harper's shaky aim", *Globe and Mail*, 19 Dec., 2008.

[8] Les Whittington and Petti Fong, "Harper says deficit could hit $30 billion", *Toronto Star*, 19 Dec., 2008.

[9] Barbara Yaffe, "Torie's stunning reversals don't stop opposition", *Vancouver Sun*, 1 Dec., 2008.

[10] William Johnson, "How Mr. Harper was brought up right", *Globe and Mail*, 16 May, 2002.

[11] Jeffery Simpson, "How a Trudeau Liberal ended up Alliance leader", *Globe and Mail*, 11 May, 2002.

[12] Stephen Harper, "Getting back on track", *Montreal Gazette*, 22 March, 2002.

[13] Stephen Harper, *Toronto Star*, 6 April, 1999, cited in "Canadian Issues: Stephen Harper in his own words…", Canadian Democratic Movement, 11 Feb., 2006, www.canadiandemocraticmovement.ca.

[14] CBC News Online, 16 March, 2006.

[15] Lawrence Martin, "The Canadian finance minister who wasn't", *Globe and Mail*, 15 Dec., 2008.

[16] J.M. Beck and D.J. Dooley, "Party Images in Canada", in Hugh G. Thorburn, *Party Politics in Canada*, (Scarborough, ON: Prentice-Hall of Canada, 1967) 76-86.

Chapter 4
The Political Crisis and Leadership

'Politics in its more primitive and vigorous manifestations is not a game or sport, but a form of civil war, with only lethal weapons barred.' [1]

"Politics, as it turned out, lent itself admirably to storytelling. Where else can you find such a mix of greed, power, lust, conspiracy, sacrifice and secrecy?" [2]

In those eight days of debate in the House and political manoeuvring on the Hill, Canadians witnessed some of the more visible expressions of 'politics' as war by other means. Our leaders and parties put on a display of political combat using language and tactics not seen for a very long time.

We take some pride in the fact that we have a democracy and have a level of parliamentary courtesy and respect for all members who serve in government. Ours is a parliamentary democracy which has evolved over many centuries beginning with the signing of Magna Carta on the fields of Runnymede, England, in 1215 AD. We are not a 'banana republic' nor are we a dictatorship. As a parliamentary democracy, competing 'visions of society' and different points of view are recognized and accorded due respect even though we may disagree with them. By sharing our ideas with others, especially other citizens, members of the society decide who they agree with and who they want to leader them. But it should never be forgotten that this democratic process has been the result of a long and difficult struggle by many individuals and groups to gain those economic, social, political and religious rights that we now enjoy. The battle remains ongoing as exclusions and injustices are challenged. It also continues at the deepest level of basic ideological beliefs and class interests.

During this crisis, many Canadians said 'a hex on all their houses' or 'quit acting like spoiled children and get on with governing'. One joke that circulated on the internet went like this:

This test is very quick with only one question, but it is a very important one, especially considering the news of the past week.

The test features an unlikely, completely fictional situation in which you will have to make a decision. Remember that your answer needs to be honest, but spontaneous.

The Situation:

You are in Canada, Ottawa to be specific.

There is chaos all around you caused by a huge early December storm with severe flooding.

This is a flood of biblical proportions.

You are a photo-journalist working for a major Canadian newspaper, and you are caught in the middle of this epic disaster. The situation is nearly hopeless.

You're trying to shoot career-making photos.

There are houses and people swirling around you, some disappear under the water of the Ottawa River.

Nature is unleashing all of its destructive fury.

The Test:

Suddenly you see four men in the water.

They are fighting for their lives, trying not to be taken down with the debris.

You move closer… Somehow, the men look familiar…

You suddenly realize who they are … it's Stephen Harper, Stephane Dion, Jack Layton, and Gilles Duceppe!

You notice that the raging waters are about to take them under forever.

You have two options:

You can save lives or you can shoot a dramatic Pulitzer Prize winning photo, documenting the death of the countries most powerful men at possibly one of Canada's most important historical moments!

The Question:

Please give an honest answer.

Would you select high contrast colour film, or would you go with the classic simplicity of black and white?

In many ways, this summed up many Canadian's feelings about the behaviour of their political leaders.

Just what is 'politics' all about?

Politics is about the making of decisions for a group of people. Because we are all different biologically and in our life experiences, we often have different ideas of what is the best answer or solution to the challenges that face us. The more important ideas become our fundamental 'interests', that is, all those things we place value on whether they are material or non-material in nature. Consequently, we compete for the 'power' to protect those things we consider right and to decide whose values will be put into practice, how things will be done and who will make those decisions. In some societies past and present, the competition literally becomes a civil war. This is not the case in Canada. Democratically, we elect representatives to the legislature to represent and promote our 'interests'. By casting our vote for one party and leader rather than another, we choose those individuals, leaders and parties that best reflect our interests.

The eight days of political manoeuvring on the Hill took on the makings of a 'political crisis' when the question arose as to which leader would command the confidence of the House and which party would control the federal government. The parties were in disarray and the political process that would sort it all out was not clear. As an article in the **Vancouver Sun** stated "We're in strange territory without a road map." [3]

And so the October 14th federal election produced a minority parliament with the Conservatives and Harper having the largest number of elected MPs. The Conservatives got 144. It requires 155 or more MPs for a party to have a majority government. In a minority situation, the leader and party that is called upon to form a government must win the support of another party or enough MPs to be able to pass legislation. If the minority government fails to do this they will likely lose a vote of confidence and have to resign. When this happens, there usually is a new election called with the hope that it might produce a majority government. But depending upon the circumstances, other options are constitutionally possible.

The Oct. 14th election returned the third minority government in a row. The country did not come to agreement on a particular leader, party or set of policies that a majority of voters could support. The country was deeply divided along regional, class and ethnic lines. Another election would likely not change the results.

When Harper decided to include his politically contentious proposals in the Economic and Fiscal Statement, he either knew what he was doing or he badly miscalculated how the opposition parties would react. He may have believed that just as he was able to browbeat the opposition parties in the previous parliament, especially Dion and the Liberals, he could do it again and get away with it. His bare-knuckle partisanship seemed to have gotten the best of him. If successful, he would again rule the roost and deal a crippling blow to his opponents.

In any case, they reacted immediately and decided to fight it. They decided to unite in a Liberal-New Democratic Party coalition with committed support from the Bloc Quebecois. The coalition agreement would be a commitment to work together for the next 18 months or more.

This quite unexpected turn of events forced Harper and Flaherty to quickly withdraw their contentious proposals and go on the offensive against the coalition. In the ensuing 'debate' in and outside the House,

Canadians were exposed to politics at its worst. Offensive accusations were made, false charges were leveled and emotions on both sides shunted aside reasonable debate. The display of parliamentary courtesy and respect, of common civility, was sorely absent.

Canada has not had much experience with coalition governments at the federal level. Of course, the ultimate coalition government was the one that helped bring about Confederation itself, the Liberal-Conservatives between 1854 and 1864. This was succeeded by the 'Grand Coalition', 1864-67. The closest thing to one after Confederation, came in 1917 when the Conservative Government led by Robert Borden formed a 'Union Government' of national unity to carry on the war. In this case, 10 Liberals split with their party and joined the government. There have been some at the provincial level – in British Columbia, a coalition between the Liberals and Conservatives, 1941-52; a Social Credit led coalition, 1952-72; another Social Credit coalition, 1976-91; in Saskatchewan, a coalition between the NDP and the Liberals, 1999; in Manitoba, the Liberal-Progressives in various forms, 1922-1958; and, in Ontario, an 'accord' between the Liberals who formed the government with the support of the NDP, 1985-87. While not common in Canadian politics, coalition governments are fairly common occurrences in many European countries.

Reaction to the coalition

News of a possible coalition between the opposition Liberals and New Democratic Party with the support of the Bloc Quebecois spread through Ottawa and the nation like wildfire overnight Thursday Nov. 27 and throughout the following day. No one thought such an alignment of forces would be possible given past differences. But the inadequacies of the Conservative's budget and the open attack upon their funding forced this awkward alliance to come together. The shock of it all, later compounded by the heated and inflammatory rhetoric exchanged in Question Period, ignited a tidal wave of comment from voters and in the media. For the most part, media commentators were cool to the coalition, some out rightly hostile and derogatory. Among voters, as would be expected, there were both supporters and opponents of the government and the coalition.

The following statements capture the nature and tone of the comments. First, what was the media's take on these unexpected turn of events. Initially, the media commented upon what Harper's motivation was and what brought about the move to form a coalition. They often remarked on how unusual it was. But it wasn't long before the focus shifted to criticism of the coalition leaders and their party's audacity to unite and offer themselves as an alternative government.

An editorial in the **Vancouver Sun**, Nov. 29, captured the feeling of a number of newspapers when it wrote "The Liberal party, which sees itself as the 'natural governing party of Canada,' needs to give its collective head a shake and back off from its arrogant attempt to grasp power from the duly elected Conservative government. As Prime Minister Stephen Harper pointed out ... Liberal leader Stéphane Dion – who wants to be prime minister of a coalition government – was clearly rejected by Canadians, and his party had in October its worst showing in an election since Confederation. To have the temerity to try to foist himself on Canadians after getting clobbered at the polls is not just hubris; it's a slap on the face to voters who gave the Conservatives a stronger mandate than they received in 2006 to govern in a time of unprecedented economic uncertainty." [4] An editorial in the **Calgary Herald**, Dec. 2, stated that "In theory, and the charge of trying to steal the election notwithstanding, the opposition parties attempting to form a governing coalition are breaking no rules. ... Nevertheless, a government reliant upon the support of a party conceived for no other purpose than to facilitate Quebec's exit from Confederation has the legitimacy of a police force maintaining public order with the assistance of a biker gang under contract. For this reason alone, the Governor General should reject the coalition proposal." [5]

Andrew Cohen, communications professor at Carleton University, offered advice to the Liberals: "History's counsel to the Liberals? Avoid this cashew coalition. Let a wounded Mr. Harper govern. Gloat over his reversal. Let him wear the recession. Choose a new leader, renew yourselves, raise money, and await your chance." [6] Nigel Hannaford, writing in the **Calgary Herald**, Dec. 2, expressed amazement at the coalition idea stating that "How bizarre therefore to see Dion and NDP Leader Jack Layton (18 per cent of the vote) with Bloc Quebecois Leader Gilles Duceppe (10 per cent)at their side, inking an agreement designed to unseat the 143-seat Tories, so that their [Liberal-NDP] combined force of 113 MPs might command the confidence of the house. Of course, it can't. To govern, it would rely on the 50 seats of the Bloc. To put it mildly, this is not what Canadians voted for." [7] One last comment comes from an editorial in the ***Montreal Gazette***, Dec. 3, "… as Liberal and New Democratic MPs begin daydreaming about ministerial posts, it's time to remember that their two-and-a-half legged coalition received 5.2 million fewer votes than the Conservatives. Nobody voted for this. Before Canadians are saddled with it, they should be able to vote for it – or against it." [8]

The ***Toronto Star*** stood out from the others as they concluded in an editorial Dec. 2, "… a coalition government of Liberals and New Democrats is preferable at this time to a Conservative regime led by Harper, who has demonstrated that ideology and partisanship are more important to him than providing good government." [9]

The public's response to the coalition idea was more divided, perhaps reflecting the political leanings of individuals and regions of the country. Here is a representative sample of 'letters-to-the-editor'. First, the following are some supportive comments on the coalition.

"I was cheering your editorial yesterday right up until the second-last paragraph: "The unwieldy three-way alliance … is clearly not promising. Why is it we all complain about our political parties not being able to cooperate and work together, until they do – then we complain even more!"

"The government is to serve with the confidence of a majority of the House. A strong coalition with the support of the Bloc Quebecois created a clear and specific agreement that would bring immediate stable governance to our country. This was ignored."

"Anyone who lives in … and surrounding area should be applauding the idea of a coalition Prime Minister Harper has shown no interest in helping out the ailing northern economy."

"I am happy that the coalition government is a possibility. Many people are calling it a coup and the Prime Minister is saying it is illegal, but I, for one, am happy to hear that our elected representatives are for once in my lifetime actually working together for the betterment of our great country."

"A move at this time toward a coalition government is an example

of the best of democracy. The Harper government has shown itself to be arrogant and does what it can to destroy the opposition. This comes as no surprise. The Harper government is filled with many of the same people who were part of the Conservative Harris government on Ontario – Jim Flaherty, Tony Clement, John Baird and staff such as Guy Giorno to name a few – all bullying thugs who believed in creating crisis so that they could push through their hidden agendas …"

"While the proposed three-party coalition is fraught with uncertainty and tainted by shortcomings, it does seem preferable to the political incompetence and lack of financial awareness recently evidenced by Stephen Harper and his party. It is also clearly allowed by parliamentary precedent and should be preferable in the near term to another election, or to the unpalatable option of proroguing Parliament."

Now, here is a representative sample of some critical comments on the coalition.

"If the Liberals and NDP are so proud of their newfound separatist allies then let them bring that ideology and coalition forward to the Canadian voters. We will certainly then have a majority government without the Bloc in the picture."

"It is a given that the only true objective of the Bloc is to destroy Canada by removing Quebec from the country. That is their mandate and they have found support for this in Quebec. That, in my opinion, makes them the enemy. … The intended actions of the Liberal and NDP parties disgust me, as they should anyone who loves their country."

"I didn't vote for a coalition. The seizing of power is a coup, plain and simple. As costly and annoying as frequent elections are, we the people deserve a vote and voice. To topple the government and force a vote is one thing; to seize power and take over is a mockery of our democracy. … Ménage a trois takes on an even dirtier new meaning."

"I have never been a Liberal supporter, but I appreciated their spirited defence of Canadian unity. Stéphane Dion has now gone from author of the Clarity Act to author of a potential coalition with the separatists. The consequences for our country would be dire."

"In almost five decades of involvement in political life, I have never seen anything as outrageous or irresponsible as the recent actions of the opposition parties in the House of Commons. … In good times, when

the economy is in great shape, one might make allowances for partisan tomfoolery, but not now."

"The given reasons for forming this coalition are a red-herring. Although a strong federalist all of my life –voting for different political parties at one time or another – if the coalition comes to pass, I will became an active Western separatist. We'll see how the have-not provinces of Quebec and Ontario get along."

"The coalition is a group of greedy men grabbing at power in any way they can. Their coalition may be legal, but it is certainly not ethical."

"When I read the cover headline "7 Days That Shook The Nation" [Maclean's, Dec. 29], had to try not to burst out with laughter. Those shenanigans might have got the people in Ottawa all hot and bothered but it created nothing but sneers out here in the West. The only responses I heard were along the lines of 'those nitwits are at it again.' When the alleged politicians in Ottawa stop throwing their toys out of their prams and act like grown -ups, perhaps they will earn the respect of the electorate."

As the above comments indicate, many Canadians felt strongly about the turn of events in Ottawa and were activated to express their thoughts. Not unexpectedly, the 'political' leanings of a person coloured their view. Perhaps the one good thing that emerged from it all was the sudden engaging of Canadians in their political process. On the other hand, the lack of understanding of the parliamentary system and its processes on the part of many raised serious questions about the role of party leaders, political parties, the media and the educational system in informing citizens about the political system that governs their lives. How do society's leaders and institutions create an informed citizenry?

Aspects of the 'political crisis'

What was the nature of the political 'crisis' that began when the Prime Minister, at the last minute, included those contentious provisions in the Economic Statement? [10]

First, the opposition began the debate on Friday, Nov. 28, leading off Question Period in the House with a question asking "why did these Conservatives produce nothing but a pathetic scam to hide the fact that their ideology and their mismanagement put Canada back into deficit before any stimulus package could even be contemplated?" [11] The

Conservatives answered by suggesting that the "economic statement seems to be misconstrued by the opposition as an actual budget. We will be delivering a budget early in the new year that will talk about the plans that we are now putting in place." [12] The question and the answer were civil and not unexpected. But thereafter, the exchanges began to reflect the tensions being felt as news of a possible Liberal-NDP coalition circulated. Neither the Prime Minister nor the Leader of the Opposition were present.

The opposition then began to make its case and repeat its themes. The Liberals claimed the Conservatives were "going in the wrong direction" and that instead of helping Canadians, were "picking scapegoats and trying to create victims. They are attacking women, pay equity, public servants, collective bargaining and programs and services that help the most vulnerable Canadians. They are engaging in a fire sale of assets." [13] Gilles Duceppe accused the Prime Minister of using "his economic update to silence political parties, union, artists, women, and every other type of opposition. The government presented an ideological update, not an economic one." [14] Thomas Mulcair of the NDP wondered why the Conservatives were the only government "in the world to still believe that the problems facing the world economy will solve themselves?" [15] To all these questions, the Conservatives responded by claiming much had already been done – increased infrastructure expenditures, reduced its value added tax, various tax cuts – that they were providing leadership and that any plan needed to be coordinated with our biggest customer, the United States.

For the rest of Question Period, similar questions and themes were repeated. The tone of the exchanges was not particularly heated or emotional.

On Monday, Dec. 1, everything changed. Over the weekend, the government had withdrawn its offending proposals, rescheduled the confidence vote to Dec. 8, and began to portray the opposition's actions, especially the emerging coalition, as undemocratic and illegitimate. When Question Period began that afternoon, all leaders were present and expecting their exchanges to be particularly heated. They were and got progressively bitter as the afternoon wore on. Things continued to deteriorate over the next two days. Dion began accusing the Prime Minister of 'deciding to play politics', asking "Does the Prime Minister still believe that he enjoys the confidence of this House?" [16] Harper responded citing actions the government had already taken and then stated that "When the hon. Gentleman speaks about playing politics, I think he is about to play the biggest political game in Canadian history." [17]

From there the opposition reminded the prime minister of statements he had made in 2004 that "defined the rule of conduct for a minority government as follows: if the government wants to govern, it must demonstrate that it is capable of obtaining the support of the majority of members. To date, they have made no such effort. Will the Prime Minister admit that he has failed to observe his own rule of conduct?" The prime minister responded that he would not want to be governing and having to "follow socialist economics and to be at the behest of a veto of the separatists." [18]

Thereafter the opposition repeatedly followed up their particular question by asking 'Why in the world would Canadians put any trust in him now?' A variety of accusations flew across the House: 'deal with the devil', 'traitor', 'double talk', 'deal with the separatists', 'can govern only with the veto of the people who want to break up this country', 'a finance minister who cooks the books', 'the secret Bloc-Liberal-NDP cabal is plotting behind closed doors to plunge Canada into a political crisis. The opposition plotters, composed of socialists and separatists and led by a rejected Liberal leader'.

Second, the proposal to eliminate the public subsidies to political parties clearly had a partisan political purpose. Under the guise of demonstrating leadership and expenditure restraint, the Prime Minister saw the opportunity to pull the rug out from under the opposition, especially the Liberals. If he succeeded in getting this enacted, he would likely be able to win his coveted majority government in the next election. And if it did not pass, the opposition parties would be vulnerable to charges of protecting their own 'entitlements' at the expense of showing belt-tightening leadership which the Conservatives were claiming to do. Either way, the opposition parties would lose. Strategically, it was a good plan. Tactically, it failed miserably.

Financial support for political parties changed in 1974 when the Election Expenses Act came into effect. It was intended to bring party financing into the open, place upper limits on the amounts candidates and parties could spend, and encourage the parties to broaden their fundraising appeal to individual Canadian voters. Previously, the parties were largely dependent upon a small number of major contributors (Conservative and Liberal parties – corporations and the business and professional community; NDP – unions). Since parties kept their finance records secret, there was always the suspicion that they were beholden to their contributors.

Other changes since 1974 further made the parties dependent upon the funds they receive through the public subsidy process. The changes had the intent of 'democratizing' the process and making it more transparent. In 2003, the Chretien government "dramatically changed the rules for political fundraising by outlawing corporate and union donations. Individuals could make contributions up to a maximum of $5,000. The money lost would be compensated for by new payments for every vote a party received, adjusted for inflation."[19] Then the Conservative Federal Accountability Act further limited donations to a maximum of $1100. The Conservative party adapted to the new rules better than the other parties. If subsidy support was eliminated as proposed in the Economic Statement, the Conservatives would be the one party financially secure.

Parties need significant funds in order to continue their efforts to represent their supporters. Primarily, parties need funds for 1) run election campaigns which are increasingly very expensive operations; 2) establishing and maintaining a small permanent staff between elections; and, 3) to support research and advisory services for the party leader and elected representatives.

As well, with the costs of running for office so high today, many capable individuals would abstain from seeking to be a candidate and running for Parliament. By assuring a candidate and party that they will be able to qualify for the public subsidy, it encourages participation.

Generally, Canadians have given little thought to the provision of public funding in support of political parties. But this Conservative proposal to remove funding drew widespread public support. One critic described it as a 'racket' and questioned its validity because public funds were supporting the separatist Bloc Quebecois.[20] On the other hand, Duff Conacher of Democracy Watch argued that there was a sound democratic argument for having a base amount subsidy: "Party funding is democratic because it encourages people to vote, and it is based on votes received and therefore somewhat balances the fact that Canada's electoral system does not dole out seats on a proportional basis." [21] He suggested a $.90 subsidy rather than $1.95 per-vote.

Whether there should be a public subsidy for political parties is a question that can be debated. Generally, the case for is stronger than the case against. What would be the appropriate amount is also a question that can be debated. By inserting the issue into the economic statement, Harper and the Conservative government sought to gain political advantage over their opponents.

Third, the question of how a prime minister is chosen was used by Harper and the Conservatives to discredit the coalition. Initially, Harper said "The opposition has every right to defeat the government, but Stéphane Dion does not have the right to take power without an election. Canada's government should be decided by Canadians, not backroom deals. It should be your choice – not theirs." [22] Harper later stated that "the highest principle of Canadian democracy is that if one wants to be prime minister one gets one's mandate from the Canadian people…" [23] In one sense, he was right given the prominence that party leaders have in elections and generally in representing their political parties. His claim had resonance with voters who think that they in fact are electing a prime minister when they cast their ballot.

But this interpretation is also a distortion of the parliamentary system we operate under. The Westminster model is based upon the principle that voters elect a representative to represent their constituency in Parliament. Their choice may be made on the basis of which party leader they want to be prime minister, but, it may also be made on the basis of which local candidate they prefer, or which particular policies they support, or which party they want in government. It is the leader of the party with the most elected representatives that is asked by the Crown to form a government.

If the governing party loses the confidence of the House, then they resign. Of course this rarely happens when a party has a clear majority of members. But when there is a minority parliament, where no one party has a majority, and the governing party loses the confidence of the House, then it is perfectly democratic and legitimate for members to form an alternative majority and be called upon to form a government.

The Liberal-NDP coalition, with the Bloc's commitment to support it, that is not support a non-confidence motion for at least 18 months, is entirely constitutional and within the parliamentary tradition. As some have noted, the turning to an alternative coalition of members to form a majority is exactly how the system is intended to work. This is especially so so soon after an election and with the prospects that a new election would be unlikely to give any one party a majority.

Canadians do not directly vote for prime minister. To believe that they do confuses our system with that of the American republican system. There they do directly vote for a candidate for president. There they can and often do elect a president from one party and a legislature that is controlled by the other party. Votes of confidence are not part of their system. They are elected for fixed terms and barring serious indiscretions or criminal activity, they are not removed from office.

Fourth, the Conservative claim that the path to becoming prime minister is through the ballot box was further distorted when John Baird stated in a CBC interview that the Conservatives would "go over the heads of parliament, over the Governor General and appeal directly to the people". [24] Again, this is a statement that distorts the parliamentary process and represents a serious threat to the democratic process. This is the solution employed when a leader and party plan to circumvent the democratic process and conduct a take-over of the government. It is the appeal used by dictators and other authoritarian leaders who claim the will of the people as their justification for holding power. This action would certainly be an abuse of power and a violation of democratic principles.

Fifth, Harper and the Conservatives claimed that the opposition had cooked up a "backroom deal to overturn the results of the last election. One of his minions called it 'a raw grab for power and entitlements". [25] Other Conservatives described the coalition's uniting to present an alternative possible government option to the Governor General as a 'coup d'état', a 'seizure of power'. Instead of recognizing the parliamentary right of other parties and members to form a coalition, the Conservatives used these inflammatory terms to demonize the opposition leaders and parties. Aside from the fact these accusations were false; the Conservatives again demonstrated either an ignorance of parliamentary practice or had decided to employ such charges for political effect and advantage. If said often enough and with enough conviction, an unsuspecting public could be persuaded to believe them.

There was no 'backroom deal'. There were discussions and negotiations and they obviously would be conducted in private. It would not be unusual for party leaders to carry on discussions regarding working together to achieve some agreed upon goal. This is especially so in minority situations. While Harper accused the Liberals of a 'deal with the devil', he conveniently ignored the fact that just such discussions were conducted when Stockwell Day was leader of the Alliance. They were willing to join with the 'socialist' NDP and the 'separatist' Bloc Quebecois to topple the Liberals. "... it is confirmed in a letter: in 2004, the Prime Minister was prepared to go to the Governor General, with support of the Bloc Quebecois. The willingness of the former Reform members to associate with separatists, ... , is not recent. In fact, the very day of the November 2000 election, a detailed proposal for a coalition was sent to the Bloc Quebecois on behalf of the leader of the Canadian Alliance." [26] While these efforts may not have led to a 'coalition' in the same sense as the one agreed to here, it did involve Conservative cooperation with the 'socialists' and 'separatists'. It is hypocritical for Harper, Day and the Conservatives to claim the Liberal-NDP coalition is a 'backroom deal with the devil'.

The Conservative charge that the opposition parties had not campaigned in the recent election on a coalition platform and that to enter into one now was to have misled voters. Here again the Conservatives were playing fast and loose with the truth for political advantage. Every party enters an election campaign to win votes. To talk of willingness to enter a coalition with another party sends a clear signal that it doesn't expect to win. As well, it runs the danger of alienating some voters who may not like the other party. To show confidence in their own party and its policies, leaders reject such talk. And so the Conservative charge, while having a kernel of truth, was a bushel of half-truths concocted to discredit the coalition's validity.

Sixth, Harper and the Conservatives played loose with the truth when Harper accused Dion, Layton and Duceppe of hiding the Canadian flag when signing the coalition agreement at a nationally televised press conference. He said "... Those pictures are all there.

They will show those flags put away off to the side where they are out of the camera angles." [27] Harper repeated these claims again during his Wednesday evening address to the nation. But they are totally false. Not knowing Harper's intent, it would be unparliamentary to say he outright lied but it isn't unparliamentary to say that he, knowingly or unknowingly, 'misrepresented the facts'.

Other examples of 'misrepresenting' the truth include the claim that the separatists are part of the coalition and that they have a veto. Both are patently false. The coalition is between the Liberals and the NDP only. The agreement binds the Bloc to vote with the coalition on all matters of confidence for a minimum of 18 moths. Conservative MP Bob Dechert claimed the Bloc obtained a promise of Senate seats for the Bloc. This too is totally false. Dechert also charged that the arrangement with the Bloc was equal to 'sedition and treason' but as Dan Leger of the ***Halifax Chronicle Journal*** wrote "Dechert stands out for the faintness of his stature and his utter moral vacuity. His claim ... was just the most disgusting of many similar comments last week." [28]

Seventh, the question of a government governing with the confidence of the House is fundamental to the Westminster parliamentary system. The government's accountability to the elected representatives and thereby to the people is at the core of the democratic idea and should not be easily tampered with. Because Harper and the Conservatives found themselves facing defeat on a confidence motion, they put the vote off for a week to Dec. 8. When this failed to avert defeat, Harper sought and obtained proroguing of parliament from the Governor General. Everyone recognized these moves as an attempt to avoid facing the House. These actions were unprecedented in Canadian political history. This political manoeuvring by the government and the opposition became the basis for a 'constitutional' crisis that divides and destabilizes Canada's political system.

Eighth, the pitting of one group and region of the country against other groups and regions as Harper and the Conservatives did in their attacks upon the opposition leaders and parties threatened to open old ethnic and regional tensions within the country. By doing so, a 'national unity' crisis became an additional threat to the political stability of the country.

Where has public opinion been in all this?

Virtually from the first day that 'all hell broke loose on the Hill', Nov. 27, 2008, Canadians have been engaged in the political process. Many wrote letters to newspapers, called radio talk-back programs, followed events closely and debated with their fellow citizens. Whether the government fell and a new election or a new government was installed, it would be public opinion that would ultimately decide the fate of the leaders and parties. Recognizing this reality, each leader and party kept an eye on the public opinion polls that were gauging the public's reaction to events on the Hill.

Early on an Angus Reid poll released Wednesday Dec. 3 revealed that 35% believed the Conservatives deserved to continue governing and that 40% were opposed.[29] On Thursday, an Ipso Reid poll indicated that 75% of Canadians were 'truly scared' for the future of the country.[30] A solid majority would prefer another election than have the Conservative government replaced by a coalition led by Dion. A Canwest commissioned poll indicated that Stephen Harper would win a majority government if an election were held then. On Friday Dec. 5, a Strategic Council/Globe and Mail poll indicated that 58% opposed the coalition replacing the Conservatives and 37% supported the coalition.[31] On Dec. 8, a Harris-Decima poll indicated that even with Michael Ignatieff as leader, support for the coalition wouldn't greatly improve (Dion 32%, Ignatieff 38%).[32] It reported 70% in favour of the Conservative government staying in office; 51% favouring Harper remaining as prime minister; 41% blamed the Conservatives for the crisis; and, 39% feeling Harper should resign.

Other polls showed similar overall support for the Conservatives: Ekos had Conservative support at 44%; Ipsos at 46%; Praxis at 47%; and, Compas at 51%. While many political observers were saying Harper and the Conservatives had a 'bad week', the polls appeared to tell a different story.[33]

Canadians were fascinated by events taking place but were deeply upset with the way their political leaders were behaving. They hoped that things would settle down and attention would return to finding ways to ease the economic problems they and the country faced. As the Christmas season descended and MPs returned to their constituencies, everyone would be assessing the public's mood.

Early in the new year, a new Nanos Research survey reported by the Canadian Press Jan. 10, indicated that public opinion may have shifted over the holidays. "The Liberal party has bounced back into contention with Michael Ignatieff at the helm." Liberal support now stood at 34 %, one point ahead of the Conservatives. While 23% felt Ignatieff would make the best prime minister, double Dion's support, he was still 12% behind Harper.[34]

The battle for public opinion remained fluid and awaited the results of Jan. 26 and 27 when the new Throne Speech and budget would be presented and voted upon. Then Canadians would get some indication of how the parties have gauged their support among voters.

Summing up the 'political crisis'

If the Conservatives can produce a budget that meets the conditions set out by the Liberals, then the Conservatives will likely win the January vote of confidence. But if they fail to propose an agreeable budget, they will lose that vote of confidence. This will further create political uncertainty and instability as the Conservatives will probably argue that a new election should be called. But the option of a coalition government being formed remains available to the Governor General. A change of government is in itself a significant political event signifying a major shift in political forces within the society. For a coalition of parties to form a government, especially the particular parties and agreements underlying this coalition, is unprecedented.

A 'political crisis' occurs when the competing forces for power are in disarray and leadership of the government is unclear. Unquestionably, Harper and the Conservatives were scrambling to hold onto power. They were trying to pull together enough of the elements of an acceptable budget to win the confidence vote scheduled to follow the delivery of the budget by Flaherty, Jan. 27, 2009. They clearly were willing to backtrack on often stated fiscally conservative economic fundamentals. This indicated just how desperate they were to hold onto power.

The opposition parties were in a state of suspended animation not really knowing what the Conservatives would propose and not knowing whether their 'grand alliance' coalition would hold under the pressures of judging the acceptability of the proposed budget, the replacement of Dion by Ignatieff who was not a keen supporter of the coalition idea to begin with and who has given the Liberals a new sense of purpose and backbone, and, the knowledge that many Canadians reject the coalition idea.

The opposition parties also demonstrated how desperate they were by forming the coalition. They recognized the threat to their political viability and decided that they could work with their often disparaged adversaries. For the Liberals to truck and trade with the NDP and especially the Bloc, was an indication of how alarmed they were at Harper's proposals. As well, the unprecedented nature of the coalition was an indication of political opportunism. For each leader and party, there were political advantages to be gained if the coalition was to form a government. This would especially be true for Jack Layton and the NDP and Gilles Duceppe and the Bloc. In the immediate situation confronting them Nov. 27th, they opted for the coalition. Whether they foresaw the political costs of uniting together was not clear but can be assumed set aside because they did reach an agreement, did announce it publicly and continued to express their commitment to it.

The Governor General was drawn into this political quagmire as the person and office that is ultimately responsible for seeing that there is a government in place. By the actions of the Conservative government and the subsequent efforts of the opposition to form an alternative government, the Crown found itself in a difficult position. It had to make one important decision in granting prorogation of parliament under the request of Harper. Would it have to make another important decision if the January 27the budget was defeated? These are difficult decisions in difficult times. The decisions ultimately affect the political balance of forces within the country and have repercussions for future political crises.

Endnotes

1 John Dafoe, Editor and publisher, *Winnipeg Free Press*, 1931.

2 Val Sears, "Hello sweetheart…Get the rewrite: Remember the Great Newspaper Wars", (1980), cited in Robert Columbo, ed., *The Dictionary of Canadian Quotations*, (Toronto: Stoddard, 1991) 429.

3 Barbara Yaffe, "We're in strange territory without a road map", *Vancouver Sun*, 3 Dec., 2008.

4 Editorial, "It's the economy stupid. Cooler heads must prevail in Ottawa for everyone's sake", *Vancouver Sun,* 29 Nov., 2008.

5 Editorial, "Monstrous result of an ill-conceived political coupling", *Calgary Herald*, 2 Dec., 2008.

6 Andrew Cohen, "A giant political gamble", *Ottawa Citizen*, 2 Dec., 2008.

7 Nigel Hannaford, "Monstrous result of an ill-conceived political coupling", *Calgary Herald*, 2 Dec., 2008.

8 Editorial, "Ottawa coalition is short on principles", *Montreal Gazette*, 3 Dec., 2008.

9 Editorial, "Coalition deserves a chance", *Toronto Star*, 2 Dec., 2008.

10 Jeffery Simpson, "After the storm", *Globe and Mail*, 6 Dec., 2008.

11 Ralph Goodale, *Debates*, House of Commons, 28 Nov., 2008: 398.

12 Ted Menzies, *Debates*, House of Commons, 28 Nov., 2008: 398.

13 Goodale, 398.

14 Gilles Duceppe, *Debates*, House of Commons, 28 Nov., 2008: 399.

15 Thomas Mulcair, *Debates*, House of Commons, 28 Nov., 2008: 400.

16 Stéphane Dion, *Debates*, House of Commons, 1 Dec., 2008: 456.

[17] Stéphen Harper, *Debates*, House of Commons, 1 Dec., 2008: 456.

[18] Dion, 456.

[19] *Ottawa Citizen*, 28 Nov., 2008.

[20] Nigel Hannaford, "Vote subsidy was a racket to begin with: let it go. Canada had funded separatism to tune of $5,970,311", *Winnipeg Free Press*, 29 Nov., 2008.

[21] Duff Conacher, "Parties 'entitled' to half rations", *Winnipeg Free Press*, 29 Nov., 2008.

[22] Brian Laghi, "Harper buys time, coalition firms up", *Globe and Mail*, 29 Nov., 2008.

[23] Stephen Harper, *Debates*, House of Commons, 2 Dec., 2008: 528.

[24] John Baird, CBCNews, 29 Nov., 2008.

[25] Editorial, "Harper to blame for political crisis", *Toronto Star*, 1 Dec., 2008.

[26] Duceppe, *Debates*, House of Commons, 3 Dec., 2008: 569.

[27] Harper, *Debates*, House of Commons, 3 Dec., 2008: 569.

[28] Dan Leger, "The critical shortage on Parliament Hill: Truth", *Halifax Chronicle Journal*, 8 Dec., 2008.

[29] Angus Reid poll cited in Barbara Yaffe, "A Nation Divided", *Vancouver Sun*, 4 Dec., 2008.

[30] Ipsos Reid poll cited in Barbara Yaffe, "Breathing time comes with a political price", *Vancouver Sun*, 5 Dec., 2008.

[31] Strategic Council / Globe and Mail poll, *Globe and Mail*, 5 Dec., 2008.

[32] Harris-Decima poll, *Globe and Mail*, 8 Dec., 2008.

[33] Rod Breakenridge, "Bad week for Harper? Not according to the polls", *Calgary Herald*, 9 Dec., 2008.

[34] "Ignatieff vaults Liberals into tie with Tories: poll", Canadian Press, 10 Jan., 2009.

Chapter 5
Canada's Constitutional Crisis

"This request [to prorogue Parliament] puts the Governor General in an invidious position." [1]

"It is a time of unprecedented constitutional drama." [2]

Canada has a parliamentary system of government based on the British Westminster model. It is also a constitutional monarchy meaning that the Crown is historically and legally the source of all political power. Section 9 of the *Constitution Act, 1867*, recognizes this stating that: "The Executive Government and Authority of and over Canada is hereby declared to continue and be vested in the Queen." [3] The Queen is the living symbol of the Crown and as such retains the traditional powers and prerogatives of the Crown. Over time, changes were made involving the exercise of those powers by others in the name of the Crown. In 1848-49, the principles of 'responsible government' were instituted in the colonies of Nova Scotia and the United Province of Canada. The most important principle was the requirement that the Prime Minister and Cabinet must come from and have the confidence of the elected members in the Legislature. This accountability is central to a democratic system.

And now a 'constitutional crisis'

When the possibility of an alternative government began to emerge following the economic statement, Thursday, Nov. 27, the makings of a constitutional crisis began. The minority Conservative government's right to govern was threatened by the opposition parties who declared that they no longer had confidence in the Prime Minister. "Something snapped in Parliament last week. It clearly isn't possible to work with this political party".[4] Over the weekend, the opposition parties moved to consolidate a Liberal-New Democratic Party coalition that would be supported by the Bloc Quebecois for a minimum of 18 months. With this threat to the survival of his government, Harper quickly moved to defuse the situation. Friday evening, Nov. 28, the Conservatives announced that the confidence vote scheduled for the following Monday, Dec. 1, would be moved to Monday, Dec. 8. Then over the next few days, they withdrew the offending proposals and hoped that an appeal for cooperation would derail the coalition's resolve. It didn't and so they began a concerted public relations campaign to influence public opinion in favour of the government. As the opposition's commitment to the coalition gelled, the Conservatives adopted an aggressive campaign to discredit the parties, their leaders and the very idea of an 'alternative government'.

Harper and the Conservatives questioned whether the coalition was 'democratic'? Whether it was 'legitimate'? Whether it was constitutional for parties that had run separate election campaigns vowing not to join a coalition with the others to now combine for the purpose of defeating the party that had 'won' the recent election? Whether a soundly defeated Liberal leader had the right to now become prime minister?

The Prime Minister's and Conservative's questions not only challenged the opposition coalition's legitimacy, but it mixed constitutional practice with political considerations. It is one thing to apply constitutional law as written and developed by convention and another to use those rules to manage a highly explosive political crisis. But all is fair game in political warfare.

What does the constitution say?

What exactly does the constitution say on matters such as these? Were there precedents that would give guidance to the leaders and parties? What 'prerogatives' did the Governor General have? Was she bound to follow the 'advice' given to her by her First Minister? If asked by the Prime Minister to dissolve the House and call a new election, was she bound to take that advice? Did she have other options and under what circumstances would they apply?

The importance and role of the Governor General in our parliamentary political system came to the fore with this political drama unfolding on the Hill. While remaining in the background and performing a variety of ceremonial political and social tasks most of the time, in situations such as this, the Governor General's role becomes critical. The Governor General had the power to decide the fate of the government and the opposition. If, as Cabinet Minister John Baird bellicosely proclaimed to the CBC that fateful weekend, the Conservatives would "go over the heads of parliament, over the Governor General and appeal directly to the people",[5] was attempted, it in itself would constitute a violation of our constitution. Even more damaging, it would constitute a 'putsch' more commonly associated with dictators and authoritarian political movements. Governor General Michaëlle Jean's decision, depending on which option she chose, would both soothe and aggravate the clash between the government and the opposition. One side's fortunes would be boosted. In doing so, it would contribute to already existing regional and ethnic tensions in the country.

The position of Governor General is meant to be above the daily political fray that the leaders and parties participate in. As head of state, it is intended to be non-partisan. "*The role of a constitutional monarchy is to personify the democratic state ... The Crown reigns. The Queen, the Governor General and the Lieutenant Governors sit above the government, at the head of the state. Because they are not elected to speak for the majority, in a democratic country such as Canada they cannot wield political power in practice. Yet they are the source of the government's power. Although the ruling government can dictate how the power of the state is used, that power never actually passes to the government, but remains with the Crown. The signature of the Governor General or the Lieutenant Governor is required to make legal every piece of legislation the government wishes to put into effect. This means that the power of the state is held in a non-partisan office above the conflicts and divisions of the political process. Thus the Crown is a unifying force."* [6]

Under the 1947 Letters Patent, the Governor General, as the representative of the Queen, exercises the powers of the Crown when the Queen is not in Canada. The Letters Patent provide the Governor General with all the powers of the Queen in respect of Canada. "Part VI of the Letters Patent vests a very important and most controversial power in the Governor General. It provides that the Governor General will have all the traditional powers of the monarch, 'in respect of summoning, proroguing or dissolving the Parliament of Canada." [7]

It was the exercise of this power of dissolution that gave rise to the Bying-King Affair in 1926. On September 5, 1925, Prime Minister Mackenzie King asked for and received dissolution of Parliament and a new election. The results returned fewer Liberals than Conservatives but Mr. King chose to remain in office and meet the House. He remained in power with the support of the Progressives. By June of 1926, as a Customs scandal confronted King and a vote of no confidence in the House, Mr. King asked the Governor General to dissolve the House. Governor General Bying refused. Mr. King handed in his resignation claiming that "he was entitled, by convention, to dissolution" and that the Governor General "was not entitled to exercise any option on this matter". [8]

The Governor General then asked the Conservative leader, Arthur Meighen, to form a government. Meighen felt duty bound to try. After three days in office, Meighen's government fell, the House was dissolved and a new election took place. King won the election arguing that a Governor General was bound to follow the 'advice' of his First Minister, the Prime Minister. Did this case resolve the question? In the minds of some, yes, but many would claim that it did not. Cheffins and Tucker argue that because of the 'uniquely powerful' position of

Prime Ministers and Premiers in the Canadian constitutional system, there are definite advantages to having "some element of countervailing power to protect us from an excessively ruthless and ambitious Prime Minister, or one who seeks an endless number of dissolutions, in order to achieve his political ends." [9] As with so many other things politically, a cautious and reasoned approach is needed. Under certain conditions, this power should be available to the Governor General: first, there should be a real possibility of an alternative government being formed; and, second, an election had recently been held. The argument here is that it would be damaging to the political system to hold frequent elections. The public's response to the idea of another election to resolve the present standoff generally was a resounding 'no'.

In this particular dispute, the Governor General was drawn into the politically contentious clash between the government and the coalition. What would she be asked to do by the Prime Minister? Was she bound by convention to accede to his request or could she assess the situation and call upon the coalition to form a government? How much discretion did she have? First, there was the immediate question of whether to grant prorogation. If she agreed, should she place any restrictions on the Prime Minister and the government? If she granted prorogation, then a second situation could occur when the House resumed sitting and the Conservative government again faced the House on a confidence motion. If the government was then defeated, what options would she have then? On the other hand, if she refused dissolution, if asked, or prorogation, if asked, and called upon the Liberal-NDP coalition to try to form a government, it would generate a considerable public outcry, particularly in the West. [10] If the coalition government soon failed for whatever reason, what then? The only choice would be dissolution of Parliament and a new election. Governor General Michaëlle Jean's decision would not be an easy one and was bound to be controversial.

"This request [for prorogation of Parliament] puts the Governor General in an invidious position. Many legal and constitutional experts say she should reject Harper's request as it is clearly designed to avoid a non-confidence vote next week. But if she did, she would expose her office to accusations of partisanship." [10]

On Dec. 4, former Governor General Edward Schreyer (1979-1984) went public. He encouraged Michaëlle Jean to not be an accomplice to Prime Minister Harper's evasion of Parliament's will. He made a point to be as clear as he could stating that "Nothing should be done to aid and abet the evasion of submitting to the will of Parliament. ... No governor-general should be seen to be in the business of closing down Parliament for the crassly political reason of saving a government from almost certain defeat on a confidence motion." [11] Mr. Schreyer's very public 'advice' seemed to be an exception to the generally practiced behaviour of former Governors General to keep their counsel private if given at all. As a former NDP premier of Manitoba and an acknowledged supporter of the NDP, his comments were open to question as to whether they were entirely neutral. Mr. Schreyer claimed that he was speaking strictly from the point of view of his experience at Rideau Hall.

While these questions were politically tricky and potentially explosive, they are part and parcel of the role of being Governor General. Canadians should be thankful that there is an office above partisan politics that can provide leadership when the normal leadership is unable to. In this situation, the Governor General's decision gave the Conservative government a 'second chance' to reassess its budget priorities and tone down its highly partisan and divisive approach to the opposition parties and their members. Everyone awaited the delivery of the new budget Jan. 27 and the opposition's response. Would an uneasy truce keep the Conservatives in government or would part two of the constitutional crisis begin?

Political manoeuvring by the political parties

No one denied that the government had the right to re-schedule the confidence vote for a week later. It was clear that they did this to avoid meeting the House and being defeated. What was questioned was for how long they could constitutionally avoid meeting the House. When the Conservatives delayed the confidence vote for a week, the opposition parties were quick to accuse the government of being 'afraid to face the House'. And this was true, but it was also true that the government was buying time. The week's delay would enable the government to rally public opinion to its side.[12] It would also give those who were uneasy with the coalition's strange bedfellows a chance to reassess their position. The question that hung in the air was 'what then?' if the coalition agreement held and confidence vote day arrived Dec. 8.

Harper and the Conservatives didn't wait to find out. When it became known that the government had asked the Governor General to cut short her European tour and return to Ottawa, speculation was rampant around Ottawa that Prime Minister Harper would request Parliament be prorogued. Some wondered whether he would request dissolution of the House and the calling of a new election. This possibility was not given much credibility since there had just been an election a short two months ago. The public was strongly opposed to another election. As well, all the parties publicly declared their aversion to having one so soon. If any party was willing to go to the polls again, it would be the Conservatives who felt public opinion was on their side and who had abundant funds to fight another election.

All talk centred on the possibility of Harper requesting prorogation of the session. By mid week, speculation on the Hill was everywhere. Harper's Wednesday evening televised 'address to the nation' said nothing about his intentions. While his declaration that the government would "use every legal means" at its disposal to prevent the coalition from taking power sounded ominous, it was interpreted to mean he would request the Governor General to prorogue Parliament. Not knowing for sure what the Prime Minister would ask for meant that the media and other observers debated the merits one way or the other of such a possible request. Suspense was noticeably building. What would the Prime Minister do? What would the Governor General do? Would her decision set a new precedent or find a way to defuse the tense situation?

Would he or wouldn't he ask for prorogation? How would she respond?

When Stephen Harper pulled up in front of the entrance to Rideau Hall at 9:30 am Thursday morning, Dec. 4, the media were ready to record the event and report to the country Governor General Michaëlle Jean's decision. Would it be an election or prorogation? Everyone waited, and waited, and.......waited. While waiting in the chilly weather, the media mused about the long wait – did it mean Harper was having a hard time convincing the Governor General to grant his request?; did it mean the Governor General was taking this very seriously and was discussing the options thoroughly before making a decision?; was the Governor General deliberately stretching the meeting out to show Harper that she should not be taken lightly since he had scheduled himself to be at a car plant in southern Ontario at mid-day? Speculation ran amuck! Added to all this was the fact that the front doors to Rideau Hall opened and closed a number of times suggesting that Harper would be emerging momentarily. But no, he didn't appear. A little later, the doors opened again; the wood podium was uncovered and put in place; a small silver platter with a glass of water on it was placed at the stand; the microphones were checked and the spotlights adjusted; and then an aid of the Prime Minister explained that reporters would be allowed to ask four questions, two in each official language. Shortly after, Stephen Harper came out the door and announced that Parliament was prorogued. At the same time, the skies clouded over and it began to lightly snow and then turned to hail. In all it had taken about 2 ½ hours for the Prime Minister to appear and quietly and briefly state that Parliament would resume again Jan. 26.

Now the question on everyone's mind was what had gone on inside? Had there been talk of alternative solutions? Had the Governor General pressed the Prime Minister over the developments that had led to this meeting? Had she at any time consulted with the opposition leaders? Had she considered calling upon the coalition to try to form a new government? Were there any restrictions placed upon the Prime Minister until the House met again in January?

Since such conversations between the Governor General and her 'First Minister' are private, no details are known of what they discussed. We only know what the decision was and what the Prime Minister stated in his brief announcement following the meeting. But one piece of information did become known, that is, that at one time during the meeting, the Governor General had left the room to confer with her advisors. Beyond that, their discussions remain secret.

What of the decision to prorogue? How does it fit with constitutional practice and what, if any, are the political consequences? Proroguing parliament normally occurs when a session of parliament reaches the end of its legislative agenda and the government wants to pause before starting a new session with a new Speech from the Throne. It's a formality and the Governor General grants permission. But in this case, the session had hardly begun and no business had been conducted other than the opening of the 40th Parliament with a Throne Speech and the delivery of the Economic Fiscal Statement. An election that produced a third minority government in four years had been held October 14, just seven weeks before. Prospects that another election, so soon after the last one, would return a majority seemed unlikely. In this context, agreeing to prorogue parliament seemed a reasonable response.

Another factor to consider was the fact that this constitutional crisis had developed because of the actions of the Prime Minister. If he had requested dissolution of Parliament and a new election, the Governor General would have to consider whether he was abusing his right to 'advise' the Crown. Was he attempting to force an election in which Canadians might give in in order to finally get some political stability in Ottawa and vote the Conservatives in with a majority? In these circumstances, it would have been appropriate for the Governor General to consider whether other viable alternatives existed, and, if they did, should she pursue them.

A further factor to consider was the circumstances surrounding the coalition alternative to the Conservatives. It was formed in desperation as each saw the writing on the wall – Harper and the Conservatives intended to govern as they had previously, bullying the opposition, especially the Liberals, forcing them to twist and turn in their agony but in the end allowing the government to get its way. Harper was quite correct to assume that the three opposition parties would not be willing to join in a coalition; that the Liberals would never agree with a lame-duck leader and a depleted bank account; and, that the Liberals and the NDP would never agree to align with the Bloc Quebecois who advocated sovereignty for Quebec. But he was wrong and his government had a 'near death experience' as a consequence.

The commitment of each opposition party to the coalition could be questioned. Was this a scheme cooked up by the leaders or was there strong support from each's caucus members? How likely was it that their new unity of purpose would last under the pressures of governing?

While little was heard about NDP or Bloc members dissenting, it was known that some Liberals were not happy with the decision to link up with the Bloc never mind the NDP. Unrest over Dion's leadership and role surfaced immediately and word quickly spread of efforts to have the leader replaced. Nonetheless, the coalition agreement did hold and was cleverly being used by the coalition to keep Harper and the Conservatives on edge. Because it didn't collapse, the opposition parties were able to keep pressure on the Conservatives to deliver a budget acceptable to them. This was good political tactics.

Certainly dissolution was an option available to the Prime Minister and Governor General. Under normal circumstances, it would have been the normal solution to the deadlock on the Hill. But, as already noted, this was not an ordinary situation. There had just been an election 7 weeks before. To call another would have meant Canadians trudging off to the polling station for the 4th time since 2004 and few looked forward to that. The $300 million cost of the last election didn't sit well with voters then and another one would be even less accepted. Besides, the chance of one party getting a majority this time around wasn't any better than before. To go through it all another time and not get significantly different results would heighten voter discontent with the parties and the political system generally. So it was not really an option for the Governor General at this time. Perhaps later after all other options had been considered and tried.

A final consideration widely discussed by commentators was whether a decision to prorogue would set a precedent. Some argued that by agreeing to a request for proroguing Parliament, a future unscrupulous Prime Minister, who wished to avoid facing the House fearing a defeat, could expect a Governor General to grant a similar prorogation. On the other hand, some argued that each situation was unique and that to grant such this time would not set a precedent that future Prime Ministers could claim automatically. The power to decide would remain with the Governor General and would be dependent upon the circumstances of the day.

Where does that leave the decision to prorogue?

The Prime Minister asked the Governor General to prorogue Parliament and she granted such. The alternative of dissolving Parliament and calling for a new election was really not a viable option at this stage in the dispute for reasons previously discussed. Calling upon the coalition was not really a viable option either since its leadership, stability and durability was questionable. Perhaps, given time, it might have become a more viable option to be considered but, on Dec. 4, it wasn't.

"What happened Thursday has never happened before. Harper asked Jean to instead [of dissolution] suspend Parliament, presumably to give him time to recoup his government's standing through a pitch to the people. Jean, whose tenure ultimately is dependent on the PM, granted the request, setting a constitutional precedent. The worry is that in the future, whenever a PM faces a non-confidence vote, he might just seek a prorogation, citing the Harper precedent of 2008." [13] It should be noted that it is really the other way around. The Prime Minister serves at the discretion of the Governor General even though the results of an election usually determine the choice.

A **Halifax Chronicle Journal** editorial, felt that "…this time-out comes at a considerable cost. The extraordinary measure of proroguing a Parliament that has just convened and hasn't done any work – just so a minority government can avoid being held to account for bad judgment – is a worrisome precedent. The right of Parliament to express its will and to hold the government responsible to a majority of elected legislators has been weakened on this 250th anniversary of the achievement of responsible government in Canada. The hand of the prime ministers who wish to evade parliamentary accountability … has been subtly strengthened. " [14]

The **Globe and Mail** editorialized that "Yesterday, the Governor General acceded to Prime Minister Stephen Harper's request to prorogue Parliament, an act that, if anything, increased the likelihood of an election before the Liberal's leadership convention in May. Michaëlle Jean helped Harper to buy some time. But she cannot prop him up indefinitely, and with the Liberal-NDP coalition unstable, it seems likely that sooner, rather than later, Canada will be into another federal election." [15] The Liberal leadership issue quickly sorted itself out a few days later. The dynamics of the situation quickly began to change as Michael Ignatieff's leadership boosted public support for the Liberal party to the point where polls in mid-January showed the Conservatives and Liberals in a virtual tie.

Proroguing Parliament was the best decision the Governor General could make. It would give time for things to settle out and the situation be clarified. It would enable Harper to get a proper budget prepared to meet the needs of the country and to satisfy the opposition party's demands. It would give the Liberals time to get their leadership problems sorted out and to clarify their real intentions in this situation. And equally important, it would give time for the coalition partners to solidify their commitment or collapse under the weight of their different interests and situations. In this way, the Governor General would have a clearer idea of whether she in fact had an option other than proroguing or dissolving Parliament.

Reaction to the Governor General and her decision

Most media commentators accepted the decision as being the best of the alternatives before the Governor General. But not all agreed and some reacted with strong criticism of her and her decision.

An editorial in the **Calgary Herald** made highly questionable insinuations about Ms. Jean when they stated that "The alternative, [refusing dissolution and calling upon the coalition to try to form a government] that Gov. Gen. Michaëlle Jean would hand them the government for free, was never likely: Given her past association with separatism, it would have created a crisis of another sort had she allowed Layton and Dion to govern with separatist support. Now, the furious public reaction to such a possibility would be all the warning she needed to permanently exclude the option." [16] Perhaps more than anything else, the tone and nature of these remarks says more about the Alberta mindset than the decision itself. As will be seen in the following chapter, Harper's inflammatory rhetoric inflamed feelings in the West towards the Bloc and Quebec.

Andrew Cohen wrote in the **Ottawa Citizen**, that "Then there was Michaëlle Jean. Of all the roles in our little melodrama, hers was the most critical and the least scrutinized. It was the role of a lifetime and Ms. Jean made the least of it. She didn't look like an independent, de facto head of state. Rather, she looked vulnerable, exposed – even intimidated – by a pushy, uncompromising prime minister." [17] He further stated how she should have handled the prime minister and exert the authority of her office. "In deciding to grant the request to prorogue – difficult as it was – she could have given Mr. Harper a time-out of two weeks. That aside, she missed a chance here to legitimize her office, explain its purpose, give it new relevance." Perhaps from his Ottawa perch, Mr. Cohen could detect all this but, from a practical perspective, a 'two week time-out' would have achieved nothing but to delay the inevitable decision given the circumstances.

Perhaps the most vitriolic and miss-informed comments came from a well-known conservative with Bush Republican credentials. David Frum, writing in the **National Post**, stated that "The only way the Liberals can prevail is if the current Governor General disregards constitutional precedent and democratic practice to transfer power without an intervening election. Lord Byng could not get away with that in 1926 – and Byng was a governor-general who owed his office to the neutral British Crown. Michaëlle Jean, by contrast, was a patronage hire by one Liberal prime minister who now (under this scenario) will have repaid the favour by delivering up power to another. It will look like the most squalid political deal in Canadian history." [18]

As with public reaction to the opposition parties forming a coalition alternative government, many Canadians felt strongly about the decision to prorogue Parliament. Through letters-to-the-editor and phone-in radio programs, Canadians expressed their support for and criticism of the Governor General's decision. Many supported her as the following letters-to-the-editor illustrate:

"The Governor General's statesmanlike decision has provided time for sanity to return to Parliament."

"Our Governor General, Michaëlle Jean, holds a Masters degree in comparative literature, speaks five languages and is an award-winning journalist. Much wisdom can come from this sort of broad exposure to different cultures and ways of thinking. We can trust Her Excellency to remain calm, assess all options, and steer us out of this mess in a manner that is for the good of the country, something the children in Parliament

seem incapable of doing." And of course there were many who disagreed with her decision. Here is a small sample:

"*The Governor General has demonstrated that the Queen's representative in Canada holds nothing but a hollow, ceremonial position, reading throne speeches and doing the bidding of sitting prime ministers. Canada faces a profound economic crisis, yet the G-G gives Mr. Harper a two-month holiday.*"

"*Italy has its pizza parliament; we now have our perogie parliament.*"

"*In true Canadian fashion, grounded on policies of compromise, Governor General Michaëlle Jean has granted Prime Minister Harper his request. ... This way, if the Harper government comes down when its budget is presented, no one can accuse her of partisanship. Skillfully done, indeed.*"

"*The decision by Governor General Michaëlle Jean to suspend Parliament ... is ridiculous. ... The GG, with no political experience, in what has been a symbolic position, has singlehandedly decided that a vote of non-confidence will not be taken and Mr. Harper can now buy time to make things work.*"

As the above comments illustrate, the decision to prorogue Parliament generated relief for some and anger for others. Any decision would have produced similar responses. To provide leadership is to make decisions knowing that you can't please everyone. Contentious issues by their very nature mean that already existing political divisions will likely produce a similarly divided response.

Perhaps a word of wisdom on the art of governing: "*The art of governing is conducting business in such a manner as to satisfy the irritated without irritating the satisfied.*"[20]

Concluding observations

The situation that unfolded on Parliament Hill that contentious week was bound to land at the doorstep of Rideau Hall. The government and opposition parties were caught in a political showdown that now required a non-partisan referee to intervene. Each side had set out their case and neither was willing or could easily back away. As Prime Minister, Stephen Harper was the only one who could constitutionally 'advise' the Governor General on a course of action. Under normal circumstances, the 'advice' given would be accepted without much controversy but this was not a normal situation. The events that precipitated the standoff and the various claims and accusations made by each side elevated the political crisis into a 'constitutional crisis' It required the Governor General to actively intervene and make a decision that had important political consequences. At a time of serious economic challenges, Canada needed a stable, secure government to guide the economy. It did not need uncertainty and instability. Both the Conservative government and the opposition coalition alternative were plagued with leadership problems. The ability of both to provide a sure hand on the economy and give political leadership to the country was questionable. In this environment, the Governor General had to navigate through the political and constitutional options available to her.

All of the options before the Governor General had both positive and negative consequences for each side. There were also important consequences for the office of the Governor General and for the current holder of that office. Whichever request her 'first minister' made to her, whether for dissolution or prorogation, would need to be carefully assessed. Each option would provide a solution, but which would be the best to resolve the political standoff, provide some breathing space for the contending parties to get their affairs in better order, and, be constitutionally appropriate.

In this context, the prorogation of parliament was deemed to be the best option. It would stick with the existing Conservative government thereby retaining continuity and the stability that comes from being familiar with the government's operations. It would give the Conservatives a chance to construct a budget that would gain the support of the opposition parties and respond to the public's desire to see vigorous action being taken to combat the trying economic conditions many individuals and regions of the country were facing. For the opposition parties, it would allow them time to reassess their situation and decide on their best course of action. The Liberals changed leadership and needed time to reorganize and clarify their views. Under Ignatieff, they appeared to be more cohesive and able to articulate their views more concisely and strategically. Ignatieff early on signaled that the Liberals would wait to see what the new budget would contain before deciding whether to support it or not. As he frequently stated, 'A coalition if necessary, but not necessarily a coalition'.

It would be the decision of the Liberals that would decide the fate of both the Conservatives and the coalition. The NDP and Bloc remained committed to the coalition accord. Both saw advantages to keeping the coalition idea alive as it kept pressure on both the Conservatives and Liberals. With regard to the Liberals, if they voted for the budget, they would be fingered as the ones who deserted the coalition. They would be the ones incurring the wrath of all those who believed Stephen Harper and the Conservatives forfeited their right to govern by their economic and political mismanagement of the country's affairs.

In the circumstances, the position of the Governor General was crucial. Under our constitution, there are both written statute laws and unwritten conventions that guide the procedures and choices available to a Governor General. It would be unimaginable that Michaëlle Jean did not consult with her advisors before making a decision on the Prime Minister's request. Having done so, and having assured herself of where her decision would lead in the coming days, weeks and months, she chose the best option available, that of proroguing Parliament. Now it would be a case of waiting to see what happened next when the government presented its new budget to the House. If it was defeated on a confidence motion, then Ms. Jean would have to decide whether to agree to dissolution or ask the coalition to try to form a government. Again, in either case, there would be controversy surrounding her decision.

Governor General Michaëlle Jean's decision to grant prorogation of Parliament was constitutional history. However this 'drama on the Hill' would eventually be resolved, this being only the second time Canadians had faced a situation like this, and some aspects of it were uniquely different than 1926, it was important constitutionally and historically. It also was a precedent in its particular context. What would not be known would be its significance in the longer term.

Endnotes

[1] Editorial, "Harper adds fuel to fire", *Toronto Star*, 4 Dec., 2008.

[2] Marilla Stephenson, "Who's laughing now, Mr. Harper?", *Halifax Chronicle Journal*, 4 Dec., 2008.

[3] *Constitution Act 1867*, III – Executive Power, Section 9.

[4] Barbara Yaffe, "Tories' stunning reversals don't stop opposition", *Vancouver Sun*, 1 Dec., 2008.

[5] John Baird, CBC News, 29 Nov., 2008.

[6] Jean Monet, *The Canadian Crown*, (Toronto: Clarke Irwin and Company, 1979) 17.

[7] Carla Cassidy, Phyllis Clarke, Wayne Petrozzi, eds., *Authority and Influence: Institutions, Issues and Concepts in Canadian Politics*, (Oakville, ON: Mosaic Press, 1985) 21.

[8] Cassidy, 24.

[9] R.I. Cheffins, R.N. Tucker, "The Crown and Perogative Power in Canada", in Cassidy, et al.: 25.

[10] Nancy Macdonald, "Will the West revolt?", 3 Dec., 2008, www.Macleans.ca.

[11] Editorial, "Harper adds fuel to fire", *Toronto Star*, 4 Dec., 2008.

[12] Ed Schreyer cited in Lawrence Martin, "One governor-general to another: Don't aid in evading Parliament's will", *Globe and Mail*, 5 Dec., 2008.

[13] Brian Laghi, et al, "Harper buys time, coalition firms up", *Globe and Mail*, 29 Nov., 2008; "Tories reverse decisions on political subsidies", *Globe and Mail*, 29 Nov., 2008; Tamsyn Bergman, "Thousands attend rallies across country", *Globe and Mail* 6 Dec., 2008.

[14] Barbara Yaffe, "Breathing time comes with a political price", *Vancouver Sun*, 5 Dec., 2008.

[15]   Editorial, "Harper buying time to wise up", *Halifax Chronicle Journal*, 5 Dec., 2008.

[16]   Editorial, "Time for a real leader", *Globe and Mail*, 5 Dec., 2008.

[17]   Editorial, "All quiet on the eastern front – for now", *Calgary Herald*, 5 Dec., 2008.

[18]   Andrew Cohen, "Failures all around", *Ottawa Citizen*, 9 Dec., 2008.

[19]   David Frum, "The poisoned chalice", *National Post*, 2 Dec., 2008.

[20]   Jack DeBloske.

Chapter 6
A National Unity Crisis

"Talk about an Alberta nightmare: Ottawa run by a Quebec Liberal with the support of the commies and the separatists. It certainly got Western Canada all riled up." [1]

"It's not Liberals verses Conservatives, or left verses right: They've snookered an elected government from Western Canada, with the interests of Western Canada at heart. ... This is a fight between central Canada and us. [From Calgary it] looks like Ottawa and Quebec just want to screw the West – period." [2]

What qualifies as a 'national unity crisis' in Canada? Historically, the term is used in reference to serious cleavages/fault lines/divisions/ tensions between either regions or ethnic groups. Historically, there have been regional tensions between the 'West' and central Canada meaning Ontario and Quebec; between the 'North', whether within a province or in the country as a whole, and the southern strip of settlement and population concentrated along the Can-Am border; or, between 'Atlantic Canada' and central Canada. Some might be more familiar with the description of these tensions as between the 'hinterland and the metropolis'.[3] Ethnically, the primary historical tension has been between French-speaking Canadiens, primarily living in Quebec but also in other parts of the country, and, English-speaking Canadians, primarily living outside Quebec but also in Quebec. Canada's many other citizens who immigrated to Canada through the years from other ethnic societies have joined these 'two founding nations' and have generally taken on the language and culture of whichever part of the country they reside in.

In this current parliamentary confrontation, the 'national unity crisis' involved both regional and ethnic tensions being aggravated by both the Conservative government's arguments defending their right to govern and, if defeated, a new election, and, the opposition party's coalition accord involving the Bloc Quebecois. Perhaps more threatening is the fact that the 'political crisis' aggravated and linked both these tensions by aggravating the West as a region against Central Canada, Ottawa and Quebec. And within Quebec, Conservative rhetoric fanned relatively dormant Quebecois feelings that the rest of the country just doesn't accept them as being rightfully French or having a right to elect who they wish and have them accepted within the political system. Perhaps it was inevitable that regional and ethnic fault lines would be drawn into the debate. On the other hand, could this situation have avoided resurrecting these two important societal divisions?

What are the issues involved? How seriously have they affected these underlying tensions of Canadian Confederation?

What was said and done to create this 'national unity crisis'?

The first development that ignited disbelief and then outrage was the formation of a coalition agreement between the three opposition parties. From the very first rumour that the three opposition parties were negotiating a coalition accord, many in Ottawa and across the country expressed surprise and concern. Any development such as this would naturally arouse concerns because the defeat of a government and its replacement by a coalition of parties or a new election are exceptional events and creates uncertainty. But it was the role of the Bloc that created the most concern and confusion as many Canadians outside Quebec regard it as a 'fifth column' within Parliament acting not in the interests of Canada but of assisting the separation of Quebec from Canada. Many did not understand the nature of the coalition, that is, that it was between the Liberals and New Democratic Party only with the Bloc agreeing to support the coalition for an 18 month period or longer. The intention of the three opposition parties was to assure Canadians of a year and a half of stability in government. Their accord was in two parts, first, "An Accord on a Cooperative Government", and, second, "A Policy Accord to Address the Present Economic Crisis".

The fact that the BQ came into being as a Quebec based party concerned for the interests of that province and ultimately committed to Quebec's separation from Canada, made any cooperation such as that entered into by the coalition agreement contentious. This was especially so since the Liberal and NDP parties are strongly federalist and the BQ strongly separatist. The Liberal party's history has been one of bridging the French-English divide and especially fighting separatism since the 1960's. While the coalition accord was between the Liberals and the NDP, who would form the government, with a commitment from the BQ to support it by voting with it in any non-confidence vote, the coalition would be dependent upon the support of a party committed to breaking up Confederation. This anomaly did not escape the Conservatives or many voters. To some degree then, it was a fair criticism the Conservatives leveled at the Liberals that they had 'made a deal with the devil'.

The possibility of such a coalition developing did not appear to have been seriously considered by Harper and the Conservatives. During the October election, each of the three parties had vociferously denied the possibility of such a coalition which, of course, is what anyone would expect them to say when they are each campaigning to win as many seats as they could for their own party. Each had a quite different ideology and policy orientation – the Liberals having a moderate pro business and pro social programs outlook and approach;

the NDP having a socialist outlook linked to the needs of working people and those needing social assistance; and, the Bloc Quebecois being social democratic and concerned with Quebec interests and possible separation. Harper knew where the NDP and Bloc pretty well stood but it was the unexpected willingness of the Liberals to join with them in a coalition agreement that shocked the Conservatives. Dion and the Liberals were expected to again buckle under when the crunch time came to vote on government proposed legislation. When rumours circulated of the coalition's negotiations and their intention to vote non-confidence on Monday, Dec. 1, the Conservatives withdrew their offending proposals and tried to diffuse the threatening situation.

A third factor here is that for the most part, the Liberals, NDP and Bloc have most of their support in Ontario and the East whereas the Conservatives have most of their support in Ontario and the West. Given the strong feelings that Western Canada has historically not been fairly treated by Central and Eastern Canada, suggestions to dislodge the Conservatives and replace them with a coalition of 'eastern' parties was more than a burr under the saddle, it was considered a 'coup d'état', a 'seizure of power', 'undemocratic', and, 'illegitimate'.

So the coalition idea and agreement came as a shock and aroused strong feelings in Western Canada, especially in Alberta. [4]

At first, the Conservatives maintained a low-keyed approach. Friday's Question Period in the House Nov. 28 was a tame affair in comparison to the heated rhetoric that took over the following week. This was probably because neither Harper nor Dion were present and that the coalition idea hadn't become a definite reality. There were accusations by the opposition parties that the Conservatives had failed to address the economic crisis with a stimulus package but instead had chosen to attack the public service, women, the opposition parties and sell off public assets. They charged that the economic statement was more of an ideological statement than a plan to deal with the economic difficulties facing Canadians. The Conservative government responded with calm and clear statements that it had acted previously, was acting now, and would be acting in the near future with its February budget. Conservative spokespersons refrained from any inflammatory accusations in their responses. Friday's Question Period passed relatively quietly.

On Monday, Dec. 1, Dion led off Question Period by accusing the prime minister of failing to introduce an economic stimulus package and instead deciding 'to play politics'. Prime Minister Harper responded by referring to the economic statement's proposed measures. He then rebutted Dion's charge of 'playing politics' saying the Liberal leader was "about to play the biggest political game in Canadian history." [5] Dion countered that, while Harper was Leader of the Opposition, he had "defined the rule of conduct of a minority government as follows: if the government wants to govern, it must demonstrate that it is capable of obtaining the support of the majority of members. To date, they have made no such effort." [6] Harper then stated that he "would certainly not want to find myself governing this economy today in a situation that required me to follow socialist economics and to be at the behest of a veto of the separatists." [7] At this point, the opposition reverted to the question of 'why would Canadians trust the Prime Minister?'

Shortly after, Flaherty accused the Liberals of making 'a deal with the devil'. When Gilles Duceppe rose to speak, he was interrupted by cabinet minister James Moore shouting across the aisle 'Traitor!' Duceppe reminded the prime Minister that he had been willing to join with the Bloc and NDP in a possible coalition back in 2004 before the election of that year. He asked "With this kind of double talk, how can we have confidence in the Prime Minister?" [8] Harper then replied that "This party will never consider a coalition with the Bloc Quebecois." [9]

On Tuesday, Dec. 2, the exchanges in Question Period heated up. Dion's first question was in the unusual form of a question. He quoted a statement and asked the Prime Minister who had said it. Harper ignored the question and stated that "if one wants to be prime minister one gets one's mandate from the Canadian people and not from Quebec separatists. The deal that the leader of the Liberal party has made with the separatists is a betrayal of the voters of this country, a betrayal of the best interests of our economy and a betrayal of the best interests of our country, and we will fight it with every means that we have." [10] When Jack Layton indicated that he was willing to work with other parties and the prime minister was unwilling to do so and therefore should turn over the government to the coalition, Harper responded that "yesterday, as part of the culmination of the machinations of the leader of the NDP, we had those three parties together forming this agreement, signing a document and they would not even have the Canadian flag behind them. They had to be photographed without it. They had to be photographed without it because a member of their coalition does not even believe in the country. As Prime Minister, it is not my responsibility to turn the keys of power over to a group like that. It is up to the Canadian people." [11] On this point, Harper was dead wrong, the Canadian flag was very visibly behind the three leaders. He was also wrong constitutionally. The ultimate determination of who becomes prime minister is determined by the elected members of the House of Commons who vote confidence or not.

When Dion and Harper repeated their previous exchanges, Dion reminded Harper that "every member of the House has received a mandate from the Canadian people to deliver a government that will face the economic crisis." [12] Harper repeated his point that "not a single member of the House, not even a member of the Bloc, received a mandate to have a government in which the separatists would be part of the coalition." [13]

On Wednesday, Dec. 3, Question Period began with Dion citing the daily bad economic news and asking "Why did the Prime Minister refuse to take action to stimulate our economy and get it back on track?" [14] Harper's response was that "this government is taking action by preparing the upcoming budget and additional measures for our economy. … [He then went on to accuse the Liberals of] signing a pact with the Quebec sovereigntists to govern the country. This is not a plan to improve the economy; it is a plan to destroy this country, which is why he should withdraw his proposal." [15] The two leaders continued in this fashion. Shortly after, in a response to Liberal Ralph Goodale, Harper stated that Dion "is proposing to govern with the Bloc Quebecois and to give it a veto over all important decisions, over all financial policies in every sector of this country. That is the price he is prepared to pay to become prime minister. That can do nothing but weaken the Canadian economy, weaken our democracy, and weaken the country." [16] When Goodale rejected Harper's claims as "absolutely false", Harper repeated his charge that "the leader of the Liberal Party sat down with the leader of the separatist party on national television. Those pictures are all there. They will show those flags put way off to the side where they are out of the camera angles." [17] Why Harper again repeated this false accusation only he knows. With these opening remarks, exchanges between the government and the opposition became more and more heated.

Duceppe then reminded Harper that he himself had been willing to 'associate with separatists' back before the 2004 election and that, prior to that, the leader of the Canadian Alliance had been ready to form a coalition with the Bloc.[18] He had copies of the letter to back up his claims. Harper denied such and Stockwell Day, who was leader of the Alliance in 2000, went so far as to say "I can tell you, Speaker, my DNA would never allow me to do a deal, a coalition, with socialists and my heart would never allow me to do a deal with separatists." [19] The opposition than pressed Harper to admit that perhaps the "current coalition is not only legitimate but that it is perfectly democratic?" [20] The Conservatives ignored the question and added that PQ (Parti Quebecois) members in the Quebec National Assembly had a "deep contempt ... for Canada".[21]

When Jack Layton began his question, Conservative MP Dean Del Mastro interrupted shouting "Jack, you're a traitor".[22] Layton didn't respond to this accusation but later an NDP member, on a point of order, asked the Speaker to ask Del Mastro to withdraw his language and apologize to members of the House for using un-parliamentary language. Del Mastro twice refused to apologize and even defended his remarks. *Maclean's* (Blog Archive) also identifies Vic Toews as calling Liberal front benchers 'traitors' though Hansard doesn't record such. The Government and opposition members continued to exchange their standard accusations until Ken Dryden prefaced his question by indicating that "it is the Prime Minister who sets the tone of the House. Respect gets respect and disrespect breeds disrespect." [23] Dryden then went on to state that it was the Prime Minister who had poisoned and destroyed the needed working relationships for cooperation in the House. He concluded with "Too late, he has broken it. How could this Parliament work with the Prime Minister?"

Perhaps the three days of heated exchanges can best be summed up by the following description of Wednesday's Question Period. "The Conservatives were primed for a show of force from the outset (and, by the sounds of it, had a bit of a pep rally in the government lobby afterwards). But it wasn't until Harper made indisputably false claims about the flag and Dion that the proceedings truly turned. At that point, for all intents and purposes, Question Period ceased, giving way to a remarkable clash between the two men who seek a claim to high office. Dion could barely maintain the control necessary to form words, screaming across the aisle at the Prime Minister. Harper challenged and goaded him on." [24]

It should be noted that backbench MPs on both sides of the House applauded and cheered whenever their respective leaders made a comment. Some observers characterize it as like a bunch of trained seals ready to cheer on one of their own at every opportunity. In this atmosphere of give and take and with the goal to largely ignore the other side's comments and try to send a 'zinger', it is no wonder that un-parliamentary language and emotions can sometimes get carried away. But in this case, claims and statements, especially by the Conservatives, were not only un-parliamentary but inflammatory. In making their respective cases and in taking the actions each took, they fuelled the underlying tensions that lurk in the background of Canadian society. Thus a 'national unity crisis' emerged from the earlier economic, political and constitutional 'crises' that the two sides were fighting.

How did the media and public react?

The public has to rely upon the media to capture and convey details of events around the country and the world. Few citizens can be witnesses to any of the events directly. The media consider themselves vital elements in that essential link and this is especially so regarding the country's political affairs. While television and radio are important components of 'the media', newspapers continue to have an important role to play in that they have a lasting presence that does not disappear once viewed or heard. So it is to the print media, editorials and political journalists, that the following comments are drawn from.

The **Toronto Star** ran an editorial refuting Harper's claim that the coalition's move to replace his government was "undemocratic and nefarious." [25] Again in a Dec. 2, editorial, it rejected the Conservative's claims that the coalition "was illegitimate and undemocratic, a coup d'état." [26] Then in a Dec. 3 editorial, it noted all the charges being made by the Conservatives against the coalition – that 'Duceppe and the Bloc would be calling the tune each and every day'; that 'the Government of Canada would be at the mercy of people committed to destroying our Confederation'; and, that 'the deal made with the separatists was a betrayal of the voters' – was "Scary, if true. But it's not. ... The Conservatives are entitled to argue that the proposed coalition government is bad for the economy and bad for the country. But to suggest, as they have, that the coalition is a conspiracy to break up the country is not just plain false. It is an insult to the intelligence of Canadians." [27] On Dec. 4, it ran an editorial titled "Harper adds fuel to fire" stating that Wednesday night's address to the country by Harper "was breathtakingly audacious, both in its twisting of the facts and its misinterpretation of our parliamentary traditions. ... If Harper gets his way [re a request for prorogation of Parliament], he will likely use the next two months to press his attack on the opposition coalition as 'separatist'. (Interestingly, in the French version of last night's speech, Harper used the softer term 'sovereignist'.) It is a dangerous tactic, for it risks stirring up anti- Canada resentments in Quebec and anti-Quebec feelings in the rest of the country. Then we might have a national unity crisis layered on top of the economic crisis." [28]

Political commentator Don Martin, writing in the **National Post**, noted that "In the course of a mere dozen sitting days, the economic crisis has been overshadowed by a Canadian parliamentary crisis that then spiraled into a national unity crisis. ... Sadly for Canada, Stephen Harper let the moment to offer his opponents an escape to safe political ground slip away amid partisan grandstanding as he wrapped himself in the Maple Leaf as Captain Canada." [29]

The **Globe and Mail** ran a series of stories highlighting the dangers of inflaming national unity. Brian Laghi's article, "Harper's attack on Bloc risks alienating Quebec" with subtitle "PM may be calculating he has to sacrifice the province in order to build support elsewhere",[30] not only speaks to the national unity division but that the PM is willing to tactically offend Quebec in order to shore up support in English-speaking Canada. Gary Mason's article the same day headlined "In the West, a deep sense of betrayal". Noting that the Liberals have been in decline for years in the West and did poorly in the recent election, he writes that the reaction in BC and generally in the West "was visceral. ... In all my years listening to talk radio in Vancouver, I have never heard such anger. Of the dozens who phoned in yesterday ... calls were running 95 per cent against the coalition. [If the coalition plan goes ahead,] There will certainly be damage done to the state of national unity." [31]

An editorial in the **Halifax Chronicle Herald**, commented that the Wednesday evening address "was an uninspired reprise of his earlier attacks on a Liberal-NDP coalition, supported by the Bloc Quebecois, as a 'betrayal' of the public interest, undemocratic and unCanadian. These are all specious arguments, but the 'unCanadian' dig is truly offensive." [32]

Another editorial the following day stated that "Stephen Harper is a lucky man. Not every minority government leader who alienates every other party with his bare-knuckles partisanship and loses the confidence of Parliament gets a seven-week time-out to show the country he has wised up. ... Hopefully, a few sober voices in his own party will have the courage to tell him that he should learn some humility from this self-made crisis that has needlessly curdled Parliament and whipped up disunity and factionalism in the country." [33]

A **Globe and Mail** editorial titled "Fanning anger towards Quebec" noted that "Prime Minister Stephen Harper has lashed out in desperate fury in an effort to save his job. He has bitterly attacked the Liberals and the 'socialists', but he has reserved particular scorn for the 'separatists.' ...He has raised the national-unity stakes by fanning anger at (and in) Quebec. ... there is danger Canadian unity will be harmed. ... There are also legitimate questions to be raised about the price the Bloc will exact from the coalition for its support. But Mr. Harper has taken it to another level entirely, suggesting it is a betrayal of the country to sign a deal with the Bloc. ... If it is 'close to treason or sedition' to connive with the Bloc, then Conservatives are as guilty as anyone. Because of the overwrought rhetoric in Ottawa, there is real potential for damage to the fabric of Canadian unity. It's not the separatist Bloc Quebecois that is responsible for that, although they may yet benefit from it." [34]

In the same day's paper, Gary Mason's article titled "National unity will pay the price for this partisan bickering", stated that "the fact is there are plenty of westerners who are now contemplating life without a governing party in Ottawa they felt finally understood their wants and needs, that appreciated the West in a way successive Liberal governments have not. ... Meantime, comments by the Prime Minister and others critical of the role that the Bloc has played in the current drama have stirred up feelings and passions in the West that are not necessarily positive." [35] He went on to quote Andre Pratte in a La Presse editorial: "Watching how the Liberal-NDP-Bloc coalition couldn't care less about the feelings of western Canadians, listening to PM Harper refer repeatedly to the threat represented by 'Quebec separatists,' gives us an idea of the damage that this crisis could inflict on the unity of the country."

Ed Broadbent wrote in a ***Globe and Mail***, article, titled "Fanning the fires of national disunity" that "I have never witnessed a Canadian prime minister consciously decide to disunite the nation. Until now. ... Stephen Harper has betrayed the fundamental obligation of a prime minister: to build and strengthen national unity in possibly the world's most difficult federation to govern. ... [Stephen Harper is] the first prime minister in Canada's history to deliberately create a political crisis and set the fire of national disunity." [36]

Finally, Rheal Seguin, writing in the ***Globe and Mail***, from Quebec, wrote that "by using the heavily charged 'separatist' term Mr. Harper has awakened a sleeping tiger. Nationalists are taking exception at being blamed for the turmoil in Parliament. ... Many [Quebecers] hold nationalist views and could react strongly against what is being perceived as Conservative Quebec-bashing, and harsh comments coming from Western Canada and elsewhere accusing the 'separatists', through their support of the Liberal-NDP coalition, ...".[37]

Don Martin wrote in the ***Calgary Herald***, that "this much is clear from a week even deans of the press gallery say was unlike any other in their memories: A three-party parliamentary rebellion was planned, threatened and, on the eve of execution, delayed as Stephen Harper ran for his life twice from a hanging-noose Parliament. In its wake, the nation became deeply polarized as the prime minister invoked and stoked fears of separatists taking over a coalition government, a move that infuriated Quebec and Alberta in equal measure for polar opposite reasons." [38]

The ***Calgary Herald***, in an editorial, wrote that "The BQ has been on the rocks for some years, lacking purpose, respect and notably financial support from its own members. It is an unfortunate consequence of the week's work that Canadian horror at a coalition involving separatists is now being played in Quebec as horror at a coalition involving Quebecers. BQ Leader Gilles Duceppe mendaciously calls it 'the worst attacks against Quebec that we have seen since the events of Meech (lake)." [39]

Political commentator Barbara Yaffe, writing in the **Vancouver Sun**, wrote that "Events of the past week have also heightened regional tensions in the country, with Albertans in particular opposing any attempt to replace the Conservative government. On the other side of the country, many Quebecers took offence at Harper's attacks on the 'separatist' role in the proposed coalition. Nearly 40 per cent of Quebecers voted for the Bloc on Oct. 14 and view it as a legitimate federal party." [40]

Andrew Cohen writing in the **Ottawa Citizen**, stated that Harper's "immoderate language set one region of the country against the other. Sure the Bloc Quebecois is secessionist and hypocritical, but it holds 49 of 75 seats in Quebec. To suggest Quebecers who voted for the BQ are all separatists is foolish; ... Quebec is complicated, and Canada's unity is ill-served by such demagoguery. In a country divided by history and geography, is this the conduct of a responsible leader? Is not the greatest mission of any prime minister to keep the fragile enterprise together?" [41]

And what of the public's comments? As indicated by Gary Mason above, the depth of angry feeling that many westerners were expressing in calls to radio talk-back shows was a clear indication of the deeper feeling in the West that it had been, and was now getting, a raw deal. While not building on a similar historic feeling of alienation, many Canadians in other parts of the country expressed strong reactions against the coalition being supported by the BQ. For them, it was inconceivable for the federalist Liberals and NDP to even contemplate such an association. These letters-to-the-editor [42] capture the broader feeling focused on the BQ and by extension to Quebecers: "It is a given that the only true objective of the Bloc is to destroy Canada by removing Quebec from the country. That is their mandate and they have found support for this in Quebec. That, in my opinion, makes them the enemy. Webster's definition of treason is 'the act or attempted act of working for the enemies of the state.' ... The intended actions of the Liberal and NDP parties disgust me, as they should anyone who loves their country." Another letter opens with the statement that "The coalition between the left and the Bloc is clearly an attack on the West." But another writer disavows the generalization that the 'west is angry'. "I am one of those people from 'the West' who are supposed to feel disenfranchised and angry about the potential for the government to be left in the hands of a left-wing coalition and those dastardly separatists. In fact, it would be thrilling to see Stephen Harper and his cronies toppled."

And finally, a letter challenging the Conservative's 'demonizing' the Bloc and their supporters: "Conservative Party ads are an affront to Quebec supporters of the Bloc, and come dangerously close to questioning the right of citizens to vote for a legal political party."

Concluding observations

Both the government and opposition parties contributed to the turning of this challenge to the Conservative's hold on power into a national unity crisis. The very act of forming the Liberal-NDP coalition and working relationship with the Bloc invited criticism and hostility. Given the choice of accepting the government's proposed removal of public funding and attacks upon the public service and women's pay equity rights or banding together to challenge the government, it was not much of a stretch to form the coalition. Supporters of the coalition would argue that by banding together, the parties were demonstrating a willingness and capability for competing parties to work together. This they would argue contrasted with the continuing practice of Harper and the Conservatives to speak publicly of cooperation while practicing the politics of division. Nonetheless, by the very act of forming the coalition, the three parties opened the door for the kinds of emotional criticism that the government and many Canadians expressed. They must share some of the blame for aggravating the 'national unity' crisis.

Many Canadians outside Quebec, especially in the West, regard the Bloc as an anomaly in that they want to break up the country yet sit in and participate in the business of the House. Earlier, when the Bloc Quebecois became the Official Opposition (1993-1997), many

Canadians couldn't fathom how the political system could allow for a party committed to breaking up the country to sit as 'Her Majesty's Loyal Opposition'. This was especially so in the Reform Party and its supporters. Nonetheless, Bloc MPs are a legitimate political party operating democratically and elected by Canadian citizens in Quebec. Not all voters who have voted for the Bloc are 'separatists'. But by implying such, the Conservatives not only branded all BQ voters 'separatists', they also tainted nationalist Quebecers. This 'branding' of the BQ and Quebecers as 'separatists' may have played well outside Quebec, especially in the West, but it angered Quebecers and may have re-invigorated separatist forces in Quebec. At the same time, it resurrected western anger towards Central Canada and Quebec. Neither of these resurrected emotions helped strengthen national unity. On this point, Harper and the Conservatives reacted to the coalition agreement in a way that damaged national unity.

Canadians generally are not aware of nor give any credit to the Bloc Quebecois' contributions to the running of parliament and the passage of legislation. The BQ is a social-democratic political party and is supportive of social policies that help those who have employment and social difficulties. In doing so, they have been constructive members of the House and its committees. On many occasions, they have voted with the government of the day, sometimes helping to keep a minority government in power. While committed to supporting Quebec's independence, it has been active in many other areas of public policy. Canadians need to recognize this and give the party its due.

Prime Minister Stephen Harper set the tone in many different ways during this crisis. On Friday, Nov. 28, he declared that the opposition did not have the right to 'take power without an election'. Simultaneously, his chief of staff was sending Conservative MPs an email 'to hit the pavement' and get the party's message out over the airwaves so as to shape public opinion ahead of a confidence vote the coming Monday. Nothing wrong with that per se but it was part of a larger strategy to discredit the opposition coalition by making a variety of questionable claims that were later followed by outright false statements.

On Tuesday and Wednesday, Harper added fuel to the fire by repeating false accusations and characterizations of the coalition. He continued to claim the coalition was 'undemocratic', 'illegitimate', 'unCanadian' and beholden to the Bloc. He went so far as to accuse the coalition of being a 'conspiracy to break up Canada' and trying 'to overturn the results of the election'. As well, rather than reigning in his party members, he allowed them to make accusations that accused opposition parties and members of having sold their souls for power and being 'traitors' to the country. In making these false accusations, repeating false information, and, by misrepresenting the parliamentary process, Harper and his MPs whipped up public emotions that played upon underlying regional and ethnic tensions. In this way, Harper bears full responsibility for turning the economic, political and constitutional crises into a national unity crisis.

The reality of regional and ethnic tensions in Canada should not be underestimated. The resentments toward central Canada (Ontario, Quebec and Ottawa) by the other regions is real and longstanding. Grievances felt by various regions rest upon historical events and central government policies that are felt to have been detrimental to these regions. They have become part of the mythology of each region and are often resurrected in any dealings with central Canada or the federal government. A good example is the case of the National Energy Program (NEP) instituted by the Trudeau Liberal government in 1980. Many Albertans consider the NEP the cause of the oil industry's collapse in the early 1980's. But as Gordon Pitts writes in his recent book *Stampede! The Rise of the West and Canada's New Power Elite*, "the NEP served as a handy scapegoat for all the anti-eastern, anti-Trudeau feeling that was already rampant in the province. 'The well-intentioned NEP came along and the Albertans tend to use it as a lightning rod for their hatred'." [43] Pitt then quotes an Albertan who made the observation that "Nobody ever explained to me how the NEP crashed Texas."

While the English-French divide has been relatively quiet in recent years, no one should regard it as having disappeared. English-speaking Canadians have reconciled themselves to bilingualism in their schools and in the services provided by the federal government. But they have not embraced the reality and opportunity that having a French cultural presence in Canada presents. Canadians continue to live in relative isolation from the other culture, especially outside Quebec. English-speaking Canadians continue to be more interested in their neighbours to the south than even their own fellow citizens never mind the other ethnic group. The most disappointing fact is that there is so little concern expressed about this reality and so little being done by those that should give guidance in building a stronger relationship between the two 'founding nations'. Canadians are largely oblivious to it all except when they feel the other group is maligning them or getting some perceived advantage. This is no way to build 'national unity'.

It is therefore no surprise that when politicians use the intemperate language that was used in this brouhaha, the old feelings and grievances were aroused again. Politicians, especially leaders, must be cognizant of these historical tensions and take all needed precautions to not add fuel to the fire.

In following the strategy he did, Harper sacrificed his much sought after breakthrough in Quebec. With the problems the Liberal party faced following the sponsorship scandals in Quebec, Harper worked hard to woo Quebec nationalists away from the Bloc and disgruntled voters away from the Liberals. He had some success in the 2006 election (elected ten MPs in Quebec) and hoped to up that number in the 2008 election. He didn't make gains in 2008. In defending his government from the coalition, he appears to have willingly abandoned that effort and decided to secure his base in English Canada hoping to make gains from his demonizing of the coalition partners. Both the Bloc and the Liberals now stand to make gains in the next election.

With the Liberals deciding to support the Conservative's Jan. 27 budget, the immediate threat of another election so soon after the last one in October, 2008, passed. But it hasn't disappeared. Provided the Liberals follow through with their stated intention to keep a close watch on how well the Conservatives follow through with their proposed measures, there may or may not be an election in a few months. The government has gotten a 'yellow light' and is on 'probation' as Ignatieff phrased it. Having decided to throw a lifeline to Harper, Ignatieff may not find his former coalition partners ready to join him if he decides that the time is ripe to bring down the government. But the calling of the next election is no longer entirely in Harper's hands. When one of them feels the time is ripe to go to the polls, they will find a way to engineer an election.

Was this really a 'national unity crisis' or just an exaggerated clash between leaders and parties? No one should underestimate the fact that strong feelings were again brought to the fore. Every time they are aroused, they reinforce the already deeply and widely felt sense of grievance that activates many in their region or ethnic group. They won't easily return to the closet soon but will linger on waiting for the next episode to draw them out onto centre stage.

Canada did not need these divisive debates and should not have had to contend with them. Recent federal elections clearly demonstrate the deep regional divisions that have developed over time. While the Conservative and Liberal parties have always had parts of the country that strongly supported them, they also had support across the land. They were 'national parties' rather than regional parties. Today a glance at a colour-coded map of any recent federal election would dramatically reveal the badly divided nature of the political system.

National political parties as were known in the past are endangered today by the deep fault lines/cleavages/divisions/fractures that seriously divide the society. Canadians may be in for a long period of minority governments as a result and may have to contend with possible coalitions more frequently. What is clear is that Canada did not need this episode of renewed regional and ethnic tension. Only the future will tell how much they have contributed to the deep divisions that mark Canadian society and its politics. National unity was not well served.

Endnotes

[1] Nancy Macdonald, "Will the West revolt?", *Maclean's*, 3 Dec., 2008, www.Macleans.ca.

[2] Barry Cooper, political scientist, University of Calgary, cited in Nancy Macdonald, "Will the West revolt?", *Maclean's*, 3 Dec., 2008, www.Macleans.ca.

[3] Harry Hiller, *Canadian Society: A Microanalysis*, (Scarborough, ON: Prentice Hall Canada, 1986) 206-233.

[4] Macdonald.

[5] Stephen Harper, *Debates*, House of Commons, 1 Dec., 2008: 456.

[6] Stéphane Dion, *Debates*, House of Commons, 1 Dec., 2008: 456.

[7] Harper, 456.

[8] Gilles Duceppe, *Debates*, House of Commons, 1 Dec., 2008: 457.

[9] Harper, 457.

[10] Harper, *Debates*, House of Commons, 2 Dec., 2008: 528.

[11] Harper, 530.

[12] Dion, 528.

[13] Harper, 528.

[14] Dion, *Debates*, House of Commons, 3 Dec., 2008: 568.

[15] Harper, *Debates*, House of Commons, 3 Dec., 2008: 568.

[16] Harper, 569.

[17] Harper, 569.

[18] Campbell Clark, "Canadian Alliance could hurt Bloc Quebecois, Day won't rule out post election coalition with separatist party to boost conservatism", *Globe and Mail*, 29 July, 2000.

[19] Stockwell Day, *Debates*, House of Commons, 3 Dec., 2008:569.

[20] Pierre Paquette, *Debates*, House of Commons, 3 Dec., 2008: 570.

[21] Lawrence Canon, *Debates*, House of Commons, 3 Dec., 2008: 570.

[22] Dean Del Mastro, *Debates*, House of Commons, 3 Dec., 2008: 570; Arron Wherry, "A lot of fear and anger and hatred", Macleans.ca, 4 Dec., 2008.

[23] Ken Dryden, *Debates*, House of Commons, 3 Dec., 2008: 572.

[24] Arron Wherry, "Dion vs Harper, Crack-up in the Commons", Macleans.ca, 3 Dec., 2008.

[25] Editorial, "Harper's to blame for political crisis", *Toronto Star*, 1 Dec., 2008.

[26] Editorial, "Coalition deserves a chance", *Toronto Star*, 2 Dec., 2008.

[27] Editorial, "Harper invokes Bloc bogeyman", *Toronto Star*, 4 Dec., 2008.

[28] Editorial, "Harper adds fuel to fire", *Toronto Star*, 4 Dec., 2008.

[29] Don Martin, "Harper ditches the olive branch", *National Post*, 4 Dec., 2008.

[30] Brian Laghi, "Harper's attack on Bloc risks alienating Quebec", *Globe and Mail*, 3 Dec., 2008.

[31] Gary Mason, "In the West, deep sense of betrayal", *Globe and Mail*, 3 Dec., 2008.

[32] Editorial, "Harper seeking re-take on economic policies", *Halifax Chronicle Herald*, 4 Dec., 2008.

[33] Editorial, "Harper buying time to wise up", *Halifax Chronicle Herald*, 5 Dec., 2008.

[34] Editorial, "Fanning anger towards Quebec", *Globe and Mail*, 5 Dec., 2008.

[35] Gary Mason, "National unity will pay the price for this partisan bickering", *Globe and Mail*, 3 Dec., 2008.

[36] Ed Broadbent, "Fanning the fires of national disunity", *Globe and Mail*, 5 Dec., 2008.

[37] Rheal Seguin, "Harper boost national sentiment in Quebec", *Globe and Mail*, 5 Dec., 2008.

[38] Don Martin, "It's time for everybody to tone things down", *Calgary Herald*, 5 Dec., 2008.

[39] Editorial, "All quiet on the eastern front – for now", *Calgary Herald*, 5 Dec., 2008.

[40] Barbara Yaffe, "Breathing time comes with a political price", *Vancouver Sun*, 5 Dec., 2008.

[41] Andrew Cohen, "Failures all around", *Ottawa Citizen*, 9 Dec., 2008.

[42] Letters to-the-editor, *Globe and Mail* and Thunder Bay *Chronicle Journal*, 1-10 Dec., 2008.

[43] Gordon Pitt, *Stampede! The Rise of the West and Canada's New Power Elite*, (Toronto: Key Porter Books, 2008) 164.

Chapter 7
The Democratic Deficit

Fewer than half of young Canadians can name the country's first prime minister and only one in four know the date of Confederation, ... " [1]

"If we fail to teach our students Canadian history and contemporary Canadian affairs, fail to teach them the many ways in which Canada is different from our giant culture-and-values exporting neighbour to the south, how can we possibly expect our nation to survive?" [2]

Politics is not front and centre on the minds of most citizens. Other daily affairs take precedence such as family, work and play. In fact, many citizen's regard politics and politicians as a plague that must be endured from time to time, but hopefully not often. But political events or personalities occasionally do command attention from citizens and, to varying degrees, voters get involved. Certainly elections and leadership campaigns are of interest to many as is the kind of political meltdown that breezed into Ottawa at the end of November, 2008. Canadians were transfixed to their newspapers, radios, and televisions to follow the dramatic clash on Parliament Hill. Canadians were engaged in ways not seen for a long time.

As the drama unfolded on the Hill, it became clear that not only were many citizens ill-informed about the parliamentary political system that operated in Canada but that their political leaders were also. The Prime Minister, cabinet ministers and backbench MPs made statements that indicated either a lack of understanding of the political system or a deliberate misrepresentation of the system. Many citizens' views, as stated in letters-to-the-editor in newspapers across the country, also indicated a lack of understanding.

Why was there this confusion and misunderstanding about how the political system is structured and operates? Is this normal and not unusual by comparison with other countries? Is it healthy for Canadian democracy? Can it be improved?

Examples of confusion and misrepresentation

When Prime Minister Stephen Harper stated that the forming of a coalition government was "overturning the results of an election"; was "undemocratic, illegitimate and a betrayal of the country"; and, that "if one wants to be prime minister one gets one's mandate from the Canadian people and not from Quebec separatists", he was misrepresenting the Canadian parliamentary system.

The Canadian parliamentary system is based upon the fundamental principle of 'responsible government' introduced in Canada in 1848-49. This means that 1) 'advisors' (PM and Cabinet Ministers) to the Crown are drawn from the members of the elected legislature; and, 2) all money bills to raise or spend public money must be approved by a majority of members in the House of Commons. These two fundamental principles ensure that the government of the day governs with the 'confidence' of a majority of the elected representatives of the Canadian people. If a government does not have the confidence of a majority of members (usually determined by a vote of confidence), it is required to tender its resignation to the Crown. It is the prerogative of the Crown to decide whether a new government could be formed by another individual or group within the House or whether a new election should be called. The Crown is obligated to consider alternatives when a situation such as this one where there had recently been an election and an alternative government was prepared to assume office.

Democracy in the Canadian parliamentary system is based on regular elections where voters have the opportunity to assess leaders, parties and their policy proposals. Voters vote for a local candidate and through them for party leaders and party policies. If enough candidates from one party wins (currently 155 or more), then there is a majority government. The last three elections (2004, 2006, 2008) did not return a party with a majority of elected members. In each case, a minority parliament was elected. In order to govern, the party called upon to form a government needs to build support from a number of individual members or another party(s) to have majority support and therefore the 'confidence' of the House. Consultation and cooperation is required on the part of the governing party.

When a minority government loses the confidence of a majority in the House, the Prime Minister can request that the Governor General dissolve Parliament and call for a new election. Normally dissolution would be granted. But the Governor General is not bound to follow the advice of her First Minister. The Crown's prerogative powers enable it to consider other alternative possibilities. When unusual circumstances are involved, as in this case, the Governor General is obligated to consider whether there is a reasonable chance of another individual or party being able to form a government that would command a majority in the House.

It follows therefore that the Liberal-NDP coalition, with support from the Bloc, was entirely democratic and not the "seizing of power in a coup d'état worthy of a banana republic". It also follows that, while Canadians elected a larger number of Conservatives than any of the other parties, they elected in good faith the particular members that won in their constituencies.

No matter how much a particular party and its members are disliked, they have been duly elected by legitimate Canadian voters. It is wrong to dismiss them out of hand as 'socialists' or 'separatists' and therefore have no right to participate in the affairs of the House, and, if called upon, to be part of a government. All elected members of the House are legitimate representatives of the citizens in their constituencies. To accuse other MPs of being so tainted, such as Stockwell Day did when he said that his "DNA would never allow me to do a deal, a coalition, with socialists and my heart would never allow me to do a deal with separatists", [3] that they are totally excluded from playing their rightful role, is quite undemocratic.

Finally, when a minister of the crown, John Baird, publically proclaims that "the Conservatives will go over Parliament, over the Governor General and go to the people",[4] he is talking in a very undemocratic way. In fact, it smacks of sedition!!!!

Our political system has placed more emphasis upon party leaders in elections and generally in modern times. It is therefore not completely inappropriate for Harper and Conservatives to say that voters decided in the election who they wanted to govern the country. But it is quite inappropriate to make this the overriding basis to defend the Conservative's claim to be the legitimate government of Canada. Canada does not have a presidential system like their neighbours to the south. There they do vote directly for President as well as many other elected offices including local dog catcher in many cases. Therefore to suggest that Canadian elections are the singular route to becoming prime minister is false and misleading.

Was this a case of misunderstanding the fundamental principles and processes of the system, or, was it a calculated decision designed to bolster the Conservative case and discredit the coalition's case? It is unimaginable that educated, experienced politicians such as Stephen Harper and members of his cabinet would be that unaware of the traditions of parliamentary government. It is unimaginable that they were not properly advised of these traditions by their public servants in the Privy Council Office. It leaves no other explanation than they consciously and deliberately misrepresented the workings of the parliamentary system for their own ends, survival of the government "by all means available".[5]

Examples from the public's statements

The foundations of a democracy rest upon the ability of its citizens to participate knowledgeably in the on-going affairs of the political system. When citizens are not well informed about the nature of politics in general and the workings of their own political system in particular, then leaders and parties that wish to are able to manipulate events and voters perceptions in ways which may not be in the interests of the wider society. Photo-ops and media messaging are two examples of practices employed by leaders and parties to 'influence' public understanding of events, policies and personalities. They use modern marketing techniques to shape the public's perception. In short, the political system is vulnerable to abuse.

Politics is a natural consequence of living with others. Our innate biological differences combine with our diverse situations and experiences to produce a wide variety of ideas and beliefs about how life should be led. Which ideas and beliefs become the dominant ones followed by the group/society? How is it decided which ideas and beliefs will be adopted? Who will implement the ideas and beliefs? All of these questions suggest the need for someone or group to give leadership. In doing so, those who hold an opposite set of ideas and beliefs will likely challenge the dominant group for the right to decide the affairs of the group. This creates the 'struggle for power' that is at the heart of 'politics' for it is the power or ability to influence or control people, objects and situations in ways favourable to one's own interests that is at the heart of 'politics'. It therefore follows that politics is present in everything we do and that politics at the higher levels of government are central to which ideas and beliefs will guide the society.[6]

This struggle for power is at the core of 'politics' and while it is often referred to as a 'game', it is a deadly serious game. History reveals the deadly nature of this struggle in the tales of war and intrigue that litter popular literature and today's mass media. The 'normal' approach taken by competing political forces is to resort to physical violence to determine who will hold political power. This is why the real benefit of a working democratic system is that it removes the literally deadly part from the 'game' and puts in place the rule of law and means by which the issues of the day can be resolved peacefully.

Letters-to-the-editor and phone-in calls to radio stations have been of a mixed nature. Some have demonstrated a general knowledge of how the political system operates but some have demonstrated an emotional or ill-informed understanding. The following are some examples that capture both the emotional and ill-informed understanding.

"*They are all a bunch of nitwits!*"

"*This ridiculous, immature game-playing has to stop. These 'leaders' are being paid to run the country but are doing nothing other than fighting among themselves with our money as their means.*"

"*She broke the parliamentary process by saying the opposition parties have no voice. She should have recalled Parliament and have the Tory government face a non-confidence vote.*"

"*I hope Mr. Dion stays on as Liberal leader and a federal election is called. I hope that the Conservatives slaughter them. If they have any guts, let them run as a coalition. But the cowards won't.*"

"*She broke the parliamentary process [decision to prorogue parliament] by saying the opposition parties have no voice. She should have recalled Parliament and have the Tory government face a non-confidence vote.*"

"*Canadians normally vote with the assumption that the party winning the most seats will govern with its leader as prime minister. This new coalition is inadvertently trying to prove that, with the election over, it really doesn't make any difference what ordinary Canadians thought.*"

"*The coalition between the left and the Bloc is clearly an attack on the West. There was a time when I voted Liberal federally, but if this coalition seizes power from our rightfully elected government, it will be the saddest day in Canadian history.*"

"*OK, let me see if I get this right. Canada had an election, Canadians freely voted as to who they want to run this great country and now what – we have a bunch of bullies who didn't get their way and have now grouped together to gang up on the Canadian people and force them into doing things their way. Wow! Never in my life have I been ashamed to say I am Canadian until now.*"

Generally, individual citizens are not actively involved in the political system other than casting their vote at election time. They may pay some attention to public affairs and may from time to time become more active. The central question is where and from whom do they get their information about politics and the political system?

This begs the question of how well citizens are introduced to politics and whether more could be done. Since a democracy, unlike an authoritarian or dictatorship system, is founded on the principle that individuals have the right to participate in deciding who governs them and which policies they will support, it is essential that the citizens be knowledgeable about the workings of their political system. Yes, Canadians have varying degrees of knowledge about politics and their political system but many have only a rudimentary knowledge that does not serve them or the country well. Why is this so?

Influences on citizen's knowledge about the society and political system [7]

Citizens are first introduced to politics and their politicians through their family. If they have parents who are relatively knowledgeable and take an interest in the day-to-day politics of the society, then they will likely develop a base of knowledge and an interest in political affairs. On the other hand, if one's parents have little understanding and consider politics and politicians as a bunch of crooks and working for other people's interests, then they will probably be turned off and will tune out. We learn a great deal about authority and authority figures from our family experiences.

Next to have an influence on a citizen's interest and understanding of the political system is the educational system. Schools across the country come under provincial jurisdiction and therefore reflect the importance each province places on having political studies in the curriculum. Often it is part of the study of Canadian history. As Andrew Cohen recently noted in his book *The Unfinished Canadian*, "On the whole, the fact is that most provinces do not teach Canadian history. ... the Dominion Institute has found that only three provinces require high school students to study Canadian history." [8] As a consequence, study after study reveals how utterly unaware Canadians are since most citizens have but a high school diploma.

In 1975, Mel Hurtig published a report based on a survey he had conducted among senior high school students. It was titled *Never Heard of Them ... They Must Be Canadian*. [9] Without going into details, he was 'stunned and dismayed' by the ignorance displayed by students across the country. Since then there have been many other such surveys testing the general knowledge of students and citizens at large and the results are all similar. Canadians have an appalling knowledge of who they are, where they come from, and where they are heading. Fundamental to this ignorance is the failure of our school systems to include a reasonable amount of the country's history in the curriculum. That history would include the social, economic, cultural, geographic and political features and development of the country.

Anything less than a good basic introduction to Canadian society, including its political traditions and system, is an abdication of educational leadership. If Canada has a weak civic culture, it can be directly attributed to this failure of the schools to teach future citizens about their society.

Finally, what part do the media have in this failure to develop a civic culture and an awareness of the parliamentary political system? The media, especially television today, is where most citizens learn about events and personalities happening in their community, province, country and the world. The media are intermediaries who select and interpret what is happening every time they present the day's stories. They are critical to shaping the understandings citizens develop of the world around them.

Today, in Canada, the media is more of a vehicle for importing American events and personalities into Canada. One only has to check program line-ups for the national television networks to see the extent of exposure to American life, values and beliefs paraded before Canadians. Private radio is little better. It is overwhelming!!!! The same is true for movies, magazines and other sports and entertainment shows. The private networks, CTV and Global, are the worst culprits. Their programming schedules, aside from news programs, are loaded with American shows making them prime purveyors of American events, behaviors and values.

Standing apart from the private, commercial networks is the public broadcaster, the Canadian Broadcasting Corporation (CBC/Radio Canada). It provides extensive Canadian content on all its various systems and is to be commended for this. But, Canadians are generally attracted to American shows. Many have developed a mind-set that consistently rejects Canadian produced materials as 'inferior' and 'boring'. Having been raised on American movies, music, radio and television, Canadians have become accustomed to the glitz and glitter of American material and find the Canadian product lacking. Without big budgets and marketing promotions, Canadian productions appear pale by comparison. The end result has been a citizenry that knows little of its own experience and prefers that of another society. A classic example is the fall 2008 release of the film Passchendaelle. Here was a major Canadian production starring well-known Canadians in a quintessential Canadian war story. It received some attention but it soon faded into distant memory. Given this reality, it is amazing then that Canadians have as much understanding and interest in Canadian affairs as they do. This hardly bodes well for Canadian society and democracy.

Another factor that undermines the ability of citizen's to better comprehend political events is the tidbit nature of reporting the news. There is an information overload due to the constant barrage of 'up-to-the-minute' news reporting. Most citizens aren't able to pull all the snippets of information into a comprehensive overview of the event and put it into a wider context. While there are programs on both the public and private networks that try to do this, they don't attract the larger audiences that other entertainment programs are able to attract.

Then there is the question of media perspective. Due to the nature of the medium, Canada's media are controlled by an increasingly small number of owners. As private businesses, owned and operated by businessmen, they tend to take a pro free enterprise view of public affairs and the role of government. They aren't particularly supportive of active government intervention in the economy, except of course when it is advantageous to their interests. Nor are they very supportive of an active social policy regarding health care, social assistance, social housing and minority rights. As members of the upper middle and upper class, they reflect the interests of their class. This puts them in opposition to an interventionist government approach to governing society. As members of the business elite, the owners set the tone for coverage and reporting of the news. In this they tend to favour a conservative approach to government and public services. "You have a bit of a problem here, [said a European diplomat]. Your media are not representative of your people, your values. So many of the political commentators are right of centre ... while Canadians themselves are in the moderate middle. There's a disconnect." [10] For the most part, this is done subtly rather than directly.

This translates into political perspectives that express themselves in the staff that is hired to run the various businesses. Some editorial writers and political commentators have identifiable perspectives on public issues, politicians and political parties. For example, the **National Post** is right of centre in its political leanings whereas the **Toronto Star** is regarded as one of the few centre-left papers left in the country. The **Calgary Herald** has a strong Albertan, Western and pro-business emphasis. As one national political commentator recently said while commenting on a day's events in Ottawa, "I better not get too liberal here, it won't sit well with my newspaper'.

If a person is regularly exposed to a particular news source, they come under the influence of that source and its political perspective. They come to see the world from that perspective. In this way, the media influences citizen's knowledge and understanding of the political system and events and, in doing so, influences their feelings.

Given the vast amount of news material that the media has to process, it is a wonder that they do the quality job they manage to do each day. From a citizen's perspective and from a democratic perspective, the wider the exposure to different media sources, the better informed a citizen should be. Exposure to different points of view allows citizens to better understand the thinking of others who may not share their take on events and personalities. Democracy is dependent upon the working through and tolerating of differences rather than the division of society into watertight political enclaves.

Canada does have a 'democratic deficit'. The knowledge and understanding of Canada's experience as a nation and its politics and the political system is inadequate. Our educational and media institutions could do more to better prepare citizens for participation in the political life of the country. Decisions in the past do not suggest that there will be much change in the future to overcome this deficit. Canada and Canadians will continue to be the worse off for it.

Endnotes

[1] Caroline Alphonso, "Canadians flunking history lesson", *Globe and Mail*, 9 Nov., 2008.

[2] Mel Hurtig, "Never Heard of Them…They Must Be Canadian", (Toronto: Books for Canadian Education, 1975).

[3] Stockwell Day, *Debates*, House of Commons, 3 Dec., 2008: 569.

[4] John Baird, CBC News, 29 Nov., 2008.

[5] *Debates*, House of Commons, 2 Dec., 2008; Editorial, "Harper adds fuel to fire", *Toronto Star*,

[6] Dec., 2008; Barbara Yaffe, "A Nation Divided", *Vancouver Sun*, 4 Dec., 2008; Brian Laghi, Steven Chase, Daniel LeBlanc, "Harper plays patriot game", *Globe and Mail*, 5 Dec., 2008.

[7] Thomas Joseph, *The Essentials of Canadian Politics and Government*, (Scarborough: Pearson, 2001) Ch. – The Nature of Politics: 3-30.

[8] Joseph.

[9] Andrew Cohen, *The Unfinished Canadian*, (Toronto: McClelland and Stewart, 2007) 59.

[10] Hurtig.

[11] Lawrence Martin, Its not Canadians who've gone to the right…just their media", *Globe and Mail*, 23 Jan., 2003.

[12] Martin.

Chapter 8
Stephen Harper's Political Beliefs

"We must continue to be guided by our founding vision of conservatism."
... We will never abandon our principles and policies."
Stephen Harper [1]

"He's a true-believing conservative. ... he really does believe in minimal
government, although he's shrewd enough to know he can't do too much
about this until he's won a majority." [2]

From the very beginning of Stephen Harper's ascendance to the
leadership of the Canadian Alliance Party and eventually to the office
of Prime Minister, Canadians have pondered the question of "who
really is this man?"

Early on in his leadership of the party and then the government, he
visibly tried to present an altered version of himself to Canadians. This
only served to create more uncertainty among Canadians. Questions

remained: what are the man's essential characteristics and what 'vision' does he have for Canadian society?

As chief policy officer for the Reform Party (1987-91), he crafted statements that denounced the wishy-washy, mushy centralist tendencies of the Progressive Conservative Party and condemned efforts to accommodate Quebec as 'appeasement'. But as Prime Minister, he has moved towards the 'mushy' centre on many issues and openly courted Quebec and its nationalists.

As a Reform MP (1993-97), he advocated for a 'decentralized' federalism that would respect provincial jurisdiction under the constitution. In 2001, he co-signed a letter urging Alberta to build a 'firewall' around itself by getting out of the Canada Health Act and create its own pension plan. This would free the province from a 'hostile' federal government. As Prime Minister, he has kept this view of federal-provincial relations in his management of the government.

As Vice-President and then President of the National Citizen's Coalition (1997-2002), he was a prominent opponent of the Calgary Declaration on national unity (1997) drafted by nine premiers to appeal to moderate Quebec nationalists. He described it as an 'appeasement of separatists'. But as Prime Minister, he has taken steps to woo Quebec nationalists, even having the Quebecois people recognized as a 'nation'.

In his capacity as president of the NCC, he delivered a controversial speech to the conservative American think tank, the Council for National Policy, in which he described Canada as "a Northern European welfare state in the worst sense of the term, and very proud of it" and "the NDP [New Democratic Party] is kind of proof that the Devil lives and interferes in the affairs of men." [3] As Prime Minister, he cancelled programs initiated by the previous Martin Liberal government – Aboriginal and child care – and held the line on others.

As leader of the opposition, Harper roundly criticized Liberal government practices as misguided and corrupt. He promised changes to clean up government and immediately implemented accountability legislation as promised in the election. But from the moment of becoming Prime Minister, he frequently abandoned those changes and conducted business no differently than previous governments.

He continues to follow this pattern to this day of 'talking the talk but not walking the walk.' Is he a ferocious partisan in the guise of a cuddly 'blue sweater'? Is he an ideological right-winger as some believe, or, is he a pragmatic practitioner of the art of politics? Is he a politician seeking to govern in the interests of Canadians or is he bent upon converting by stealth Canada into a 'truly conservative' society?

So the question remains, '**who** *really* **is Stephen Harper?**'

Stephen Harper's Formative Years: [4]

1. He was born and raised in Toronto. His father was an accountant at Imperial Oil and the family lived in a white, middle-class neighbourhood – Leaside then Central Etobicoke. He attended Northlea Public School in Leaside. Later, he attended John G. Althouse Middle School and Riverview Collegiate Institute, both in Central Etobicoke, Ontario. He was an excellent student graduating in 1978 at the top of his class with a 95.7% average earning his school's gold medal. His admiration for Pierre Trudeau led him to join the Young Liberals student club a friend had formed. He was a member of Richview's *Reach for the Top* team.

2. He then enrolled at the University of Toronto but dropped out after two months. He moved west to Edmonton and got work in the mailroom at Imperial Oil. Later he moved up to work on the company's computer systems.

3. He soon enrolled in the University of Calgary graduating with a BA (1985). As a student, he immersed himself in the Canadian equivalent of the U.S. Young Republicans (calling themselves 'Tiny Tories') and became an avid fan of intellectual conservative William F. Buckley and his weekly television debate show "Firing Line". As a graduate student, he often debated free-market theory and political theory with fellow students. The growing popularity of Margaret Thatcher in Britain and Ronald Reagan in the U.S. made him wonder why their brand of 'strident conservatism' was not catching on in Canada. The shift from being a 'Trudeau Liberal' to a 'libertarian' conservative was underway.

4. He married Laureen Tetsky in 1993. They have 2 children.

Political Activism: [5]

1. When Trudeau brought in the National Energy Program (NEP) in 1980, his admiration for Trudeau ended. As well, the Keynesian approach to economics – a belief that activist governments could and should macro-manage the economy by regulating spending and influencing demand – was coming under more and more criticism. This viewpoint held that it was the 'large, postwar, big-spending state [that] was the problem'. For Harper, his increasingly free-market economics beliefs, combined with his exposure to Western Canadian alienation from Central Canada and Ottawa encouraged him to join the Progressive Conservative Party.

2. While a student at the U. of Calgary, he worked to elect Jim Hawkes, the Progressive Conservative candidate in Calgary West in the 1984 federal election. In 1985, he went to work for Hawkes as chief legislative aide in Ottawa.

3. After a year and disillusioned with the Mulroney Progressive Conservative government and Ottawa political power games, he returned to Calgary and enrolled in a master of economics program at the U. of Calgary. He graduated in 1991. There he immersed himself in the works and thinking of Adam Smith and Friedrich Hayek. He developed a strong belief in the workings of a free- market economy and the neo-conservative beliefs being espoused by Margaret Thatcher in Britain and Ronald Reagan in the United States.

4. Believing that the existing parties couldn't be reformed, he became interested in the new political movement being promoted by Preston Manning. This movement became the Reform Party of Canada. Manning invited him to give a speech at Reform's 1987 founding convention in Winnipeg. He then became the Party's Chief Policy Officer and a major influence on the 1988 election platform. He is credited with the Party's campaign slogan "The West wants in!".

5. When Deborah Grey became the first Reform MP in 1989, he accompanied her to Ottawa to help write her speeches. He continued to be Reform's chief policy officer.

6. In 1988, he ran unsuccessfully for Parliament. In 1993, he ran again and won this time defeating his earlier boss, Tory Jim Hawkes, in Calgary West. He was seen as one of the party's bright lights with

prospects for a bright future. But again he became dissatisfied with politics in Ottawa and the leadership of Preston Manning. Specifically, he disagreed with Manning's handling of the national unity debate. In early 1997, he left Parliament and resigned his seat as an MP.

7. He moved over to the National Citizen's Coalition (NCC) first as vice-president then as President. The NCC "is a non-profit corporation, independent of all political parties … [with] thousands of members from across the country that share in the belief of 'More freedom through less government'." [6] While there, he spoke out in defence of taxpayer's rights; penned articles calling official bilingualism 'the god that failed'; criticized federal politicians for their 'appeasement' of Quebec separatists; and fought against limits on third-party election campaign spending.

8. When Manning transformed the Reform Party into the Canadian Alliance Party in 2000 and Stockwell Day became its leader, he again considered becoming actively involved. On March 20, 2002 he defeated Day and assumed leadership of "a party that was battered, broke, and discredited." [7] In June 2002, he won the federal constituency of Calgary Southwest. He soon set about to 'unite the right'.

9. In October 2003, he successfully concluded a merging of the Canadian Alliance with the Progressive Conservative Party, then led by Peter MacKay. In March 2004, he defeated Belinda Stronach and Tony Clement and became the first leader of the new Conservative Party of Canada.

10. In the 2004 federal election, the Conservative Party made gains in Ontario and became the Official Opposition. But efforts to make a breakthrough in Quebec failed. Paul Martin and the Liberals were returned with a minority government.

11. In the 2006 election, Harper was able to capitalize on the 'sponsorship scandal' that hounded the Liberals, and Paul Martin's weak performance in the campaign. The Conservatives won a minority Government .

12. In the 2008 election, Harper defeated the Liberals under their new leader, Stéphane Dion. While the party increased its number of seats from 124 to 144, it again fell short of a majority government.

Media characterizations of Stephen Harper

Before Stephen Harper became Prime Minister, his personal and political character was closely scrutinized. The media and Canadians wanted to know just who this new party leader was and what his political views were. Was he a neo-conservative right-winger as some claimed or a moderate conservative? Would he be able to unite and moderate the fractious right-of-centre factions that had plagued conservatism and the Reform Party since the mid-1980's? What was he '*really*' like?

When Harper first assumed the Canadian Alliance's leadership on March 20, 2002, he was still a relatively unknown personality. The **Ottawa Citizen** captured this with the headline "Harper unknown to most Canadians".[8] In the media coverage following his victory, he was portrayed as:

- 'fluently bilingual'

- ' polished, cerebral and able to articulate ideas in French or English'

- 'small 'c' conservative policy has consumed much of his adult life. It dominates his thoughts, his reading, his jokes.

- 'a formidable strategic thinker'; 'a gifted strategist'

- 'a strong ideologue focused on a specific set of principles'

- 'intelligent, articulate and surprisingly charming'

- 'smart…serious…humourless'

- 'He is bilingual, telegenic, and that unusual combination, a thinker who does things'

- 'methodical'

- 'An intensely private man, … abhors stunts, photo-ops and what he calls "circus behavior" to gain public attention.'

- 'criticized for being inflexible in his views'

- 'reputation for petulance – someone inclined to retreat into churlish snits when things don't go his way'

- 'Frontline politics doesn't come easily … a policy wonk who is more comfortable in the company of economic textbooks and flow charts than in a roomful of potential voters'

- 'a policy wonk and research guy'

- 'too intelligent, too bookish, too wonkish and lacking fire in the belly'

- 'a man who appears to dislike public life'

- 'a guy more wedded to purity than pragmatism'

- '[he] practices a florid partisanship reminiscent of Brian Mulroney. The good thing and the bad thing about Harper is that he appears to believe every word of it, has for a very long time, and will not easily add water to his whine.'

- 'a cerebral policy wonk not willing to bow to populist sentiment'

It is obvious from the above descriptions of Stephen Harper that he has many commendable traits but that there were others that raised concerns about his suitability to hold high public office. It was also obvious that a 'make-over' was needed if Harper and the Conservatives were going to be able to win the majority government that they cherished. From the very start of winning the Alliance leadership, the campaign to 'soften' the hard edges of his persona began. The **Globe & Mail** ran an article "Makeover tip for the earnest young man from Alberta: Look warm and caring".[9] A number of image consultants offered suggestions – cut the hair, lose the part and chop the bangs; fix the 'helmet hair' so that it moves more; 'add a little salsa to loosen up his straight-laced demeanour'; he may be smart but he plays 'dull and boring', even 'aloof, sullen and cool' so become more 'warm and fuzzy'; and, 'bounce your eyebrows' so as to look animated when talking'.

Ever since, Stephen Harper has tried a variety of ways to soften his image, the latest effort being in the 2008 election where he frequently appeared wearing a light blue sweater and an open necked shirt. When Harper was first elected to Parliament as a Reform Party MP (1993), he went public with criticisms of Preston "Manning's use of a personal expense account provided by the ... party for its leader. Manning had used some of the money to enhance his wardrobe and appearance. (As Prime Minister, Harper has had a make-up artist and image consultant, apparently on the public payroll.)" [10] If Harper felt it was inappropriate for Manning to use party funds for this purpose, then why does he feel it appropriate for him to use public funds to do so now that he is prime minister?

When Harper led the Conservative Party to Official Opposition status in the 2004 election, he had become better known to Canadians but questions remained as to his 'real' political beliefs and agenda for the country. Many Canadians wondered how deeply he was committed to the Reform agenda that he had been so instrumental in writing. Many wondered about the statements he had made as spokesman for the National Citizens Coalition. Both Reform and the NCC were regarded as 'far right' in their positions on tax reduction, deficits, bilingualism, Quebec, social and health programs and the role of government generally. Would he continue to espouse these views as leader and in office if he were to win an election? The Liberals and NDP frequently played upon this uncertainty portraying Harper and the Conservatives as being 'scary' neo-conservatives having a 'hidden agenda' that would emerge only after the Conservatives won a majority government.

When Harper's Conservatives replaced the Liberals in January 2006 with a minority government of their own, Canadians had opted for the only viable alternative available. The Liberals had been in power since 1993 and were fending off accusations of corruption surrounding their handling of the sponsorship program in Quebec. The Gomery Commission's first report in November exposed criminal corruption by some Liberal organizers in Quebec and a 'culture of entitlement' in the Liberal party. Many Canadians were angered to learn of these activities and abandoned the Liberal party. When the RCMP announced late in the campaign that it was investigating the Finance Minister for income trust tax change violations, Liberal support in the polls declined further. Added to these problems was the weak performance of Liberal leader Paul Martin. When *The Economist* magazine labeled Martin as 'Mr. Dithers',[11] the contrasting clear and concise style of Stephen Harper was appealing for many voters. Liberal attempts to again raise the specter of a Conservative 'hidden agenda' failed because they did little more than make the charge but added no details. Canadians weren't yet ready to fully embrace the Conservatives but they had become more comfortable with Stephen Harper.

While the media acknowledged a number of strengths and accomplishments in the first Harper minority government, they nonetheless still characterized him in largely negative terms. Political commentators captured this as illustrated in the following observations.

- "The new 'positive' Stephen Harper played the Goodale news [RCMP investigations of possible income trust violations] exactly right. … If he had gone on a harangue, it would have reinforced his too negative image, which is already a problem for him. … Harper has been fighting the angry-right-wing-guy factor throughout the campaign." [12]

- "the clue to his behaviour may be that Harper really wishes that he were president of Canada. … Harper takes the U.S. presidency as his model, where the president is both head of government and head of state, and has a power and deference unknown and inappropriate to parliamentary governments.' …

  [again showing his preference for the American approach of invoking the deity and always assuming that God is on one's side] 'Harper ended many of his early public speeches with a "God bless Canada" invocation" [13]

- "…it's becoming increasingly clear that we have undergone the most radical political change in decades … Harper is a conservative Conservative. That doesn't mean he's a raving neo-con. It does mean he's a true-believing conservative. … We won't know Harper's full agenda until after the next election, when and if he wins a majority.' …

  There's a steeliness about him we aren't accustomed to in our leaders. … And an unrestrained arrogance …" [14]

- "he has so far exhibited a sure-footedness that sets him apart from many of the more experienced hands who reached higher office over the past decade. ... After three months in office, he is the most popular federalist politician in Quebec. As those who have covered Harper for a while now, it is an acquired rather than a natural skill and a sign of his capacity to grow in office." [15]

- "Three times this week, he showed that he will not compromise, that he will have things his way or not at all. ... Sometimes when he refuses to budge, he looks smart and tough. At other times, though, you have to wonder whether he is making decisions based on tactical considerations or is driven by a reflexive cussedness. ...

  [When the Commons rejected his nominee to head a new committee, Harper dropped the idea of an appointments committee.], Mr. Harper reacted with anger. ... [he] looks like a schoolboy who takes his ball and goes home when the other boys won't play by his rules.

  When politics really connected with the public this week, Mr. Harper looked tough, not petulant." [16]

- "But the purpose of this exercise was not to have a considered debate on Afghanistan. Harper simply wanted to embarrass the Liberals... As a partisan ploy, it succeeded. As a contribution to public policy-making, it was a cynical failure. We have a right to expect more from a man who wants us to give him a majority government." [17]

- "... Canadians are becoming more comfortable with Harper. ... People are taking a look and they kind of like what they see. They do see him as a breath of fresh air and a significant change from the previous administration. ... In its first 100 days, Harper's government has surprised many with its unconventional, but disciplined approach to power." [18]

- "But Harper holding Parliament in contempt is a legitimate public concern – and he does. And it will worsen. In just three days this week, there have been three examples of Harper's churlish disregard for a democratic institution he repeatedly pretended to value during his stint in official Opposition. ... We witnessed the return of the angry Albertan, the bitter and hard-done-by personality his image-enhancers thought they'd licked into likeable submission during the last election campaign. ...

From afar, Harper might look decisive and principled. Up close, he looks angry, unparliamentary and, if he persists in scrumming on stairs instead of running up them, chunky." [19]

- "There are things even the most authoritarian prime minister can't control. ... There's an obvious parable here for a prime minister whose control-freak tendencies are raising even supporter's eyebrows: Unpredictable events unfold while politicians conspire over perfect plans. ...

  Those Machiavellian manoeuvres, ... foster a doubt. Is Harper smart, or is he too smart by half? ... Yes, Conservatives won the last election and Harper continues to impress with a fast climb up a steep learning curve. But he could easily spook voters by treating Parliament as a prop and the mini-universe around him as a clockwork toy." [20]

- "Stephen Harper says journalists on Parliament Hill are biased against his government so he'll be avoiding them. ... One prominent media analyst said Wednesday the prime minister was being paranoid..." [21]

- "Stephen Harper's mistake – it may well turn out not to be fatal but it most definitely is serious – is to think he can get away with governing as if his single most important job is to get himself a majority. ... Harper's objective was, of course, to improve his future electoral prospects ... [in reference to the appointments of Liberal David Emerson to cabinet, party organizer Michael Fortier to the Senate, and, former defence lobbyist Gordon Connor as Minister of Defence] ... So much for all that stuff about integrity and accountability." [22]

In the aftermath of the October 14, 2008, federal election, the media's characterization of Stephen Harper had changed little.

- "...Stephen Harper has definitively emerged as the most polarizing figure Canada has seen in almost two decades, eliciting negative emotions of a visceral strength not registered on the federal political scale since Brian Mulroney. ... What makes the phenomenon striking is that it is so uniquely personal. ... Harper and his brain trust seem to equate meanness with leadership." [23]

- "Our work has only begun and we will have to be both tough and pragmatic, not unrealistic or ideological, in dealing with the complex challenges before us." That, surely, isn't the same Harper who, during a recess from federal politics, led the uncompromising National Citizen's Coalition or once advised Alberta to build firewalls against an intrusive Ottawa." [24]

- "[Evident in the Throne Speech's bleak assessment of the immediate future] ... is the Prime Minister's commitment to suspend the politics of division in favour of partnership. That [is a] seismic shift in the way Conservatives have conducted Canada's business since taking power in 2006 ...". [25]

When viewed as a whole, the above descriptions and comments about Stephen Harper are of a mixed bag. On the one hand, they recognize his intelligence, strategic thinking abilities, discipline, decisiveness, sure-footedness, capacity to grow in office, and 'a surprising air of maturity and confidence'.

On the other hand, they continue to portray a person who exhibits traits considered immature, petulant, arrogant, excessively partisan, "can't resist the urge to point fingers...digs like these are needless and damaging ... taking cheap shots", "a leader obsessed with destroying opponents couldn't forego a hazardous lunge at the jugular", "his voice dripping with scorn", "Harper demonstrated his tin ear again", "Regrettably, Harper's conciliatory tone proved an aberration at best and, at worst and most likely, a sham and a crass political ploy."

Canadians have sensed both these positive and negative character traits in Stephen Harper and while turning to him and the Conservative Party in both 2006 and 2008, are not yet ready to give him the majority government that is said he desperately seeks. Both minority government victories in large part came because of weak Liberal leaders and their poorly organized election campaigns. If given a reasonable alternative, will many Canadians abandon Stephen Harper and the Conservatives?

Sources of Stephen Harper's political views

Much has been made of the 'conservative' beliefs of Stephen Harper. But equally, there seems to be considerable uncertainty as to just what kind of a conservative he is. He began as a 'progressive' conservative but became disillusioned with it's seeming lack of fundamental principles and inability to follow sound fiscal practices. It was 'too mushy centrist' for his liking. He embraced the Reform Party and was an important contributor to its principles and policies. While Harper frequently encouraged moderation, many Canadians considered Reform's policies "extreme, on the fringe, right wing, and potentially racist and separatist." [26] When Harper sought the leadership of the Canadian Alliance Party, he was described as a 'libertarian' conservative by various observers. As well, during the leadership campaign, he spoke encouragingly of 'social conservatism'. Others have described him as a 'neo-conservative'. Stephen Harper is all of these variations of conservatism yet likely none of them exclusively.

Putting a defining label on any politician may be a mugs game as any politician worth their salt has to 'play' to many audiences in order to gain the support needed to win office. But just as a politician must emphasize different 'shades' of their party's beliefs and policies depending upon the issue, the audience and the times, the influences that shaped Stephen Harper's conservative beliefs have come from a variety of sources and express themselves in different 'shadings' at different times. Nonetheless, given the various individuals and groups that Stephen Harper has been associated with, a clearer understanding of his conservatism can be identified. He unquestionably is a conservative the likes of which Canadians have not had to contend with for a very long time.

Influence of William F. Buckley, Jr.

Early on Mr. Harper was attracted to the ideas and policies expressed by American conservative William F. Buckley, Jr. Buckley's advocacy of conservative views began with his founding of the **National Review** magazine in 1955. He had become aggravated by the liberal policies of the Eisenhower administration. Over the years he was able to fuse traditional American conservatism with laissez-faire economics and vociferous anti-communism. He was 'the preeminent voice of American conservatism' when Stephen Harper began to follow his *Firing Line* television show (1966-1999).

Influence of Ronald Reagan and Margaret Thatcher's 'neo-conservatism'

The 'neo-conservatism' of Reagan and Thatcher coincided with a growing desire to reduce the size and role of government in citizen's daily lives, reduce state intervention in the social and economic affairs of society, increase support for free markets and entrepreneurialism, follow monetarist economic policies, privatize government services and de-regulate business activities, opposition to unionism, and, reduce the size of the welfare state. As Andrew Kopkind expressed in a November 3, 1984 article in **The Nation**, under Reaganism "the first targets of choice are clear: all those liberal institutions that have defined and shaped American culture for fifty years or more – the press, the churches, unions, academia, local public education, urban government, philanthropic foundations, the artistic establishment, Hollywood, publishing, Federal service, the liberal professions and their organizations. They will come under increasing pressure to redirect their orientation along lines that have already been drawn, to change their social roles, to reassess their values. Even the term 'liberal' has been dropped from political discourse. A major ideological conflict is underway." [27] Philip Resnick expressed similar thoughts when he wrote that Thatcher and Reagan's victories "unleashed a frontal attack on government spending and social priorities. It placed some of the familiar values of western society, such as equality and social justice, into jeopardy. It entailed a re-definition of the relationship between private and public goods." [28]

Both Thatcher and Reagan came to power at a time when their respective countries were experiencing serious self-doubt. Britain's economy and standing in the world was in decline while the United States was reeling from defeat in Vietnam and the recent hostage taking and occupation of the U.S. embassy in Tehran, Iran. Each provided strong leadership and set about to change the course of social and economic practices in their respective countries. Kopkind noted that 'Reaganism lack[ed] sharp ideological definition and programmatic coherence." Milton Friedman, prominent American economic monetarist, once said that most "people do not recognize that Margaret Thatcher is not in terms of belief a Tory. She is a nineteenth-century Liberal." [29]

Influence of Friedrich Hayek

Another important influence upon Stephen Harper was the writings of Friedrich Hayek, an Austrian economist who many consider one of the most important economists and political philosophers of the twentieth century. He strongly presented the case for classical liberalism and free-market capitalism against socialist and collectivist thought. Thatcher was an 'outspoken *devotee* of Hayek's writings' while Reagan was advised at times by followers of Hayek.

By the time Stephen Harper began working with the Progressive Conservative Party in Canada, he was already deeply immersed in the ideologically driven conservatism of the times. Reaganism and Thatcherism were ascendant political personalities and prescriptions for governing society. Harper's experience with conservatism in Canada had both disturbed him and puzzled him. Why was there no equivalent resurgence of a 'neo-conservative' movement in Canada?

Influence of Preston Manning and the Reform Party

Disillusioned with the Progressive Conservative Party under Brian Mulroney, he turned to the new political movement and party being created by Preston Manning. Manning brought him in as Reform's Chief Policy Officer. In this capacity he played a significant role in shaping the party's Principles and Policies *Blue Book*. The *Blue Book* emphasized a variety of 'reforms' suggesting it was following in "the 'reform tradition' of Canadian politics." [30] This linkage to the reform movement in the 1840's (advocated for democratic and responsible government and the removal of the privileges and power of the old Family Compact and Chateau Clique) is a bit misleading. Yes, Reform advocated change, and yes, some of those changes would extend greater individual freedom and independence from government.

But its proposals were a frontal assault on the existing approaches and practices of government as they had developed since WW II. Reform wanted 'a united Canada that included Quebec' but only if Quebec would accept that it was but one of 10 equal provinces, drop the idea of Canada as a partnership between the two founding nations of French and English, give up any claims to 'special status' and commit to freedom of expression in its language policy. Another example concerned social policy. Reformers acknowledged societies collective "responsibility to care and provide for the basic needs of people unable to care and provide for themselves." [31] But they believed that families, charities and community groups should do the job rather than governments. They did not believe in universal social programs. Instead programs should be targeted to those who need help. EI benefits should not be different across the country regardless of the differing regional unemployment rates. They would keep Medicare but would turn it over to the provinces who could each decide whether to impose user fees, allow doctors to extra-bill their patients or allow a two-tiered system. Immigration would be tailored to admitting those who had the skills needed by Canada and who could adjust easily and independently to Canadian society. Those needing assistance with language instruction, job training or social services would be discouraged. Closer relations with the United States would be encouraged including a realigning of Canadian industrial, tax, transportation and fiscal and monetary policy with that of the United States. Bilingualism would be restricted to the federal institutions of Parliament, Supreme Court and critical federal services where need is sufficient to warrant provision of minority services on a cost-effective basis. With regard to multiculturalism, the Reform Party would do away with the department of multiculturalism, end all funding for multicultural programs and encourage immigrants to integrate into Canadian society. Efforts to preserve a group's cultural heritage would be dependent upon the group and financed by the group. On questions of Aboriginal affairs, the Reform Party would move to replace the Department of Indian Affairs with Aboriginal managed agencies accountable to Ottawa. The preservation of Aboriginal cultural heritage would be similar to that for other cultural groups, that is, they would be free to do so but at their own expense. Finally, and perhaps telling a great deal about the party and its supporters, the Reform Party would not permit changes to the dress code of the RCMP due to 'religious or ethnic reasons.'

As the above strongly indicates, Reform clearly stood in opposition to much of what Canada had become after WW II. By challenging and rejecting many of those 'socially progressive' changes, Reform was capturing and expressing the conservative feelings of many dissatisfied and alienated citizens particularly in the West but also in other parts of the country. Manning's strategy was to give voice to the irritants that various citizens had and 'ride these successive waves' to political power. Perhaps these supporters understood the larger political agenda that Manning and Reform wished to implement but perhaps not. Supporters of Reform were 'conservative' in that they wished to return to an earlier time when society was not so complicated and diverse. Reform's agenda would have dramatically changed the nature and character of Canadian society.

Essentially, Reform policies reflected a deep unhappiness with the way society had developed since the 1960's – the expanded size of government and government intervention in the social and economic affairs of society. It was an unhappiness with the 'sexual revolution', the counter-culture morality and behaviour of youth, the growth of government affirmative action programs, and the increasing efforts of federal Liberal and NDP provincial governments to change the traditional social institutions of the family, church, schools, class system, and business market. It was a rejection of the rationale for this expanded role of government based on the recognition that, through no fault of their own, many individuals and groups did not have a fair opportunity to develop their abilities and compete in the society (for example, access to higher education, access to needed medical care and access to legal assistance), and, that there were aspects of the free market that needed regulation and supervision (for example, workplace safety and environmental standards). Reform policies sought to reverse those changes or, at the least, insulate individuals and regions from federal government interference. Reformers professed an abiding faith in "the common sense of the common people" and "the inherent wisdom of the free market" and therefore wanted to 'get government off the backs of individual citizens and businesses'. In this way, the Reform Party was a radical conservative party.

Reform Party election platforms built upon these strong feelings of dissatisfaction and alienation felt by Westerners, the middle class, seniors, caucasians, males, and religious and rural people outside the urban centres. Popular issues were pledges to 'reduce the size of government', 'cut taxes', 'make families a priority', 'make our streets safe again', 'repair the social safety net', and, 'end the uncertainty caused by the national unity crisis'.[32] Preston Manning's strategy was to 'ride the wave' of whatever popular grievance was hot at that moment hoping to build enough momentum to win power. Stephen Harper, on the other hand, believed that success would need to be built on more than a grab-bag of grievances, that success would come only if there was also a core of conservative principles guiding the party. These issues continued to activate Reformers/Canadian Alliance/Conservatives as evidenced by the five priorities that the party emphasized in the 2006 federal election campaign: cleaning up government with a Federal Accountability Act; tax relief by cutting the GST; making streets and communities safer by cracking down on crime; help parents with the cost of raising their children; and, establish a Patient Wait Times Guarantee.

Stephen Harper was Chief Policy Officer and greatly contributed to these policies. While he may have had some reservations with some of them, he was generally in agreement.

Influence of the National Citizens Coalition

When Stephen Harper moved over to the National Citizens Coalition becoming its President and public spokesperson, he embraced the strong free market and conservative views of its founder Colin Brown. The NCC argued against the Canada Health Act, the Canadian Wheat Board, Canada Post, unions, accommodation with Quebec, social assistance programs and women's rights. It argued for greater privatization (especially health care) and smaller government. "Government is still too big. Taxes are still too high. Public spending is still too wasteful. If anything, the Common Sense Revolution [Mike Harris and the Ontario Conservative Party's election platform 1995] needs to be expanded. ... Privatization, ... is the quickest and most cost-efficient way to reduce the size, scope and costs of government." [33]

Harper acknowledged the close relationship between Reform and the NCC when he stated that "The agenda of the NCC was a guide to me as the founding policy director of Reform." [34] In 1994, Harper told a NCC meeting that both the NCC and the Reform Party could claim credit for the rightward shift in Canadian politics.

In addition to these public issues, the NCC was an important contributor to a variety of conservative candidate and party election campaigns including that of Harper's in 1993. In that election, the NCC spent about $50,000 on attack ads against Harper's opponent, Jim Hawkes, in the Calgary West constituency.[35]

Influence of the Canadian Alliance Party

When Stephen Harper campaigned for the leadership of the Canadian Alliance Party in 2002, he recognized the strong support for social conservatism among Alliance members. In an article titled "No time for social conservatives to retrench",[36] he stated that "Social conservatism – particularly regarding the family as central to the fabric of society – is in the ascendancy. ... social conservatives have provided the intellectual and political common sense that Canada needs." He also expressed support for a stronger government "role safeguarding the right of Canadians to express and practice publicly their religious beliefs"; opening up more opportunities and financial support for home schooling and private education; limiting government intrusion in the way families raise their children; tax deductions for middle-income families; raising the age of consent for sexual activity back up to 18 years of age; and, parent's rights by decriminalizing spanking – "criminalizing spanking extends the long arm of government too far into the private activities of families." Finally, he questioned the wisdom of human rights commissions and the broadcast regulation of religious programming.

Another important policy issue that Stephen Harper spoke to in his campaign for the leadership concerned the state of Canadian federalism. Harper believes that returning to the federal division of powers outlined in the original 1867 British North America Act (now titled the *Constitution Act, 1867*) would best enable Canada to operate in a changing world. "It is time to recognize the wisdom of that original design in a country as geographically and culturally heterogeneous as Canada." [37] He argued that two central forces are at work – 'globalization' meaning the developing of a truly international market place and continental integration, and, 'localization' or the regionalization of economic hubs. In this newly emerging world, "Federalism, with its constitutionally autonomous national and local governments, is ideally suited to react to this combination of global pressures and local concentration." The trouble, he stated, is that the more or less 'watertight' compartments identified in the BNAA have become blurred as the federal government intervened into provincial jurisdictions in order to implement national programs. Various social assistance programs and the Canada Health Act are two good examples of federal interventions. Both were listed as provincial responsibilities in the BNAA.

Decentralization giving the provinces more autonomy to carry out their constitutional responsibilities is the direction that Canadian federalism should go in according to Harper. "Policy competition in a federation results in better outcomes in the political market – something I have argued for in the particular case of Canada's health care system." [38] The federal government's core functions, according to Harper, are defence, justice, solicitor general and immigration.

In the 2004, 2006 and 2008 federal elections, Stephen Harper and the Conservative's presented variations on these conservative themes: reduction of taxes, balanced budgets, control over government spending, assistance for families, strengthening the criminal justice system, and, taking a more active role internationally. In each election the underlying theme was 'standing up for change' and 'standing up for Canada'. Given the quality of the Liberal leadership and campaigns, these themes and campaign slogans had appeal with the voters. Nonetheless, it did not have enough appeal to deliver a majority government. Canadians weren't yet ready to embrace the conservatism of Stephen Harper and the Conservative Party.

Stephen Harper's 'political beliefs'

From the above look at the issues and policy positions taken by Stephen Harper over the years and in the various positions he occupied, a clearer picture emerges as to his political philosophy and 'vision for

Canada' that he is attempting to implement. He is determined to change Canada and move it towards a right-of-centre conservative society. Shortly after Harper and the Conservatives became the government in 2006, columnist Richard Gwyn made the following observation: "it's becoming increasingly clear that we have undergone the most radical political change in decades, and, arguably, although only potentially, the most radical in our entire political history." [39] To support this strong claim, he stated that "Harper is a conservative Conservative. It doesn't mean he's a raving neo-con. It does mean he's a true-believing conservative. ... Harper comes to the office with an ideological belief in conservatism." In addition, "we are making a switch from ... waterbed politics to Procrustean bed politics." Here Gwyn is saying that the 'mushy', hard-to-pin-down policies and practices of past Liberal and Progressive Conservative governments – much like a waterbed where when you press down in one place it pops up somewhere else - is going to be replaced by a government with clearly identified and articulated polices demanding 'conformity by violent or arbitrary means'. Harper's practice during his first minority government of making many bills before the House a confidence motion reflected this determination to gain approval by 'violent or arbitrary means'.

So just what is Stephen Harper's political philosophy and where would he lead Canada under a Conservative Party of Canada majority government?

Stephen Harper as 'progressive' conservative: As a teenager in high school, Harper joined the Young Liberals. He abandoned his liberal leanings when Trudeau's Liberal government introduced the National Energy Program (NEP) in the early 1980's. Alberta's oil and gas economy experienced a serious decline at that time and, rightly or wrongly, blame was placed by Albertans on the NEP. Harper soon began to associate with the Progressive Conservative Party (PC's) working to elect Jim Hawkes in Calgary in the 1984 federal election. After working for Hawkes as a legislative assistant in Ottawa, he left Ottawa disillusioned with the Mulroney conservatives who seemed without real conservative principles, failed to abide by any fiscal discipline, and, was unable to revoke the NEP until 1986. The PC's were 'too centrist' and too willing to 'blow with the wind' on issues. Harper's beliefs demanded more of a 'conservative' party.

Eventually, he would come to believe that the 'progressive' policies of the PC's were part of the wider problem created by the application of Keynesian economic interventionism in the social and economic affairs of society. While Liberal and NDP governments were more strongly committed to such intervention, the PC's had moved to the left in an effort to be more electorally competitive. This began when John Bracken, Progressive Party premier of Manitoba, became national leader in 1942. Harper came to believe that a truly principled conservative party was needed to offset the destructive policies and practices of Liberal and NDP (socialist) led governments.

Stephen Harper as an 'economic conservative': At the University of Calgary enrolled in the economics program, Harper read and discussed all the major works of political economy, especially the ideas of Adam Smith, Friedrich Hayek and William F. Buckley, Jr.

As a convinced 'economic conservative', Harper came to believe in the "primary value[s of] individual freedom, … private enterprise, free trade, religious toleration, limited government and the rule of law." [40] The Liberal acceptance of the 'positive state' as a means to achieve greater equality of opportunity through an active, interventionist state was seen as a serious threat to society's wellbeing. "…there are still lots of statist economic policies and people dependent on big government. But the modern left-liberal economic philosophy has become corporatism. Corporatism is the use of private ownership and markets for state-directed objectives. Its tools are subsidization, public/private partnerships and state investment funds." [41] He therefore has consistently challenged Liberal and NDP social and economic policies and programs that have intervened in the affairs of society.

Stephen Harper as 'libertarian': "Libertarian Harper will strike new tone" read the headline of a ***Globe and Mail*** article the day after he won the leadership of the Canadian Alliance party, March 20, 2002. "Edmonton MP James Rajotte, a key supporter, said Mr. Harper is a libertarian – believing that governments govern best that govern least – rather than a social conservative who aims to impose Christian values on a secular society." [42] During the leadership contest, Harper had indicated he would not promote the social conservative agenda, particularly the anti-abortion and anti- gay positions favoured by many of the party's supporters. He had indicated this view on a number of occasions but many wondered whether he would stand by while others promoted such legislation. Obviously, Harper needed to maintain support from his fundamentalist religious and socially conservative base. While those voters have little option but to support Harper and the Conservatives, they could not be ignored entirely.

Others have also labeled Harper as a 'libertarian' conservative. Soon after Harper won the leadership, Faron Ellis, political scientist at Lethbridge College, stated that "Harper is libertarian conservative. He wants to get the government out of people's lives as much as possible and stop it there. He has no interest in seeing left wing social engineering replaced by a right wing version of the same thing. That's where he draws the line in the sand with Day and the special interest groups, such as anti-abortionists, who support Day. ... People can be socially conservative in their private lives but their libertarian attitudes – the desire to get government further removed from their lives – overrides it." [43] Given the far right nature of libertarian views, Harper faces the difficult task of projecting "his libertarian economic ideas and larger principles in a rhetoric that can inspire the Canadian electorate." [44]

Just what are 'libertarian beliefs' and how do they fit with Harper's beliefs? The following is taken from a description written by a life-long libertarian who served as Chairman of the Ontario Libertarian Party from 1976 to 1979.

"Today we live in a world in which virtually all countries are rushing headlong toward some form of statism, whether in the form of Communism or the welfare state. ... The very concept of the 'individual' is becoming obsolete. Libertarianism challenges the basic premise behind this trend – this view that what the state perceives as 'the common good' should be forced on the individual – and it challenges the idea on two fronts. In the civil area, Libertarianism supports all civil liberties and opposes all attempts by government to reshape its citizen s lives. In the economic area, Libertarianism challenges the right of government to restrict trade in any way, or to force citizens to support through taxes projects they will not willingly support on the free market." [45]

Libertarians are strongly opposed to the progressive, left of centre policies that have been adopted since the end of WW II. They see state intervention in the economic and social affairs of society as an infringement upon the rights of the individual to make their own choices and lead their own lives as they want to. As well, the growth of the welfare state is damaging traditional social institutions such as the family. Thus Keynesian economics and interventionist governments seeking to implement various social programs are a threat to individual liberty and must be vigorously challenged by conservatives.

Harper has said that "I tend to come from the small end of conservatism. I would not describe myself as a libertarian, by any means. But the kind of conservatism I stand for is one that I view as completely consistent with the Reform agenda of significant democratic change." [46] On another occasion, Harper stated that "I'm very libertarian in the sense that I believe in small government...". [47] It is not difficult to see why some have described Harper as a libertarian. His strong commitment to economic conservatism whose "primary value is individual freedom,, and to that end it stresses private enterprise, free trade, religious toleration, limited government and the rule of law", [48] is a comfortable fit.

Stephen Harper as 'social conservative': In seeking the leadership of the Canadian Alliance Party, Harper proclaimed that "Social conservatism – particularly regarding the family as central fabric to society – is in the ascendancy." [49] He claimed that welfare reformers of all ideological positions have now come to believe that family break-up is the key factor contributing to impoverishment. Therefore governments should 'favour policies that assist families to make up rather than policies that subsidize family break ups'. "The primacy of families in education is also gaining adherents – witness the new tax credit for private education in Ontario, and the expansion of funding to home schooling in Alberta. There is a growing backlash against government intrusion into the way families raise their children." Harper then indicated his support for "citizen-initiated referendums on issues of personal conscience." He went on to identify "a generous, universal, per child tax deduction, raising the age of sexual consent", and repeal of the criminal code provisions criminalizing spanking. Each of these issues resonates strongly with socially conservative individuals and groups in Canadian society, that is with fundamentalist Christian and other religious groups, older citizens, recent immigrants, and rural parts of the country.

In 2003, as leader of the Canadian Alliance, Stephen Harper

delivered a speech to the conservative interest group, Civitas. John Ibbitson, writing in the ***Globe & Mail***, observed that "Any citizen who reads it will fully understand the Conservative Leader's deep commitment to a carefully implemented, socially conservative agenda, despite his election promises of moderation and non-interference." [50] Harper spoke of the 'conservative coalition of ideas' that is centred on 'economic conservatism' and 'Burkean conservatism'. Burkean conservatism's "primary value is social order. It stresses respect for custom and traditions (religious traditions above all), voluntary association, and personal self-restraint reinforced by moral and legal sanctions on behaviour." [51]

The essence of this conservatism is "the preservation of the ancient moral traditions of humanity. Conservatives respect the wisdom of their ancestors; they are dubious of wholesale [social change]. They think society is a spiritual reality, possessing an eternal life but [having] a delicate constitution; it cannot be scrapped and recast as if it were a machine." [2] What this means is that conservatives resist social change preferring to protect and defend existing institutions such as the traditional family, church, class system and governmental authority. Conservatives fundamentally distrust the rationality of the individual and want to retain strong hierarchical institutions to contain what they believe to be humanity's inherently disruptive nature.

Harper believes these two streams of thought, economic conservatism and Burkean conservatism, merged in the 20th century in reaction to the threat of socialism. He argues that the socialist threat has now passed and that middle-of-the-road parties like the Liberals have moved right on the political spectrum and now accept the fundamental principles of conservative economics which is really classical liberalism economics. To put this in context, when liberalism shifted to the left ideologically from classical liberal economics which advocated for the limited state and unfettered free markets to modern liberalism which considers the state as having a positive role in managing the social and economic affairs of society, conservatives became defenders of the older liberal economic beliefs. Thus, various business organizations, think tanks and conservative politicians such as Margaret Thatcher and Stephen Harper are in fact arguing for 'classical liberal economic' positions. For them, the interventionist state/government is a negative force in society interfering in the freedom of individuals to decide for themselves how they wish to live. The state/government should mind its own business by being limited to defence of the nation, maintaining law and order, and, providing internal transportation and communication infrastructures.

Harper believes that the political centre has shifted to the right, as witnessed by socialists and liberals now "stand[ing] for balanced budgeting, the superiority of markets, welfare reversal, free trade and some privatization, ... [t]he real challenge is therefore not economic, but the social agenda of the modern Left. ... [The Left] has moved beyond old socialistic morality or even moral relativism to something much darker. It has become a moral nihilism – the rejection of any tradition or convention of morality, a post-Marxism with deep resentments, even hatreds, of the norms of free and democratic western civilization. ... [S]erious conservative parties simply cannot shy away from values questions. ... social values are increasingly the really big issues." [53]

From the above statements by Harper, it is clear that he is strongly committed to a social conservatism that would reverse the progressive social values and programs that Liberal and New Democratic governments brought into being since the Depression of the 1930's and WW II.

Stephen Harper as a religious conservative: No mention has yet been made of the influence Harper's religious views may have on his support for social conservatism. Harper is a member of the Christian and Missionary Alliance denomination. He is the first evangelical prime minister since John Diefenbaker. "His church follows in the traditions normally associated with American evangelism" [54] which gives him more in common with born-again Christians like George W. Bush. "The church looks and sounds nothing like the ornate, staid Catholic churches attended by past prime ministers. ... There is a strong emphasis on the certainty of one's faith and on the authority of the Bible... [and] on the physical healing powers of Jesus Christ (at the end of the service the pastor asks the sick to come up to be anointed with oil)." [55] In the church lobby, pamphlets opposing stem cell research and outlining the dangers of abortion are available for parishioners. And as with many other religions, the church opposes gay marriages.

Harper "is a fairly devout religious person" says Lloyd Mackey, author of the recent book *The Pilgrimage of Stephen Harper*.[56] Though having early roots in the Presbyterian and United churches, Harper moved over to the evangelical faith under the influence of Preston Manning and Diane Ablonzy. His reading of C.S. Lewis and Malcom Muggeridge also had an influence on him, particularly their disdain for politics and that they came to their Christian faith as adults.

While Harper takes his faith seriously, he does not follow it blindly. He is not unlike many other politicians and leaders who have reflected their faith in their politics but have not made it a central part of their politics. As Harper wrote in *Faith Today*, it "does not mean that faith has no place in public life or the public square." [57] Harper's ending of speeches with 'God Bless Canada' may or may not reflect his religious faith. It may be a necessary political acknowledgement to the evangelical Christians in the party.

It is therefore fair to say that generally Harper's evangelical, fundamentalist religious beliefs support his efforts to raise social value issues and argue for a more traditional and religious, socially conservative, approach to social questions.

To sum up the varied influences that have shaped the political beliefs of Stephen Harper, all of the above have combined to shape his conservatism. As an individual, he was deeply affected by personal experiences such as the visible affects on fellow workers and the province of Alberta when the NEP took effect, and, when he witnessed "the Mulroney government's fiscal irresponsibility ... the posturing and adolescent antics he saw daily in the Commons ... and the influence special interest groups had on governance." [58] His belief that conservatism must be guided by fundamental principles reflects these unhappy experiences.

As a student studying for his BA and MA in economics at the University of Calgary, his readings of the classical writings on capitalism and free markets combined with the electoral successes, policies and programs of Reagan and Thatcher. His underlying belief in economic conservatism reflects the influence of these experiences.

As Reform Party Chief Policy Officer, he had the opportunity to insert his conservative views into the party's statement of principles and policies. He benefited from being so intimately involved in Manning's and Reform's pragmatic political maneourvrings and witnessing the politically disruptive statements some social conservatives were prone to make. The necessity of establishing and maintaining tight message control over the party's members resulted from these experiences.

As President of the NCC, Harper was able to publicly express his economic and socially conservative views. The strong free market and small government views of the NCC reinforced his already strong commitment to economic conservatism.

As leader of the Canadian Alliance and then the Conservative Party, Harper has promoted both economic conservatism and social conservatism. There is little doubt about his strong belief in the benefits of the free market and the need for government intervention to be kept to a minimum. While his social conservatism is tempered by a belief that moral issues such as abortion and same-sex marriages should not be matters of party policy, he does believe that issues of faith must be part and parcel of what guides legislators.

On the expression of these beliefs, he has not been hesitant to exert tight control over the party, its elected MPs and members of his cabinet. Given the repeated embarrassing and politically damaging public comments made by various Reform and Canadian Alliance supporters and members over the years, it is no wonder that Harper instituted a gag order on all party announcements. On the other hand, it would appear that Harper is by nature a control freak and is in fact exerting tight control as an extension of this authoritarian nature. All political leaders want to minimize damaging comments made by others in their party but in this regard Harper appears to be excessive. He has been able to manage the messages conveyed to Canadians and therefore been able to implement economically and socially conservative policies. Canada is unquestionably under the influence of a 'conservative' government and leader.

Stephen Harper's vision for Canadian society

It is no secret that Stephen Harper wants to make the Conservative party Canada's 'naturally governing party' replacing the Liberals in such a role. From 1896 to 2009, the Liberals were in power federally 79 out of the 113 years. They therefore were able to set the tone and direction for Canada's economic and social development. For Harper to achieve his goal, he must shift the Conservative Party towards the centre of the political spectrum and move the centre towards the right.[59] He has been successful with the first as the party has adopted more moderate right-wing positions on a variety of issues. On the second, he benefited from the ideological shift to the right that occurred with the Reagan, Thatcher and Mulroney governments in the 1980's. The Chretien-Martin Liberals adopted deficit reduction, balanced budgets, deregulation, limited privatization and social program cuts as the means to reduce the national debt and eliminate the annual deficits which they had inherited from the Mulroney conservatives. Conservatives saw the Liberal's adoption of their policies as a vindication of their beliefs and the essential movement of the political spectrum's centre to the right.

Liberal ascendancy through the 20th century was based in part on a shift to the left in fundamental political philosophy in the 1920's and 1930's away from classical liberalism/'laissez-fairism' with its strong commitment to free trade, free markets and free individuals. This earlier view considered the state/government as a barrier to individual freedom and economic growth thus the idea of 'the negative state' and 'the government that governs best is the government that governs least'. This view of the role of government, that it should be limited so as to give individuals maximum freedom to fully apply their skills and abilities and that as the individual thrives so will society, was the philosophy of classical liberalism. It came into being to challenge the existing conservative, traditional, aristocratic, hierarchical society that existed in the late 1700's and through the 1800's.

But as society developed and the industrial revolution took hold, liberalism began to recognize that there could be a 'positive' role for the state/government to play. Freer markets undoubtedly unleashed the creativity, efficiency and energies of society. As western economies developed in the 19th and 20th centuries, it was recognized that 'laissez-faire' economics not only brought prosperity, it also brought inequalities and injustices. There was a need for state/government intervention in the economic and social affairs of society. Liberals began to see the state/government could and should provide some regulation over economic activities and provide some social programs that would ensure greater 'equality of opportunity'. Thus began the shift towards the left, towards a 'positive state'. Keynesian economics, also known as counter-cyclical economics, reinforced this new understanding of the role of governments.

With this shift, conservatives became defenders of the earlier classical liberalism that promoted the idea of 'the government that governs least governs best'. They became committed to the free market ideology and 'classical economics' that liberalism had tempered with its shift towards the activist state. For Harper and conservatives, this shift by the liberals towards the left on the political spectrum was wrong. By embracing the interventionist government approach, conservatives believed that liberals had unleashed other forces that have resulted in the economic and social problems society faces today.

Harper believes that government intervention distorts the marketplace by placing unnecessary restrictions and burdens upon businesses. He believes that the 'self-regulating'/'invisible hand' identified by Adam Smith will ensure that the market doesn't stray too far off the just and moral path and is better at monitoring the market. Combined with his strong religious belief that it is the individual who must seek and achieve salvation through their own efforts, so too is it the responsibility of the individual to ensure their own economic and social wellbeing. The state/government should be supportive but not unduly active in the economic and social affairs of society.

What would Canadian society look like under a conservative government? What would a Harper majority conservative government do to shift Canadian society back to the right after fifty plus years of left-leaning Liberal governments?

Perhaps the primary observation to be made is that conservatives of all stripes believe the embracing of Keynesian counter-cyclical economics that encourages government intervention in the social and economic affairs of society is a fundamental mistake. What began in the 1930's in response to the Great Depression and was adopted by governments after WW II, has distorted society's natural growth and development.

Economic conservatives attribute many of current economic and social problems to this misguided belief that governments are able to manage the economy well and engineer social change so as to 'better society'. By fundamentally rejecting this belief, Harper and economic conservatives are determined to roll-back the interventionist state and restore what they believe to be sound economic practices – balanced budgets, limited government, greater reliance on individuals and groups to provide for themselves and to resolve difficulties, and greater respect for and influence of traditional social institutions and practices – family, church, social class and governmental authority.

Social conservatives attribute the moral chaos that burst forth with the hippie generation in the 1960's and the moves towards legislated affirmative rights legislation thereafter on the false belief that human beings can be morally and socially responsible without strong outside influences. Conservatism believes that human nature is essentially guided by emotions, instincts and impulses and that our selfish and aggressive behaviours can only be held in check by strong traditional social institutions such as the family, church, social class and government. Respect for traditional authority whether within the family, schools, church, class or government is important to the establishment and maintenance of a civil society. Changes made by Liberal and NDP governments over the past fifty years, guided by their belief in the need for 'progressive' social change – various social assistance programs, human rights tribunals, affirmative action programs, etc. – are weakening the relationships and institutions that are essential to maintaining the social order. For Harper and social conservatives, they seek to reverse or temper these 'progressive' changes and reclaim a more conservative society.

Therefore, significant changes can be expected from a majority conservative government led by Stephen Harper. Without a majority government, Harper must move cautiously and prudently on situations and issues that conservatism would like to change. Changes that are made, such as tax cuts, increased spending, support for the military, tougher stances on justice issues, and, shifting universal social programs to needs based programs for example, are done in a 'moderate' way so that they are not likely to arouse strong public resistance. They can be presented and defended without appearing to be ideologically conservative based. Harper learned well from Preston Manning that it is important to capitalize on any wave of popular protest.

It should also be said that a 'conservative' view of society is not in itself mistaken. Conservatism began in reaction to the enlightenment shift towards liberalism and socialism after 1700 in Europe. The feudal order based on land and a landed aristocracy, the church and its hierarchical authorities, the family and its traditional structures, and, government under the control of the aristocracy was being challenged by new liberal and working classes. Over the past 300 years, this struggle continued to unfold in many parts of the world and continues in our present day societies. Many changes were made to extend democracy and alter economic and social relationships in society. These were positive changes but along the way they also created new problems and it was these that conservatives have focused on.

Chris Axworthy , NDP activist and former MP captured this problem well when he wrote *"Taken together, the initiatives the Left championed – from universal health care to assistance for the jobless and even family allowances – constituted a community insurance policy against the worst vicissitudes of life. They were not a replacement for hard work, individual initiative, and self-sufficiency – just a safety net for when things went wrong. The idea was to enhance family life within a supportive community, and build social cohesion. But with those gains made, we put them in a box on the lowest shelf of our policy closet, where they were crushed by [years] of fuzzy, unthinking social liberalism. We've been seen to champion social programmes that confer rights but demand no responsibilities. Blaming 'the system,' we've sloughed aside valid criticisms that social programmes do sometimes create dependency. We've been soft on crime. We've been too timid to criticize parents who don't take their obligations seriously. We've been too 'caring' to criticize a welfare system that rewards recipients for having more children when they can't properly feed and clothe the ones they have. We've been too accepting of children who don't go to school at all, who are told that they, too, can collect welfare at sixteen if they leave home."* [60]

In the above context, Harper and Conservatives have a case to be made for a more 'conservative' approach. But if it is their intent to 'reverse' the direction taken since the 1930's and restore society to a modern version of conservative ideological values, then there is something for Canadians to be concerned about. A conservative society emphasizing social order, hierarchical social, religious, economic and political structures and relationships is not in the 'reform tradition' of the 1840's but a retrograde move back towards a society long ago abandoned by progressive forces in society.

What then are some of the specific changes that Stephen Harper and a majority Conservative government are likely to make?

Since forming his minority Conservative government early in 2006, Harper listed his government's achievements as "Lower taxes and prudent spending focused on the priorities of Canadians. A commitment to free enterprise, free markets, and free trade. The belief in a government more responsible, more transparent. A justice system that puts the welfare of law-abiding citizens before the interests of criminals. Strong support for rebuilding the country's too-long-neglected Canadian Forces. An unwavering commitment to asserting our sovereignty over the Arctic. A belief in a foreign policy that is both strong and independent. And a passionate belief in the unity of this country!" [61]

In addition to the above list of Conservative successes, what would his conservative principles and program mean for Canadian society?

- **Smaller, more limited government:** Harper believes that the federal government should be downsized. It has expanded its programs into areas best left to private individual and community attention. Many social programs would be targeted, re-structured and delivered by those closer to the need. Universal social programs would be restructured to focus on the needs of those most in need and not delivered as a universal program to everyone.[62] This it is believed would be more efficient, save taxpayer's dollars and ensure that dollars weren't spent on programs taxpayers disagreed with.

  Federal intrusions into provincial jurisdictions, such as welfare and health care, would be significantly reduced. A return to a federalism closer to the original 1867 design was better because it would weaken the federal ability to promote national programs and strengthen the ability of the provinces to develop programs tailored to their particular province. As Harper stated "The trouble is, jurisdictional boundaries in Canada have become blurred. As originally conceived, Canadian federalism was a unique effort to create absolutely clear boundaries between areas in which provincial governments would exercise sovereignty, and areas in which the federal government would be paramount. Clearly defined barriers were established between the powers of the two levels of government, with the clear understanding that neither level could legislate in those areas falling under the competence of the other." [63] The federal government would restrict itself to control over currency, monetary policy, trade, national defence, immigration and citizenship.

The state/government would reduce or privatize many of the regulatory functions it performs – regulatory functions such as food safety and inspections, environmental protection and inspections, workplace health and safety protections and inspections, labour-management protections, broadcast systems and Canadian content regulations, and, transport safety and inspections to name but a few.

Critics would argue that there is a need for regulatory inspections. At the very time that the Maple Leaf Foods meat packaging plant was announcing it had a lisoteria bacteria contaminated meat problem, Harper's Conservative government was turning over meat inspection duties to the company. Food safety inspection would in future be handled by companies under the belief that they would act responsibly and ensure that their facilities and products were safe. Similarly, the Walkerton, Ontario, contaminated water supply problem developed in part because the Harris Ontario Conservative government had gutted the water quality inspection system and turned it over to the municipalities and private testing agencies.

Privatization and deregulation are two ways conservatives favour in their drive towards limited government and expanded private ownership.

- **Smaller government through tax cuts:** The state/government would cut taxes believing that by leaving more money in the pockets of businesses and individuals, the economy would benefit. Businesses would have more to invest and individuals would have more money to do the things they chose to do rather than government chosen social and economic programs and their attendant public bureaucracies that they might disagree with. As Flaherty said January 2, 2009, "he's reviewing options for putting more money in people's pockets through tax cuts…" [64]

Critics would argue that the reality of who really benefits from these tax cuts, which unquestionably are attractive to voters, suggests a different effect and perhaps a different agenda. Lisa Philipps, associate professor of law at Osgoode Hall Law School, has written that the Conservative's Jan. 27th stimulus budget reflects a 'split personality'.

"Behind a thin veil of rhetoric about helping those most in need is a set of long-term tax cuts that seek a much diminished role for governments in the future. … The broad personal income tax cuts are not well targeted to lower and middle earners, … The expansion of the [tax] brackets gives nothing to those earning less than $35,000 [mainly women] who are already taxed at the lowest rate of 15 per cent. … The largest cut will go to those earning more than $80,000 … [who] are the top 8 per cent of tax filers, most of them men. [These tax cuts] only make sense if the goal is to diminish, over time, the government's role in moderating income inequalities.

… Tuesday's budget shamelessly massaged numbers and tables to give a false impression that the tax cuts favour low-income earners. In true form, Stephen Harper has used the budget as cover to advance the Conservative's vision of a good tax system – one that is less redistributive, and encourages heavier reliance on private savings to meet citizen's needs." [65]

As Rick Salutin, a left-leaning political journalist has described it, once you make serious reductions in the tax base and put an emphasis upon spending what tax revenues that remain on debt reduction, "public services inevitably erode due to the lack of funds. Then, … market forces move in to fill the vacuum with private clinics and schools, toll roads, for profit water testing, etc. And the public realm can no longer afford to regulate them effectively even if it has the will." [66] Examples of this process can be seen in the actions of the Harris and Klein conservative governments in Ontario and Alberta respectively. Each offered tax cuts in their election platforms and made serious cuts to the funding of various social and health programs. The obvious result was a deterioration in those services and their regulation – health care and education for example - with the resultant pressures then to bring in more private facilities and staffing. Legal aid programs across the country would be another example. They suffer from a number of problems including inadequate funding. Rather than fix the existing systems which would involve more state/government intervention, pressures are building to permit more 'legal services plans' provided by private companies. [67]

Human rights tribunals and affirmative action programs would continue but be more limited in their scope and application. As spokesperson for the National Citizens Coalition, Harper said that "Human rights commissions, as they are evolving, are an attack on our fundamental freedoms and the basic existence of a democratic society. ...It is in fact totalitarianism." [68]

A more focused targeting of those in most need would prevail and therefore, conservatives claim, it would be more efficient. The proposal in the Nov. 27th, 2008, Economic and Fiscal Statement to remove pay equity claims from the tribunal and make it a part of contract negotiations reflected this desire to reduce the influence and interference of government agencies in the marketplace. While the government claimed it was proposing this change for reasons of costs and to reduce the time for claims to be settled, it appeared to be a move motivated by conservative ideology that governments should leave such social changing programs to the marketplace.

- **Strengthening the justice system:** Conservatives consider changes made to the justice system – for example, the Young Offenders Act, criminal offender's rights, sentencing provisions, police complaints commissions, changes to family law and children's rights – to be coddling of offenders and an unwarranted interference in the functioning of the family.

Conservatives have consistently campaigned on pledges to make communities safer and to punish offenders more severely. Harsher penalties and a restoration of respect for traditional families and authority would characterize a more conservative society.

- **Health care:** Health care is a provincial responsibility under the Constitution Act, 1867. As society developed in the 20th century, the need for a national, universal medical care program was adopted in 1966. The provinces and doctors objected to the federal government's role in establishing national standards and providing funding. Conservatives believe that the provinces should be given more latitude under the Canada Health Act to experiment with health care delivery. As Harper stated in 2002, Ottawa needs to "overhaul the Canada Health Act to allow the provinces to experiment with market reforms and private health care delivery options....[these would include] experimenting with private delivery in the public system." [69]

  Critics of Harper's approach believe it would lead to a two-tiered system of health care, one tier (private) for those who can afford the extra costs and the other tier (public) for those unable or unwilling to pay the extra fees. They also question whether a public-private system would lead to a deterioration in the public system as doctors move over to the private system for monetary advantages. Critics of a two-tiered health care system often point to wel known inadequacies of the American system where costs are horrendous by comparison and over 45 million Americans have no medical coverage.

- **Education** is also a provincial responsibility under the constitution. Under conservatism, there would be greater acceptance of religious schools, private schools and home schooling as alternatives to the public education systems operating in the provinces. These would be seen as 'complementing' the public system by providing greater 'market' choice to parents.

Critics argue that the public system brings children of all ethnic, racial, social class and religious backgrounds together thereby encouraging greater integration into society.

- **Regional development:** Conservatives believe that the various regional development programs distort the economy and the priorities of the regions they are designed to help. All provinces should be considered equal and treated equally. In Harper's words, "conservatives can lead the long-term evolution of the country if they recognize the principles of pan-Canadian federalism. This means support for provincial autonomy and jurisdictions, including differing language policies within the context of a free and democratic society, and opposition to ideas of special status and unilateral secession that only serve to inflame separatist sentiment." [70]

- **Relations with the United States:** Canada's relations with the United States would be closer under a conservative government. Harper, like Preston Manning, has a strong affinity to the American political system and to American conservatism. In a speech to a 1997 meeting of the Council for National Policy, an American right-wing think tank, Harper praised Americans and the U.S. conservative movement as "a light and an inspiration to people in this country and across the world." [71] Alberta's cattle ranching culture and oil industry connections may account in part for conservative's desire to strengthen Canada's ties to the U.S. On trade and economic relations, conservatives would be open to greater integration with the U.S. [72] Conservatives support greater 'continental economic and security integration' with the U.S. and a 'continental energy strategy' that should be broadened 'to a range of other natural resources.' On foreign policy, Harper has frequently indicated support for the U.S.

When Harper was active with the Reform Party, he supported its policy of increasing Canadian industrial, tax, transportation and fiscal and monetary policies with those of the U.S. Generally, conservatives have argued for closer alignment with the U.S.

- **Strengthened armed forces:** Under a conservative government, greater attention and resources would be placed on our armed forces and their ability to defend Canadian territory and engage in conflicts in other parts of the world. Harper has stated that "What Canada needs is a combat-capable armed military – a force able to meet reasonable commitments abroad as well as our needs at home." [73] Restoring the capabilities of the armed forces to perform their tasks is needed and will take time and resources. However, Conservatives see the threat to Canada and the world in starker terms than the Liberals and have placed greater emphasis on a combat ready capability at the expense of Canada's peacekeeping ability. Peacekeeping, a role Canadians proudly identify their country with, would be downgraded to a secondary priority. Harper and the conservatives have rejected such peace initiatives as the international land mines treaty and Canada's refusal to sign on to U.S. missile defence policies.[74]

  Canada would act in closer unison with our closest ally, the United States. Harper was very critical of the Liberals for not being more supportive of the U.S. following 9/11 and when the U.S. invaded Iraq. When Canada decided not to join the U.S. invasion of Iraq, Harper condemned the Liberals. In his view, "We believe the government should stand by our troops, our friends and our allies and do everything necessary to support them right through to victory." [75] "Where Liberals seek to make headlines by tut-tutting the slightest American misstep, conservatives want Canada to stand abreast of our U.S. allies in their time of need." [76]

- **Immigration and Multiculturalism:** Conservative election strategies have placed a great deal of emphasis upon wooing ethnic communities that traditionally support the Liberals. To this end, Conservatives introduced the Community Historical Recognition Program in 2006 and allotted $29 million to commemorate a variety of apologies for past immigration events. Since then, the Chinese-Canadian, Indo-Canadian, Jewish, and Ukrainian-Canadian communities have received apologies and funds. "The timing and motivation for the announcements are the subject of debate." [77] Critics claim the announcements are politically motivated. The comments of Tom Flanagan seem to confirm their intent is to win electoral support among ethnic communities. "The affected communities are thrilled to have received this recent recognition." [78]

Since coming into office, the Conservatives have introduced legislation, C-14 (making it easier for Canadian parents to get citizenship for their foreign-born adopted children) which was supported by the opposition parties, and, C- 50 (intended to clear up the backlog of applicants) which has been strongly criticized by the opposition. "The major reform would give the Minister of Citizenship and Immigration authority to 'give instructions' regarding the attainment of Canadian immigration goals. ... The Canadian Bar Association said '... the Tory reforms place way too much power in the hands of the minister.' ... Activists in the immigration community also see the reforms as an attempt to shift the focus of immigration policy toward allowing more so-called 'economic immigrants' at the expense of other categories, such as refugees and family reunion." [79]

Conservative policy documents refer to the need to attract immigrants who can best integrate into the 'Canadian fabric'. The question that arises is 'who' can best integrate? Who is included in this description - whites?, Europeans?, 'economic immigrants'? Harper has been quoted as saying that "West of Winnipeg, the ridings the Liberals hold are dominated by people who are either recent Asian immigrants or recent migrants from eastern Canada: people who live in ghettos, and who are not integrated into western Canadian society."

While Harper's views may well have changed from the days when he helped formulate Reform Party policies on immigration, one can only wonder. Back then he endorsed immigration policies that "would be essentially economic in nature ... Immigrants should possess the human capital necessary to adjust quickly and independently to the needs of Canadian society and the job market." [81]

On multiculturalism, he supported a policy whereby "individuals or groups are free to preserve their cultural heritage using their own resources. [Reform] opposes the current concept of multiculturalism and hyphenated Canadianism ... We would end funding of the multiculturalism program and support the abolition of the Department of Multiculturalism." [82] Harper continues to oppose multiculturalism preferring instead a greater integration into Canadian society. His government's efforts to attract new Canadian's votes away from the Liberals is motivated by immediate political considerations and not by any support for multiculturalism.

- **Bilingualism and Quebec:** Conservatives recognize that, under the constitution, "English and French have equality of status, and equal rights and privileges as to their use in all institutions of Parliament and the Government of Canada. " [83]

For Harper, bilingual efforts in Canada have been a failure. "It is simply difficult extremely difficult – for someone to become bilingual in a country that is not. ... Canada is not a bilingual country. In fact it is less bilingual today than it has ever been... So there you have it. As a religion, bilingualism is the god that failed. It has led to no fairness, produced no unity and cost Canadian taxpayers untold millions." [84]

The question of Quebec's 'special status' within Canada has been an important issue for Harper and the Conservatives. While Chief Policy Officer for the Reform Party and as President of the National Citizens Coalition, Harper advocated a 'tough love' approach to Quebec. He accused federal politicians of appeasement in their efforts to find workable solutions to Quebec's concerns. As a candidate in the 1988 election, Harper stated that "It is time for a new approach to federal language policy, one that recognizes that there is a predominantly French-speaking region of the country and a predominantly English-speaking regions of the country, that recognizes this in a way that involves no double standards, in a way that respects minorities, and in a way that is fair to all Canadians, including the vast majority of Canadians who are unilingual. I say, let Quebec be Quebec; let the West be the West." [85]

As Prime Minister since 2006, Harper made moves to gain electoral support in Quebec, such as recognizing the Quebecois people as a 'distinct nation' within Canada. Harper's efforts to woo Quebecers is politically motivated for electoral purposes and overshadows his real beliefs regarding French-speaking Canadians and the status of Quebec in Confederation.

- **Environmentalism:** Stephen Harper and the Conservative party have been quite clear about their policy towards the environment. Back in 2002, Harper wrote a letter to members of the Canadian Alliance party that "Kyoto is essentially a socialist scheme to suck money out of wealth-producing nations." [86] He went on to say that it is "based on tentative and contradictory scientific evidence ... [and that the accord] would cripple the oil and gas industries, which are essential to Newfoundland, Nova Scotia, Saskatchewan, Alberta and British Columbia." Concern for Kyoto's impact on Canada's economy is valid. As one of the major energy users on the planet, the other being the U.S., Canada must find ways to reduce its greenhouse gas emissions and keep its oil and gas industries operating. Toronto-Dominion Bank chief economist Don Drummond, along with a few other economists, shared the government's concern. [87] As to Harper's questioning of the science involved, David Suzuki noted that "Stephen Harper not only opposes Kyoto, but he refutes the science. He's back in the dinosaur era. Harper is just totally out of it." [88]

Since becoming the government in early 2006, the Harper Conservative government has effectively dismantled Canada's commitment to Kyoto and proposed instead a 'Made in Canada' policy. It has announced a number of programs and made 'adjustments and revisions' to them in a scramble to allay widespread public criticism. In Kyoto's place, Canada joined the US-led Asia-Pacific Partnership. This group, made up of the U.S., China, Japan, India, South Korea and Australia, rejected Kyoto. At various international meetings, Canada was singled out for failing to put in place effective environmental programs – at the Nairobi summit, November 2006, Canada was given the "fossil of the day" award along with Australia for contributing the least to the climate change battle.

Disclosure in the **National Post** early in 2008 that Environment Canada had instituted media message control rules for government scientists infuriated scientists who have long been encouraged to discuss their work with the media and the public. "The concept of free speech is non-existent at Environment Canada," said Andrew Weaver, a Canadian university climate scientist.[89]

Harper and the Conservatives are acutely sensitive to the American position. Under Bush, Harper had an ally but now that there is a new, more environmentally sensitive President and government in Washington, Canada must move quickly and adopt more aggressive policies. This will be a challenge for Harper and his government because it will require serious action to clean up the environmental effects arising from the development of the massive tar sands among other things. It strikes at his political base in Alberta and the West particularly.

Protecting Canada's economy is important but there are ways to do that and put the economy and the country on a more environmentally friendly basis. Given Harper's beliefs about the 'science' of climate change and the tremendous pressures from the oil and gas industry and Alberta government to disrupt the industry as little as possible, Canadians will have to wait and see what measures the Conservative government takes. Or perhaps it is more appropriate to say, wait and see what steps the American government takes before Canada follows suit.

A Stephen Harper led majority Conservative government would unquestionably change the face of Canada. Everything in his past suggests that he has arrived at strongly held beliefs that many of the directions Canada has taken in the past 50 years has been wrong. In adopting the views of Hayek and other 'liberal' economists, Harper sees *"Keynesian policies … as inherently inflationary [and rejects] the 'redistributionist' logic of social democracy and the more progressive versions of liberalism, calling for a roll-back in the functions of the state to those specified by 18th or 19th century laissez-faire doctrine (i.e., defence, the administration of justice, certain public works). ... [While Harper may not want to go back that far, he strongly agrees] "on the need to deregulate large sectors of economic life, privatize public corporations and activities, and impose strict limitations on government spending."* [90]

For all the reasons cited above, Canadians should be fully aware that Stephen Harper does have a 'hidden agenda' and that it would 'revolutionize' Canadian society. His 'moderation' of Reform/Canadian Alliance policies is but a means to achieve his end goal of 'moving Canadian society to the right' and making the Conservative party 'Canada's natural governing party'. He, and the Conservative party, need a majority government to achieve this revolution. Canadians need to be fully aware of his intentions before granting him his wish.

Endnotes

[1] Joe Paraskevas, "CA won't sell out to Tories: Harper", *Calgary Herald*, 7 April, 2002.

[2] Richard Gwyn, "Is Harper paddling with the tide or against it?", *Toronto Star*, 28 May, 2006.

[3] Stephen Harper, V-P National Citizens Coalition, Speech to the Council for National Policy, an American right-wing think tank, June, 1997.

[4] Carolyn Ryan, "Stephen Harper and the road to power", CBC News, Canada Votes 2006: Leaders and Parties, www.cbc.ca/canada votes; "Profile Stephen Harper", BBC News, 2 Nov., 2006; "Indepth: Stephen Harper" CBC News Online, 16 March, 2006.

[5] Ryan.

[6] National Citizens Coalition, "About the NCC", www.nationalcitizens.ca.

[7] Canadian Press, "Alliance back on track, Harper says", 20 March, 2002; Larry Johnsrud, "Strong and here to stay", *Edmonton Journal*, 7 April, 2002.

[8] "Harper unknown to most Canadians", *Ottawa Citizen*, 21 March, 2002.

[9] "Makeover tip for the earnest young man from Alberta: Look warm and caring", *Globe and Mail*, March, 2002.

[10] Dennis Gruending, "Preston Manning and Stephen Harper, uneasy alliance", *The House*, CBC radio, 11 April, 2009, link to "Pulpit and Politics" http://dennisgurending.ca/pulpitandpolitics.

[11] "Mr. Dithers", *The Economist*, 17 Feb., 2005.

[12] John Geddes, "Let them hang themselves", *Maclean's*, 9 Jan., 2006.

[13] Arthur Haberman, "The Prime Minister who would be President", *Toronto Star*, 19 April, 2006.

[14] Richard Gwyn, "Steely PM taking Canada down a radical path", *Toronto Star* 2 May, 2006.

[15] Chantal Hebert, "PM off to a promising start", *Toronto Star*, 15 May, 2006.

[16] Stephen Maher, "Harper will have things his way, but will we like it?", *Halifax Chronicle Herald*, 20 May, 2006.

[17] Stephen Kimber, "Harper crosses the line", *Halifax Daily News*, 21 May, 2006.

[18] Mark Kennedy, "Harper would get majority: new poll", *Winnipeg Free Press*, 23 May, 2006.

[19] Don Martin, "Up close, Harper looks less parliamentary", *Prince Albert Daily Herald*, 23 May, 2006.

[20] James Travers, "Bush too busy for Harper", *Charlottetown Guardian* 24 May, 2006.

[21] Alexander Panneta, "Harper thumbs nose at national media", *Toronto Star*, 24 May, 2006.

[22] Richard Gwyn, "Prime Minister obsessed with majority", *Toronto Star*, 10 Feb., 2006.

[23] Chantal Hebert, "Harper still draws strong emotions", *Toronto Star*, 13 Oct., 2008.

[24] James Travers, "Harper pulls shroud over Reform", *Toronto Star* 15 Nov., 2008.

[25] James Travers, "Harper spreads the blame", *Toronto Star*, 20 Nov., 2008.

[26] Preston Manning, *The New Canada*, (Toronto: Macmillan, 1992) 158.

[27] Andrew Kopkind, cited in "Reaganomics: The Legacy of the 40th U.S. President – Part 1", *Lighthouse Patriot Journal*, 4 March, 2007.

[28]   Philip Resnick, "The Ideology of Neo-Conservatism", in Warren Magnusson, et al., *The New Reality*, (Vancouver: New Star Books, 1984) 131.

[29]   Kopkind.

[30]   Reform Party of Canada, Principle and Policies, *The Blue Book*, 1991: 1.

[31]   *The Blue Book*, 2.

[32]   Reform Party election pamphlet 1997, "A Fresh Start for Canadians – A 6 point plan to build a brighter future together".

[33]   Colin T. Brown, "Guest Column", *Windsor Star*, 16 Feb., 1997.

[34]   Stephen Harper, "Glad to be aboard", NCC's *The Bulldog*, Feb., 1997, cited in www.StephenHarperSaid.ca.

[35]   "Defeat Jim Hawkes campaign", National Citizens Coalition, www.StephenHarperSaid.ca.

[36]   Stephen Harper, "Now is no time for social conservatism to retrench", www.harperforleader.com/newsroom.

[37]   Stephen Harper, "Federalism, Firewalls and Promoting Canadian Prosperity", www.harperforleader.com/policy, 19 Feb., 2002.

[38]   Harper.

[39]   Richard Gwyn, "Steely PM taking Canada down radical path", *Toronto Star*, 2 May, 2006.

[40]   Stephen Harper, "Rediscovering the right agenda", Civitas, *Citizens Centre Report*, Vol. 30, Issue 10, June 2003.

[41]   Harper.

[42]   Shawn McCarthy, "Libertarian Harper will strike new tone", *Globe and Mail*, 21 March, 2002.

[43]   Chris Cobb, "Harper unknown to most Canadians", *Ottawa Citizen*, 21 March, 2002.

[44] Neil Cameron, "Harper wise to shun the centre", *Montreal Gazette*, 23 March, 2002.

[45] Marilee Haylock, "What is Libertarianism?", www.libertarianism.ca.

[46] Stephen Harper, "Getting back on track", *Montreal Gazette*, 22 March, 2002.

[47] Stephen Harper, *National Post*, 6 March, 2002, cited in "Canadian Issues: Stephen Harper: in his own words...", www.canadiandemocraticmovement.ca.

[48] Harper, "Rediscovering the right agenda".

[49] Harper, "Now is no time for social conservatism to retrench", 14 Jan., 2002, www.haarperforleader.com.

[50] John Ibbitson, "How much social conservatism?", *Globe and Mail*, 12 June 2004.

[51] Ibbitson.

[52] Ibbitson.

[53] Ibbitson.

[54] Colin Campbell, "The Church of Stephen Harper", *Maclean's*, 20 Feb., 2006.

[55] Campbell.

[56] Lloyd Mackey, *The Pilgrimage of Stephen Harper*, (Toronto: EWC, 2005).

[57] Campbell.

[58] William Johnson, "The Outsider", *Walrus*, March 2009: 25.

[59] Paul Wells, "Harper's Canadian Revolution", *Maclean's*, 29 Sept., 2008: 18.

[60] Chris Axworthy, "Mums the word: for a long time the left has been afraid of family values. That has to change", *Saturday Night*, Nov., 1996: 33-34.

[61] Johnson, 24.

[62] Stephen Harper, Speech to Colin Brown Memorial Dinner, National Citizens Coalition, 1994: universality has been severely reduced, "it is virtually dead as a concept in most areas of public policy…These achievements are due in part to the Reform party…".

[63] Stephen Harper, "Federalism and all Canadians", www.harperforleader.com/policy.

[64] Julian Beltrame, "Flaherty hints at tax cuts in budget", *Globe and Mail*, 2 Jan., 2009.

[65] Lisa Philipps, "Tax cuts: Why the opposition should have insisted on changes", *Toronto Star*, 30 Jan., 2009.

[66] Rick Salutin, "Round up the usual suspects", *Globe and Mail*, 7 July, 2000.

[67] Kate Lunau, "How to pay for some justice", *Maclean's* 9 March, 2009.

[68] *BC Report Magazine*, 11 Jan., 1999, StephenHarperSaid.ca, 10 Feb., 2006.

[69] Stephen Harper, "Harper on Health Care", *Toronto Star*, 4 Dec., 2001.

[70] Stephen Harper, "Federalism for all Canadians", www.harperforleader.com/policy, 19 Jan., 2002.

[71] Brian Laghi, "Harper adopts strong stance in favour of the U.S.", *Globe and Mail*,29 May, 2002: "Stephen Harper adopted an aggressive pro-American policy yesterday in his first major speech in Parliament, embracing tighter ties."

[72] Andrew Potter, "It's time to talk about North American integration", *Maclean's*9 Feb., 2009: 17. Potter is a conservative leaning journalist who

advocates 'continentalism' fully recognizing that it means "integrated governance structures to enhance coordination, collective action, and mutual benefit."

[73] Stephen Harper, "Federalism, Firewalls and Promoting Canadian Prosperity", www.harperforleader.com/policy.

[74] Laghi.

[75] Stephen Harper, *Debates*, House of Commons, 1 April, 2003.

[76] Stephen Harper, "Liberal policies threaten Canadian troops and security", 4 Fed., 2002, www.harperforleader.com/policy.

[77] www.cicnews.com.

[78] Tom Flanagan, cited in Kenneth Kidd, "How Harper let it slip away", *Toronto Star*, 18 Oct., 2008.

[79] Terrence Corcoran, "Open the door on immigration policy reform", *National Post*, 13 May, 2008.

[80] "The Devil in Stephen Harper", NOW Magazine Online Edition, 3 March, 2004, www.nowtoronto.com.

[81] Reform Party *Blue Book*, 1991: 34.

[82] Reform *Blue Book*, 35.

[83] Stand up for Canada, "Founding Principles", www.conservative.ca.

[84] "Bilingualism", *Calgary Sun*, 6 May, 2001, www.canadiandemocraticmovement.ca.

[85] Stephen Harper, cited in William Johnson, *Stephen Harper and the future of Canada*, (Toronto: McClelland and Stewart, 2005) 97.

[86] "Harper's letter dismisses Kyoto as 'socialist scheme'", CBC News, 30 Jan., 2007, www.cbc.ca/canada.

[87] "Environmental policy of Harper government", Wikipedia, 4 April, 2009, http://wikipedia.org/wiki/Environmental_policy_of_the_Harper_government.

[88] David Suzuki, "In their own words", 2003, www.intheirownwords. ca/harper.

[89] Andrew Weaver, "New Harper government policy muzzles communication by Environment Canada government scientists", ClimateScienceWatch, 13 Feb., 2008, www.climatesciencewatch.org.

[90] Resnick, 133.

Chapter 9
Stephen Harper's Political
'modus operandi'

"If Harper gets elected, he'll make a [expletive] *change in this country."*
Ted Byfield (founder of Alberta Report and the 'unabashed voice of
the west') [1]

Every political leader has a style of leadership that results from their
personality development and their experiences. From a look at his
formative years, his experiences at university and as a political activist
and practicing politician, a general description of Stephen Harper's
leadership style and political 'modus operandi' can be identified.

Stephen Harper's Leadership Style

From a variety of comments and observations by family, friends, colleagues and political journalists, the following characteristics appear prevalent.

1. **Confidence in himself:** One trait that has characterized Stephen Harper throughout his life has been his determination to follow his own path. He was described by his father as "his 'headstrong' son" [2]; by friends as having a "natural inclination to lead and equally natural disinclination to be led" [3]; by a fellow Reform executive officer that "he did not like 'being told what to do'" [4]; and, by his university thesis supervisor as "a difficult student".

While being independently inclined can be a positive characteristic, it also can be a liability. Various associates have commented that "There's always been this concern that Harper believes he's the smartest guy in the room and that, no matter what, he's never wrong"; and, that "a picture emerges of a bright and driven man who does not take dissenting counsel especially well". [5]

All of this independence of nature has led Harper to follow his own path towards political success. And no one can deny that he has enjoyed considerable political success as he has developed a clear idea of his political values, contributed to the success of the Reform Party, the National Citizens Coalition and the Canadian Alliance and its successor the Conservative Party. He has gone from campaign worker to Prime Minister. That surely is success.

But his independence streak has also caused grief for himself and his party. He follows his own counsel for the most part. Many have noted that he runs a one-man government, a tight ship with everything centralized under his control. In the aftermath of the 'storm' that engulfed Parliament Hill last December, Jeffery Simpson wrote that "Mr. Harper's decisions showed a secretive, ferociously partisan leader, centralizing everything in his own hands. ... Mr. Harper makes decisions himself, or in an exceptionally closed circle. ... [The problem with this government is] the centralization of power in Mr. Harper's hands, [and] his office's fundamental distrust of most ministers and their staffs,..." [6] CTV's Craig Oliver, similarly observed that "If this thing goes down, [referring to Harper's miscues in the 2008 election] it will be the great strategist himself who will carry the heaviest load of blame. That's the way it is when you run a one-man government –especially one in which others do not feel free to offer advice or sharp disagreement." [7]

2. **Partisanship:** In addition to the tight control that Harper has placed on his cabinet and MPs, his nature is to approach politics in a highly partisan manner. He considers it a blood sport especially if it is against the Liberals. In the assessment of one Conservative insider, "He truly is ... politically brilliant, but he's also pathologically partisan. ... It's a deadly combination. You know that you're a smart guy and you're pretty sure you can outsmart everybody and you never miss an opportunity to poke an opponent in the eye. ... He cannot abide by the Liberals. He finds them indecisive, he finds them pandering, he wants to destroy them. He can't help himself." [8]

His partisanship has been demonstrated on numerous occasions when some restraint would have served him better. Some examples are: the bullying inflicted on Dion and the Liberals in the House where, contrary to tradition, Harper turned many votes into questions of confidence forcing the Liberals to abstain or face an election, and then taunting them for their weakness; when CTV ran the tape of Dion struggling to understand and respond to a reporter's question, Harper immediately went for the jugular; and, then there are the various arguments that he made during the crisis on the Hill last December. They were highly partisan and destructive of civility in the House. A final example of Harper's nature was demonstrated by the lack of any acknowledgement of his role in the crisis in his Dec.3, 2008, address to the nation. [9]

Harper's self-confidence combined with his partisan instincts led him to operate in the House as if he had a majority government rather than the minority that he had. Assessing the opposition parties, especially the Liberals, as divided, financially weak, and unwilling to force an election, Harper was not content to just use this advantage but relished every opportunity to harass and embarrass his opponents, especially Stéphane Dion. Many political observers described it as bullying. The deliberately negative ads successfully branded Dion's image in the public's mind as a weak leader. The 'puffin pooping on Dion's shoulder' TV ad in the 2008 election similarly captured this ruthless side of Harper. One final example of this ruthlessly partisan nature is evident in the conscious decision by Harper to continue to use some of his MPs, particularly Dean Del Mastro and Pierre Poilievre, to attack the new Liberal leader in the House. [10]

Finally, as opposition MPs reminded Harper during the heated exchanges last December, "There can be no substitute for responsibility at the top. The Prime Minister sets the moral tone for the government and must make the ultimate decisions when issues of trust and integrity are raised." [11] When a leader is willing to knowingly misrepresent the facts, encourage his MPs to accuse opposition leaders of treason, and, is willing to put the wellbeing of the nation in jeopardy in a desperate bid to save his government as he did during the December crisis on the Hill, it demonstrates a depth of combativeness dangerous in a national leader.

Perhaps the advice Harper gave to his son when he was stepping onto the ice for an election photo-op with the Calgary Flames captured best his no-holds-barred nature. He said "Don't take any bulls---t." [12]

3. **Petulance and profanity:** Quite in contrast to the cool and controlled image Harper portrays most often in public, Harper has demonstrated a behaviour more akin to immaturity on more than one occasion. When things have not gone well, he has a tendency to withdraw and sulk. When the 2004 election came up shorter than expected, he withdrew from public view for the summer months. Many speculated that he was in a funk brooding about his political future.

During the crisis on the Hill last December, Harper was "visibly shaken, … angrily flouncing around in his Langevin Block office, eyes reddened and battling a bad cold exacerbated by a lack of sleep. … He has displayed that almost adolescent blend of petulance and stubbornness before…" [13]

Life in the Prime Minister's office, especially during the crisis, demonstrated another side of Stephen Harper. As one Tory described it, "He is a yeller and certainly longshoremen could take language lessons from him. The backrooms are blue but it's not cigar smoke; it's four-letter words."[14] Others describe a picture "of a bright and driven man who does not take dissenting counsel especially well and is prone to profane outbursts." [15]

Relations with his staff are said to be 'delicate'. He is said to have people around him that are too obedient and are hesitant to challenge or disagree with him. While this charge can be made against many political leaders, this seems to be a valid description of Harper given the qualities identified above. As one insider phrased it, "there's no question the Prime Minister rules by fear ... at some point, ... you get up every day and you get kicked in the balls and, you know what, you get tired of it..." [16] and stop fighting back. That's a dangerous situation for decision making. Every prime minister needs people around them who can and do think independently and are willing to challenge them when they believe they are neglecting some consideration.

Another telling indicator of Harper's leadership style and relationship with party staff members comes from Rick Mercer. He writes that "junior staff members were ordered to be outside 24 Sussex Drive by 6:15 in the morning. Their job was to stand there in the dark with the temperature well below zero and wait for the PM to appear. Their instructions were to applaud, wave and sing *O Canada* loudly as the motorcade pulled out of the gates and drove Stephen Harper to work. Mr. Harper, by all accounts, actually believed that the young people were there of their own accord and represented a groundswell of love and support for his actions. Staffers in the Prime Minister's Office know that he is easier to handle when being applauded and not questioned." [17]

One final observation. Neal Carter applied a 'personality at a distance' political profiling technique to Stephen Harper. It develops a profile by applying seven traits: self-confidence, conceptual complexity, belief in one's own ability to control events, need for power, task or affiliation focus, in-group bias and distrust of others, to major interviews written up in the media. On this basis, Carter concluded Harper's profile as that of "a crafty, context-savy leader concerned with being informed about the relevant facts and the attitudes, beliefs and capacities of other players, seeking out situations where cooperation can lead to mutual gains. This is not to say that he is unlikely to make enemies: his ideological views and his reaction to constraints may make him susceptible to too blunt a use of power and lack of subtlety in dealing with others." [18]

This description seems to both describe Stephen Harper yet doesn't. Since it is based on media interviews, it may be fair to say that as a politician, Harper's responses to questions were guided by political considerations and therefore perhaps not entirely a true reflection of his views and nature.

Stephen Harper's Political 'Modus Operandi'

1. **Waiting for the Wave:** Working with Preston Manning and the Reform Party exposed Harper to the 'waiting for the wave' approach that served Reform so well in its early years. This approach sought to build broader party support by giving expression to the various political 'waves of discontent' that naturally emerge in a society. Harper questioned the long term viability of this strategy. He strongly believed that any conservative party needed to have a strong set of fundamental principles if it was to succeed in holding the disparate elements of discontented citizens together.[19] On this issue, Harper and Manning disagreed. It contributed to Harper resigning as a Reform MP in 1997.

2. **Incrementalism:** Harper has retained the idea of 'waiting for the waves' by adapting it to the idea of 'incrementalism'.[20] Both he and Manning described the 2008 election result as progress in that the Reform/Canadian Alliance/Conservative party had continually made gains over the years. Speaking to the 2nd Conservative Party convention in Winnipeg, November 13, 2008, Harper said "Five years ago this fall, … we came together as a party. We united forces and we energized our supporters. We offered Canadians a viable alternative … In short order, we faced down the Liberal juggernaut and turned it into a minority, turned it into a Liberal Opposition, and formed the first government of the new Conservative Party of Canada. And last month, Canadians re-affirmed their decision, and chose us once again… We can be proud of what we have accomplished."[21] On election eve, Manning said "They managed to get a minority last time, and they got a stronger minority this time. The graph is going in the right direction. We'd all like to see it go to a majority faster. But I don't think you can complain about the trend."[22]

Incrementalism has other political benefits that are especially important for a party like the Conservatives who want to make major political and social changes. Canadians are well aware of the party's historical roots and tumultuous political experience. In the words of Preston Manning, the Reform party was initially characterized as "extreme, fringe, right wing, potentially racist and separatist." [23] Stockwell Day's leadership of the Canadian Alliance and his publicly stated belief that the world was but 6,000 years old helped reinforce the public's feeling that the party harboured a strange collection of supporters. Finally, various statements by socially conservative members in the 2004 and 2006 elections reminded voters of why they hesitate to give their support to the Conservative Party.

And so any gradual gain is less likely to set off alarm bells with voters whereas making major changes would likely resurrect public fears. This is good change theory. It is change by a strategy of stealth rather than change up front and in your face. Canadians will be less likely to notice the incremental shifts that are happening and will have adapted to them when they combine in the end and complete the societal change the party wants. As Harper neatly put it, "My goal is not only to win an election. It's to create a natural Conservative majority in this country." [24]

3. **Tempered Idealism:** Stephen Harper arrived at his deeply felt conservative values and beliefs after much study and thought. He has time and again pronounced on those beliefs and how they must never be abandoned. He has indicated on a number of occasions that his conservative principles and values have not changed though his tactics have responded to the needs of the times. In this respect, a similar statement could be made for any practicing politician, especially a successful one. Unwavering dedication to one's principles at all costs is incompatible with the democratic political process.

Much is made of Harper's strong commitment to conservative principles. But others have qualified this by challenging the assessment that he is an "unwavering neo-conservative hampered by his ideological rigidity. ... He is a pragmatist. There is some ideology there, of course, but he's always looking ahead." [25] He has said on numerous occasions that "Leading a national conservative party is a balancing act. 'If you refuse to adjust to the wider electorate, the tendency in parties like that is not just to be locked in to your own supporters, but frankly for that support base to continue to diminish because you continue to have more and more ideological tests of purity. [But the opposing danger lies in reaching out too vigorously to every constituency.] If you don't care about your principles – which are ultimately embodied by your core supporters – you'll quickly find that you've thin and insignificant support everywhere." [26]

There have been many who have bemoaned Harper's moderation of party policies and approaches. One ardent and outspoken conservative journalist, Terrence Corcoran, writing in the ***National Post***, November 30, 2004, lamented that "Conservatism is dying in Canada. Not just dying; it is being murdered and deliberately removed from the political scene by strategists. [He placed Harper at the scene of the crime: since the June election, Conservatives have] drifted ever further away from the core conservative values that once seemed to animate Mr. Harper. [He then notes that others have also recognized Harper's moderation and centrist bent saying that they're] disheartened with Harper's attempts to reposition himself as a 'professional politician'." [27] The reference here is to politicians who have become 'mushy centrists', a characteristic Harper denounced in the past in reference to the Progressive Conservatives and the Liberals.

More recently, Harper spoke to conservatives at a conference sponsored by the Manning Centre for Building Democracy. In a reaction to "high-profile conservatives warn[ing] against watering down conservative ideas to win votes", Harper reminded participants that "compromises had to be made to face the economic reality. [Some in attendance found his remarks deeply offensive.] The treatment of classical liberals and libertarians … was nothing short of stunning. The condescension was literally dripping from his mouth." [28]

4. **Identify and target the 'loose fish':** More so than in previous elections, the Conservatives were able to identify segments of the voting population that would be susceptible to the conservative message. Having successfully discovered the key to fundraising under the new, tougher and more restrictive rules, the Conservatives had the funds to conduct the kind of socio-economic research and develop the contact and communication techniques that would enable them to target possible voters. As Tom Flanagan said "You don't want to waste your resources talking to people who won't support you. It's a kind of triage." [29]

In the 2006 and 2008 elections, the Conservatives targeted new

Canadians, women and 'bleu' nationalists in Quebec. Specific policies and specific proposals were devised knowing they would likely be well received by the targeted groups. Examples of this were the cuts to the GST and $100 a month child care benefits to families for sports in 2006 and then artistic activities in 2008. These moves were not made on the basis of any national purpose. They were made strictly for politically partisan objectives. While all parties practice such at election time, the Conservatives have turned it into an art.

5. **Control the image and the message:** One of the strongest aspects of Harper's method of operating politically is to seize control of the images and messages that the party puts out. Perhaps watching the Liberals brand Stockwell Day in the 2000 election and himself in the 2004 election, or perhaps learning from conservatives and the Republican Party in the U.S., Harper has been determined to use the media to shape his and his opponents public image and the messages the party delivers. "He learned during the 2004 election that it is a mistake to allow your opponents to define you. In politics, image matters." [30] Also, given the frequent derailing of Conservative messages in the 2004 campaign, it was wise policy for Harper to put restrictions on his members. But has he taken it too far?

As his biographer William Johnson noted, once Harper became PM, he "demanded an iron discipline from his cabinet and caucus. ... he became a control freak, restricting the public utterances even of caucus members. Whatever was not official doctrine could not be freelanced without prior permission from the Prime Minister's Office. Harper placed controls on journalist's access to ministers and information, engaging in a constant power struggle with the press gallery." [31] This tight control greatly contributed to the Harper image of a 'rigid and controlling' personality.

The use of negative attack ads characterized another aspect of this determination to control and use the media to put across his message and shape his and his opponent's images. From the moment Stéphane Dion gained the Liberal leadership, the Conservatives successfully created a public image of him as 'a wonky academic wandering in the political big leagues'. Ads during the 2008 campaign continued this approach. Nor did straying from the truth deter conservative's efforts to brand their opponents. As one Conservative spokesperson stated

"We've put the Liberals on the defensive on issues we believe will have the potential to drive votes. [Three such issues were] hiking the GST, scrapping the $100-a-month child benefit, and the imposition of a carbon tax. [These accusations were entirely false! Wells went further and stated that] On other issues Harper simply invents Liberal policy as he goes along. ... This is the worst kind of cheap politics." [32]

With Michael Ignatieff the new Liberal leader, Harper and the Conservatives are preparing to negatively brand him. Various Conservative MPs are using the member's statements time in the House before Question Period to "launch personal attacks against" Ignatieff.

6. **Policy and position reversals:** Harper frequently speaks of the need for principles and to be guided by conservative values. But whether it is pragmatism or opportunism, Harper has shown a remarkable degree of 'flexibility' when the situation presents itself. Paul Wells, writing in *Maclean's*, observes that "... to hug the centre, he will indulge in the most blatant contradictions and occasional incoherence. ... The list of Conservative U-turns and broken promises is growing longer. [fixed election law, not taxing income trusts, treatment of resource revenues in calculating equalization payments, the quick withdrawal of the '3 poison pills' in the economic update statement, the rosy financial picture followed shortly thereafter with dire predictions of economic hard times, the vow to never run a deficit followed by the most massive deficit in Canadian history, to name but a few] ... Taken together, these actions give the image, not so much of a strategic genius as a man who will throw anything and anyone overboard if it threatens his ability to hang onto power." [33]

7. **Muzzling social conservatives, economic conservatives and libertarians:** On many occasions, comments by social conservative party members have plunged the Reform Party and its successors, the Canadian Alliance and Conservative parties, into damage control mode. Their statements confirmed the belief many Canadians had that the parties attracted extreme right-wingers and fundamentalist evangelical Christians. As Harper stated while a Reformer, "They do more damage to us than any media outlet, any other party, and any real enemy can do." [34]

The need to control party members in order to attract a broader range of supporters was complicated by the very nature of the social, cultural, economic, and political policies Reform and the Canadian Alliance advocated. These policies attracted people with strongly held and more extreme views. As Harper observed, "[t]he biggest problem is when you seek input from the bottom up [as the populist approach of Reform did], often the ideas are simple and of low quality, or just slogans. ... But if people feel you're listening to them, they'll have faith in you, and then, they'll be very open to what you're trying to sell them." [35] In this respect, "Preston Manning had an uncanny ability to sound moderate and reasonable but extremists interpreted it as they wished, for example, a 'balanced immigration policy' meant to extremists 'keep Pakis and niggers' out." [36] Recognizing this problem and pattern, Manning, and later Harper, acted to moderate party resolutions and member's statements.

When Harper took over leadership of the Canadian Alliance party he had to tread a delicate line. During the leadership campaign, he acknowledged the important beliefs and role of social conservatism in the party and wider conservative movement. [37] Politically he needed their support in order to defeat Stockwell Day who was seen as a stronger social conservative. Once in the leadership, he had to keep their support (not that they had many other options) but not let them openly display their views. Harper's agile leadership managed to fairly successfully contain these elements of the party, but not entirely.

In the 2004 election, comments by Conservative candidates were given wide publicity and hurt the party at the polls. Scott Reid's comments on bilingualism, Randy White's comments regarding gay marriages and the court's interpretation of gay rights, and, Cheryl Gallant's comments comparing abortion to beheading, reminded voters of the more extreme views of party members and the possibility of a 'hidden agenda'. It hurt the party at the polls. In the 2006 election, Harper and the party were more successful. During the eight week campaign, "[t]he most right-wing elements of [the] caucus and party supporters have been held tightly in check".[38] The possibility of gaining power and, with a minority, the fragility of keeping power, were powerful incentives for the more extreme and outspoken party members to mute their voices.

The challenge for Harper during his first minority government, and now with his second, is to keep the social conservative wing happy while ensuring he doesn't offend the other parts of the coalition that has helped elect him and the Conservative Party into power. Overcoming the image of a 'scary' party with a 'hidden agenda' has been an uphill struggle that can quickly be lost with an unguarded comment.

Economic conservatives and libertarian conservatives hold strong views regarding the size and role of the state in economic and social affairs. At the core is a strong belief in individual freedom and liberty. As with social conservatives, Harper has encouraged these supporters to avoid making extreme comments and has moderated his own comments concerning Conservative economic and social policies. This has not always gone over well with these groups.

7. **Bad mouthing Parliament:** Stephen Harper has adopted a 'run against Ottawa' strategy that includes bad mouthing Parliament and its various participants. As a leader and party with an unquestionably radical agenda, he has decided that it is advantageous to portray 'the system' as a problem. As a Reform Party policy officer and MP, he championed attacks on the parliamentary process and proposed changes borrowed from the American republican political system. The proposed changes – referendum, initiative and recall, elected senate, and other changes – reflected the 'wave of discontent' Westerners felt towards Ottawa and their desire to find ways to limit the role of the federal government.

Harper's disdain for the workings of Parliament stretched back even further to his experiences in Ottawa as a legislative assistant. On each of those two occasions, he came away frustrated and cynical about the political manoeuvrings and compromises that 'doing politics' involved. Thus as a committed conservative and from his own personal experiences, he has little patience with the parliamentary process.

In his short time as prime minister, he deliberately abused the committee system by directing his party chairpersons to obstruct the work of the committees whenever they did not work to his benefit. He sprung votes in the House on important issues and gave little time for serious debate, such as extending the Afghanistan military mission with but six hours of debate and no expert witness testimony and then cavalierly suggested that he would go ahead and extended the mission even if the House voted against it.[39]

He has blamed the opposition parties for delaying legislation when in fact the legislative agenda has been minimal. He has accused the parliamentary press gallery of being 'anti conservative' and gone to war with them over who can ask questions in press conferences. When he couldn't get his way, he boycotted the press. When his nominee for chairman of the promised non-partisan public appointments commission was rejected by MPs on the grounds that as a "fierce partisan with decidedly discriminatory views towards some immigrant groups", he was unsuitable to clean up patronage appointments, Harper refused to nominate someone else. [40]

When Stephen Harper proclaimed that Parliament was 'dysfunctional' and that he 'would not use the words Parliament and reality in the same sentence', he was demonstrating his disdain for the parliamentary process. Few would claim that everything is okay with the way the House conducts its business and that some changes wouldn't be helpful. But the level of partisanship displayed by Harper and his gut level disdain towards his opponents has combined with his innate belief that Ottawa and the nation's political players are anti-conservative. He believes they should be suppressed and subjugated and that only a clear Conservative majority government will rescue the situation. It is the perfect strategy for a person whose ideological beliefs and strong personality have melded together to convince them that their mission is to save Canada. His desire to win a majority government is based on the depth to which he sees Ottawa and Canadian society as fundamentally flawed.

These then are some of the major characteristics of Stephen Harper's approach to conducting politics. Some of these methods have been forced upon him, such as the need to have tight control over what messages are sent out by the party and the government, but others reflect his very nature. All individuals are complex composites of many influences and factors. Pigeonholing political leaders can be especially difficult since they operate on a national stage and must respond to a myriad of individuals, groups and situations. In this way they are like chameleons, they often can seem to be changing colours and stripes, or, as some would accuse many politicians, of 'blowing with the wind'.

What does all of the above add up to? Can we get a better handle on just who is Stephen Harper and how does he practice politics? Perhaps, but as Reg Whitaker concluded, Harper is "an 'enigma' of 'hidden depths, concealed agendas, complex contradictions'…" [41]

Endnotes

[1] Lloyd Mackey, *The Pilgrimage of Stephen Harper*, (Toronto: EWC, 2005) 145.

[2] Mackey, 12.

[3] Mackey, 13.

[4] Mackey, 13.

[5] Robert Benzie, "PM Partisan, passionate and profane", *Toronto Star*, 6 Dec., 2008.

[6] Benzie.

[7] Jeffery Simpson, "After the storm", *Globe and Mail*, 6 Dec., 2008.

[8] Craig Oliver, "Craig's List: Conservatives can't quite believe what is happening…", CTV News, 8 Oct., 2008.

[9] Benzie.

[10] Don Martin, "Harper ditches the olive branch", *National Post*, 4 Dec., 2008.

[11] *Debates*, House of Commons, 1 & 3 Dec., 2008; 10 March, 2009.

[12] William Johnson, *Stephen Harper and the future of Canada*, (Toronto: McClelland and Stewart, 2005) 315.

[13] Tondra MacCharles, "Majority slips from Harper's grasp", *Toronto Star*, 15 Oct., 2008.

[14] Benzie.

[15] Benzie.

[16] Benzie.

[17] Benzie.

[18] Rick Mercer, "It's not the economy, stupid", *Globe and Mail*, 6 Dec., 2008.

[19] Neal Carter, "Stephen Harper, Canadian: a personality at a distance profile. (Case Study)", *Inroads: A journal of opinion*, Summer-Fall 2008: 26-30.

[20] Tom Flanagan, *Waiting for the Wave*, (Toronto: Stoddard, 1995).

[21] Tom Flanagan, "Mr. Harper's Canada", *Globe and Mail*, 17 Oct., 2008.

[22] Conservative Party of Canada, "The Conservative party is Canada's Party", 13 Nov., 2008.

[23] MacCharles.

[24] Preston Manning, *The New Canada*, (Toronto: Macmillan, 1992) 157.

[25] John Geddes, "Harper overhauling the Political Right", *Maclean's*, 24 May, 2004.

[26] Benzie.

[27] Paul Wells, "Stephen Harper's Balancing Act", *Maclean's*, 27 Dec., 2004.

[28] Terrence Corcoran, "Harper's Balancing Act", *National Post*, 30 Nov., 2004.

[29] Jennifer Ditchburn, "PM rips into Liberals behind closed doors", *Globe and Mail*, 13 March, 2009.

[30] Tom Flanagan, cited in Kenneth Kidd, "How Harper let it slip away", *Toronto Star*, 18 Oct., 2008.

[31] Jeffery Simpson, "How Harper won the election", *Globe and Mail*, 23 Jan., 2006.

[32] William Johnson, "The Outsider", *Walrus*, 2009: 28.

[33] Paul Wells, "Harper's Canadian Revolution", *Maclean's*, 29 Sept., 2008.

[34] Joan Bryden, "Tory MP faces suspension for attacks on Ignatieff", *Globe and Mail*, 31 March, 2009.

[35] Wells, 21.

[36] Murray Dobbin, *Preston Manning and the Reform Party*, (Toronto: James Lorimer, 1991) 116.

[37] Ian Pearson, *Saturday Night*, cited in Dobbin, 131.

[38] Dobbin, 120.

[39] Stephen Harper, "Now is no time for social conservatives to retrench", 14 Jan., 2002, www.harperforleader.com.

[40] Canadian Press, "Voters take a chance on change, elect Harper", 23 Jan., 2006.

[41] Stehen Kimber, "Harper crosses the line, Afghanistan vote all about politics, not Canada's role, soldier's safety", *Halifax Daily News*, 21 May, 2006; Stephen Maher, "Harper will have things his way, but will we like it?", *Halifax Chronicle Herald*, 20 May, 2006; James Travers, "Bush too busy for Harper", *The Charlottetown Guardian*, 24 May, 2006.

[42] Stephen Kimber.

[43] Carter.

Chapter 10
Stephen Harper: Master Strategist ...or Master Stumbler?

[He has] *"a rare strategic gift combined with a lot of brain power ... he can size up a situation of political conflict; he can figure out who your main enemies are, where your opportunities lie."* [1]

Repeatedly, Canadians have been told that Stephen Harper is a 'master strategist'. His record to date lends support to such a claim – his contributions to the policies, strategies and successes of the Reform Party; his analyses of key public issues such as federalism and relations with Quebec; his success in gaining leadership of the Canadian Alliance Party; his success in 'uniting the right' to form the Conservative Party of Canada; and, his success in leading the Conservative Party to form the Official Opposition and then the government. All of these are real achievements that reflect the Conservative claim that he 'knows what he believes in', 'knows what really matters', and, 'knows exactly where he wants to lead Canada.' [2]

But there is another side to this story that raises questions about his strategic prowess. Along the way to becoming Prime Minister, Stephen Harper made some strategic blunders – spending away the $13 billion surplus on politically motivated initiatives; the last minute insertion of the infamous '3 poison pills' into the November 27th Economic and Fiscal Statement; untold reversals of earlier positions, the most gigantic of which is the complete reversal on fiscal policy with the January 27, 2009, federal budget; his premature statements near the end of the 2004 and 2006 elections that may have cost him a majority victory; his injudicious statements and funding cuts to cultural programs late in the 2008 election that cost him increased support in Quebec; and, his intemperate accusations about the coalition partners, especially the Bloc Quebecois, back in early December, 2008. Each of these contributed to his failure to obtain the majority government that he is said to desperately seek. Each of these may have prevented his being able to fully implement his conservative agenda and move Canadian political culture to the right.

In this context, it could be said that Stephen Harper is as much a 'master stumbler' as a 'master strategist'.

Stephen Harper as Master Strategist

When Conservatives met in Winnipeg for their second party convention in mid November, 2008, Harper recounted the struggle the party had gone through to get to where it was today, from the wilderness of defeat in 1993, through a variety of transformations and eventual success at the polls in 2006 and 2008. *"As we gather together as a party, let us pause for a moment, and truly reflect and appreciate how far we have come, in so short a time. ... Five years ago, the Conservative movement in this country was divided, defeated, and demoralized. The government of the day ridiculed us. The pundits discounted us. And the public said, 'Don't bother talking to us until you've got your act together."* [3] Indeed the party had come a long way under his leadership.

Having a clear idea of what is happening and what you want to do to change a situation helps a person to give leadership to a political party. Harper had given much thought to a variety of ideas and committed himself to conservatism. His readings and discussions with various people – such as fellow students and faculty at the University of Calgary, Preston Manning and others in the Reform Party, members of the National Citizens Coalition – sharpened his understandings of the economy and Canadian society so that he could take an overall view of events rather than a short-term approach.

Another component to leadership is being able to determine what specific actions will bring one closer to the end goal. Harper and his advisors have been quite successful in identifying key issues, some would say 'wedge issues', that resonate with voters generally or with a particular segment of the voting population – for example, reductions in the GST tax from 7% to 5%, recognition of the Quebecois people as a 'distinct nation' within Canada, providing a per-child tax credit to parents with children under six years of age, and, tax cuts generally. Harper and the Conservatives have successfully drawn increased support from women and new Canadians. Harper's strategy has been to continue the 'wave approach' adopted by Preston Manning and the Reform Party. It was based on seizing upon 'hot button' issues of the moment and ride the wave of popular discontent until the next wave came along. It also was felt to be better to have incremental changes towards the eventual conservative society as that would be less likely to arouse a strong negative reaction from Canadians. In doing so, he successfully challenged the Liberals.

Unquestionably Stephen Harper has had considerable success as leader of the Canadian Alliance Party and the Conservative Party of Canada. He has had an important role at all stages in the rebirth of conservatism in Canada and deserves credit for this.

Stephen Harper as Master Stumbler

While recognizing the considerable achievements that Harper has had, the question continues to linger as to whether he and the Conservative Party might have achieved their cherished goal of winning a majority government if important errors had not been made at key moments along the way. Would the Conservatives have gained a comfortable majority in 2004, 2006 or 2008 if errors of strategy hadn't been committed?

In the June 28, 2004 federal election, the Conservatives were forced to fight the campaign prematurely. The party had little time to prepare a policy document following the recent uniting of the Canadian Alliance and Progressive Conservative parties and the leadership contest in which Harper had emerged as leader. Nonetheless, the Conservatives got off to a good start and seemed to be climbing in the polls. Harper's strategy was to not let the Liberals portray him as radical and scary with a hidden agenda. For example, when the Liberals tried to make health care a defining issue, Harper deftly indicated his support for the agreement reached by Chretien and the premiers in the previous year and accused Martin and the Liberals of failing to live up to it.[4] He even added a proposal to create a federal 'catastrophic' drug cost plan. Liberal efforts to use health care as a scare tactic floundered.

Early on in the campaign, statements by the Conservative's critic for official languages raised the spectre of major changes to bilingualism and the Official Languages Act; Harper's earlier comments regarding partition of Quebec if Quebecers voted for secession were resurrected by the press in Quebec; and, two Conservative candidates in Ontario made inflammatory comments concerning abortion and homosexuality. Each of the social conservative comments raised difficulties for Harper and the Conservatives even though he had publicly stated on a number of occasions that "moral issues should not be a matter of party policy, but each MP should be free to follow his or her conscience and the wishes of the constituents."[5] When Harper began musing about preparations for a majority Conservative government, conservative momentum stalled. Then came the leader's debates June 14 and 15. In the French debate, Harper did reasonably well as a CROP poll put him one point better than Martin. On June 15, the morning of the English debate, the ***Globe and Mail*** reported that the Conservatives had edged ahead in a new Ipsos-Reid poll.[6] Momentum for a Conservative victory was again building.

On June 16 however, "Harper made perhaps his biggest mistake of the campaign when he said: 'There are no safe seats for the Liberals anywhere, any more.' ... He began to talk about the transition of power from the Liberals to the Conservatives. That sent a message to the electorate of over-confidence, of presumption, even of arrogance. …Harper's boast focused attention on himself, and people were uncertain about who he was." [7] Harper's aloofness from the press and desire to control the image of himself projected to the public meant that Canadians didn't have a feel for who he was. All the old questions re-emerged including whether he was the 'anti-social extremist' that Liberals had tried to label him as. Canadians were worried.

Then Ralph Klein, Conservative premier of Alberta, announced that he would be making changes to Alberta's health system two days after the election, including more private delivery of health care. This fuelled the public's concerns as to whether the federal conservatives would defend the Canada Health Act or allow such changes. The Liberals pounced and raised the spectre of a 'hidden agenda'.

Another damaging event happened when the Conservative campaign issued a press release accusing Martin of supporting child pornography. This was a very sensitive issue for conservatives, especially in the West. An earlier 2002 British Columbia Supreme Court ruling had ruled that having written works of child pornography in one's possession was not a criminal offence because they could be considered to have 'artistic merit'. When a murder case involving child pornography arose in Toronto on June 17, the Conservatives issued a press release titled 'Paul Martin supports child pornography' accusing Martin and the Liberals of having failed to toughen the laws on pornography. Harper had not previously seen the release. When questioned by the media about it, he said the headline went too far and had it changed but he did not back away from the charges it made about the Liberals and Martin. Instead he challenged them to make it an issue during the remaining ten days of the campaign.

The media and the public reacted negatively regarding the press release as 'unfair, grievously insulting, and that Harper should have apologized.' "Harper's excess changed the public perception of Harper." [8] Thereafter, his campaign was on the defensive as reporters raised questions about child pornography, abortion, homosexuality, use of the notwithstanding clause, his refusal to apologize to Martin, and, his intentions regarding bilingualism.

Then came another bombshell when the Liberals unveiled a video clip on same-sex marriages in which Conservative MP Randy White denounced such marriages, questioned the role of the courts on such questions, and declared that the notwithstanding clause should be used to over-ride the Charter of Rights and Freedoms. He claimed that his "position and the Conservative Party's position are identical." [9] The clip was given wide play in the media and seemed to confirm the public's image that a Conservative government contained too many extremist social conservatives. White's rant, played over and over in the final days of the campaign, "had an enormous impact, especially in volatile Ontario and British Columbia." The damage was done and it was major.

One final event occurred in the final days of the campaign. Harper 'retreated' back to his earlier position as defender of Alberta and the West. By doing so and by choosing not to end the campaign in Ontario, he was sounding like a regional spokesman rather than a national leader.

The results of the 2004 election, which were a major letdown for Harper and the Conservative party after hopes had risen so high, were the result of a variety of factors. Harper was in his first national election campaign and the party was still actively integrating the Canadian Alliance and Progressive Conservative organizations. The Conservatives made gains in the number of seats and they held the Liberals to a minority government. Progress had been made.

But while statements by Conservative candidates seriously hurt the campaign, Harper's succumbing to the lure of possible victory and commenting upon it prematurely was a tactically strategic error. Given the widespread public uneasiness about him and the Conservative agenda, he should have known better than to draw attention to an expected election victory. He didn't and it opened the door to closer public scrutiny of himself and the party. The old 'bimbo outbreaks', as members of his campaign team called them, were the final torpedoes that sunk Harper's chances to form a government. [10]

In the January 23, 2006 federal election, Harper and the Conservatives adopted a strategy of announcing a different policy proposal each day. They began this early on in the campaign while the Liberals decided to wait until after the Christmas holidays thinking that Canadians would be caught up in Christmas celebrations and not tuning in to the election until the start of the new year. Conservative strategy was right on the mark. The Conservatives had the field to themselves and were able to appear prepared and ready to govern. Their daily policy pronouncements received wide media coverage without being diluted by competing messages.

A second strategic decision was to put a tight lid on what candidates could say. Lessons had been learned from the 2004 campaign. This time the lips of socially conservative party members would be zip-locked. "Harper knew he was mistrusted, and that the Liberals would again paint him as scary, so he focused his campaign not on himself, but on a daily unveiling of goodies that targeted broad clusters of voters." [11] And again, as he had done in the 2004 election, Harper countered Liberal proposals with similar or competing proposals intended to appeal to as many Canadians as possible. The strategy worked well.

Also the decision was made to 'soften' Harper's public image. In an effort to prevent the Liberals from defining him as 'scary' or 'goofy' – think of the photo of the ten-gallon cowboy hat and the too-tight western vest – the Conservatives portrayed Harper and themselves as ordinary folks, hockey dads and soccer moms, small c-conservatives who were middle class and a bit bland. The message was that Harper and the Conservatives were definitely not scary. It worked to counter Liberal efforts to again raise the spectre of right-wing extremism.

Up until the holiday break, the Liberals were holding their own in public opinion polls with the Conservatives trailing but gaining. The tide really began to turn when news of the RCMP's decision to launch a criminal investigation into the Finance Department's handling of the income trust tax decision was made public December 28. Canadians were already angry with the Liberals over the sponsorship scandal revealed by the first Gomery Commission report on November 1, 2005. Liberal mismanagement and corruption combined with Gomery's charge that Liberals had an 'arrogant sense of entitlement' had already turned many away from the Liberals. According to CTV's chief parliamentary correspondent, Craig Oliver, "this development 'changed the whole course of the campaign.' It played right into the Conservative platform to clean up corruption and increase government accountability. ... Oliver added that the news cost Martin days and days of campaigning, and allowed the Tories to continue their policy-a-day pace." [12] By the time the new year rolled around, Paul Martin and the Liberals were in serious trouble.

Martin and the Liberals desperately tried to reverse their fortunes by again turning to the themes of Stephen Harper and the Conservatives being 'scary' and having a 'hidden agenda'. But this theme had been so often used by the Liberals that its effectiveness was wearing thin.

A series of blunders compounded Liberal troubles. Communications Director Scott Reid's derogatory remark that Harper's $1200 per year per child benefit would be spent more on 'beer and popcorn'; a blog entry by an Ontario party official comparing NDP candidate Olivia Chow to a dog; and, Buzz Hargrove calling Harper a separatist, all diverted the Liberal campaign off track. "It played into another Conservative complaint about the Liberals, which is the whole business of privilege, of contempt for ordinary people – that the Liberal Party is a bunch of elites all serving each others' interests." [13] In the final days, with indications that the campaign had gone well and polls indicating a possible Conservative majority, Harper again made a strategic mistake. This time he did not muse about a possible Conservative majority government as he had in 2004. But he did say that Canadians shouldn't worry about him and his party having too much power because the Liberal dominated Senate, senior civil service members, and the Canadian court system loaded with Liberal judges would act as a check on his government. As Craig Oliver stated "It's certainly legitimate to say that the Senate is a hindrance to his government having too much power, but to suggest that judges will actively start making decisions to stalk his government, or make life difficult for him, is a really upsetting and sinister suggestion." [14]

With these remarks, Canadians had second thoughts about giving Harper and the Conservatives a strong mandate. As some stated, "just a minute now, we don't want this guy to clean up. We want a leash on him." [15] As this sentiment spread, prospects for a Conservative majority government retreated back to a minority.

Stephen Harper did win a minority government – 124 Conservative, 103 Liberal, 51 Bloc Quebecois, and, 29 NDP. This in itself was quite a feat. In four short years Harper had rebuilt the Conservative party and made it a serious contender for government. The party was back in power even if only with a minority. Incrementally the party had made continuous progress and prospects for the future looked very promising.

But it should not be forgotten that this election campaign could have given the Conservatives a majority government. The Liberals reeked like a dead skunk's odour from the various scandals that hovered around them. The strategy to go lightly until after the holidays combined with their woefully inept conducting of the campaign gave the Conservatives an important head start in defining the issues and establishing Stephen Harper and the Conservative Party as a reasonable alternative to the Liberals. The unfocused leadership of Martin had earned him the title of 'Mr. Dithers' by the magazine ***The Economist***. [16] And finally, the attempt to revise the well-worn charges of Harper and the Conservatives as 'scary', having a 'hidden agenda', and of being 'extreme right-wingers' was wearing thin with voters. Conservatives had countered that image with a more moderate and friendly image of Harper and the party.

With all these factors working in the Conservative's favour, they should have won a majority. They didn't because in the final days of the campaign, Stephen Harper made a strategic mistake. His remarks about the Liberal Senate, civil service and judges was a wake-up call to Canadians who have always had a distrust of Harper and the Conservative party he has constructed. This is the second time that Stephen Harper derailed Conservative chances for a majority government.

In the October 14, 2008, federal election, the Conservatives were in a commanding position going into the election having successfully shredded Liberal Leader Stéphane Dion's leadership credibility. In addition, by making many bills before the House confidence motions, Harper had backed the Liberals into a corner and greatly weakened their credibility as a party ready, willing and able to govern Canada. Harper and the Conservatives were clearly in the driver's seat. Throughout the campaign, Harper took the high road making few promises, avoiding unscripted public events for the security of staged photo-ops, even waiting until the last week of the campaign to announce the party's election platform. He and the Conservatives appeared on the verge of winning a majority.

Early on in the campaign, Harper stated that "*I actually think this time, we pulled together a bunch of elements from different regions of the country that actually fit together pretty well. We've got some people who are a little more on the left – but they're certainly not left-wing. We've got people who are a little more on the right – but I certainly don't think they're some of the extremes you saw in the past. In Quebec we've started to build a Conservative party that actually has a federal Conservative organization, as opposed to being just borrowed parties from the provincial level, which is what we've seen in the past. …And whether it's an agenda that has a high emphasis on tax reduction as opposed to spending increases; an agenda that focuses on delivering benefits to people and to families instead of creating bureaucracies; whether it's restoring pride in the country – not just in things like, you know, health care or various government programs, but pride in things like our institutions, our military, our history – I think we're also doing that. We're also building the country towards a definition of itself that is more in line with conservatism."* [17]

Conservatives had been planning for this election the moment the 2006 election ended. They had a master strategy and a detailed plan for victory. Their game plan included assessments of the four leading Liberal leadership candidates and how to negatively brand which ever won in the public's mind. As well, Tory strategists had built a riding-by-riding model that would bring gains in Quebec, the 905 suburbs around Toronto, and the suburbs around Vancouver. According to Tom Flanagan, campaign organizer, you conduct "a ruthless assessment of which voters you have a chance of winning over. … You don't want to waste your resources talking to people who won't support you. It's a kind of triage." [18] Married women with children, new Canadians with young families, and, Quebec 'bleu' nationalists would be targeted with Conservative policies.

"Look at the policy announcements," said Flanagan. "They're almost all directed at family-oriented women. …[for example] last election's $100 –a-month child-care allowance, followed up this time with promises of money for kids' art and dance lessons." To make gains in Quebec, Harper transferred billions to the provinces, gave Quebec a special role at the United Nations' cultural forum, and, recognized the Quebecois people as a 'nation'. To make gains with new immigrants who were seen to be family-oriented, entrepreneurial and susceptible to conservative economic and social policies, a variety of actions were taken to build support among eastern European groups and Indo-

Canadians - immigration law changes regarding citizenship for foreign-born adopted children, work visas for foreign students, and expanded trade offices in India.

And so the Conservatives had a strategic plan that this time would likely bring them a majority government. "Our approach throughout this entire campaign is just to stay on our course, stay on our own game plan. We want to have the consistency of a metronome.", a Tory strategist stated.[19] The plan called for an announcement in the morning followed by an attack on the opposition in the afternoon. This approach "all meshes with Harper's essential personality – shy, cautious, incremental and not at all comfortable with anything off-the-cuff if the stakes are high. Stephen's a great one for following the plan, [said] Flanagan."

By way of contrast, Stéphane Dion and the Liberals were in a very weak position. The Chretien-Martin divisions within the party were still active; the divisions coming out of the 2006 leadership race hadn't been resolved; ongoing staffing disruptions in his office, campaign team and party headquarters; declining party membership and wholly inadequate fundraising was added to the Conservative's successful portrayal of Dion as weak, indecisive, and as a stammering, somewhat confused leader.

Added to these woes, was Dion's commitment to what became known as the 'Green Shift' economic-environmental plan. It received widespread approval from environmentalists and over 250 economists but it alarmed farmers, truck drivers and some provinces which feared they would be paying disproportionately high fossil fuel taxes. Harper and the Conservatives jumped on the plan claiming it would 'screw everyone by imposing a tax on everything'. Dion and the Liberals spent the remainder of the campaign on the defensive trying to explain that a carbon tax would be offset by income tax cuts and other benefits. He was never able to get his message across to voters. The 'Green Shift' plan became a heavy albatross around Dion and the Liberal party's neck throughout the whole campaign.

And so the 2008 election began with Stephen Harper and the Conservatives primed to fight the election and, with good fortune, make the gains he and the party considered quite possible. It also began with Dion and the Liberals in a precarious position with a party ill-prepared, a leader badly bruised, and a centre-stage policy under serious attack. As for the Bloc Quebecois, they appeared to have lost their purpose and would likely lose seats. The NDP were hoping to cash in on the Liberal's troubles and significantly improve their seat totals, including some gains in Quebec.

When Harper called the election, he was criticized for breaking his own much touted 'fixed election' legislation. He claimed that Parliament was 'dysfunctional' due to the obstructionism of the opposition parties even though the Conservatives had contributed to any obstructionism through their own actions. By calling the election under such contrived arguments, Harper reminded Canadians of other broken commitments he had made since becoming prime minister in 2006. Various political commentators reminded voters of the long and growing list of reversals, but in the end it seemed to have minimal effect.

Conservative campaign strategy was to market a new image of Stephen Harper as a "congenial, sweater-vested uncle who spoke constantly about his family and projected an unwaveringly sunny disposition." [20] Some reporters named the Conservative's campaign plane 'Air Sweater Vest'. To achieve this 'friendly, familiar, and safe leader' image, and to ensure the Conservative message remained on track, that is "nothing unexpected, no one uninvited, [and] everything in its right place",[21] Harper's every public event was planned down to the last detail. Some reporters labeled it 'Stephen Harper's bubble'. Later on in the campaign, he even brought his mother into his speeches in an effort to demonstrate his sensitive side.

Aside from the usual campaign glitches that all parties experience, the Conservative campaign began well. When negotiations were concluded with the media for the leader's debates, Elizabeth May, leader of the Green Party, was excluded. Harper defended the decision claiming she and the party were really stalking horses for the Liberals since Dion and May had agreed not to field candidates against each other. Harper threatened to boycott the debates if she was included. After considerable public criticism, Harper and NDP leader Jack Layton agreed to let her join the debate as an equal participant. This affair didn't reflect well on Harper or Layton. Dion and the Liberals had supported May's participation. Its impact was soon overshadowed by the crumbling state of the American economy and the dangers it posed for the world economy. The tidal waves of shocking economic news soon claimed centre stage.

Canadians wondered how it all would affect the Canadian economy. Harper requested extra time be given to the economy during the debates. Expectations were that he would have something significant to say. But during the debate, Harper was strangely silent offering no new thoughts and no new government actions. Many observers wondered why he had requested extra time if he had nothing to contribute.

Shortly thereafter, in an interview with Peter Mansbridge on the CBC National News, Harper adamantly insisted that "There are a lot of people out there panicking. I think there's probably some great buying opportunities emerging in the stock market as a consequence of all this panic." [22] While possibly true, it wasn't "the message for people whose idea of liquidity is having enough pocket change for a beer after the rent's been paid and the shopping done. Or those who've been watching their retirement savings shrink like morning glories in the afternoon." [23] Harper's response struck many observers as a failure to connect with Canadians, to show he 'felt their pain' and understood their concerns. It reinforced the public image of a man who was seen by many as being 'emotionally cold', aloof and detached. He compounded these feelings when he added that prime ministers have to be 'hard-headed' in such situations. It seemed contrary to the 'friendly, blue sweater-vested' guy the Conservatives were trying to portray during the campaign.

Later in the campaign, Harper committed his most serious strategic mistake. Conservative hopes of winning a majority government depended upon a breakthrough in Quebec. Some Conservatives believed they could win upwards of 30 seats tripling their 2006 number of 10. Their hopes were dashed when Harper announced his intention to re-introduce legislation to treat violent young offenders as adults as of age 14. Quebecers reacted strongly condemning such a harsh approach. Support dropped dramatically, especially among women, after the announcement – from 32% to 18% among single women and from 32% down to 22% among urban women. Conservative strategists intended the effect of the announcement to win support among voters in British Columbia, especially among men in the 35-55 age group who their research indicated would respond well to law-and-order agendas. Taking such positions, they said, always involved a calculated risk of collateral damage. While support among women rebounded later in the campaign, aided by some late-campaign television ads targeted to women on female-focused specialty channels, damage had been done.

Harper further damaged Conservative chances, especially in Quebec, when he commented on proposed $45 million in budget cuts to arts funding. This was another strategic mistake that he compounded by commenting that "I think that when ordinary people come home, turn on the TV and see a gala of a bunch of people, you know, a rich gala all subsidized by taxpayers claiming their subsidies aren't high enough, when they know those subsidies have actually gone up – I'm not sure that's something that resonates with ordinary people." [24] Immediately the arts community responded, especially in Quebec where arts and culture has been central to Quebec's identity politics. Across the country, 'Wrecking Ball' performances featuring material written by prominent playwrights and other performers were organized. An active internet exchange sprang up to share ideas and gather national support for the arts. Margaret Atwood was so upset that she wrote a scathing article in the *Globe & Mail* and Quebec award winning playwright Wajdi Mouawal circulated his views on the internet. Canada's top film and television performers gathered in Toronto on September 24th to condemn the announced cuts. Harper's attempt to win support among ordinary working Canadians generally backfired, especially in Quebec.

Gilles Duceppe, leader of the Bloc Quebecois, cited the groundswell of anger towards Harper and the Conservatives as an important factor in his party's electoral success. On election eve, he said, "Without the Bloc Quebecois [holding onto its seats], Harper would have formed a majority government. ... The Tories began the campaign seeing Quebec as the key component in their hopes to win a majority. In the end, though, the Conservatives had to fight off a projected collapse of support in the province".[25] While the collapse didn't happen, it was enough to rob the Conservatives of any gains.

In this election, Harper and the Conservatives ran a very tight ship. Every effort was made to control every event and to ensure no one would go off message and cause trouble for the campaign. Events open to the public were kept to a minimum because they couldn't be controlled. Criticism of the 'bubble' surrounding Harper was rebutted by him as "only the 'chattering classes and the people who pay more attention to this than perhaps we should' were interested in what a party leader and prime minister might have to say spontaneously about issues of interest to the public.

But, the catch to all this was that "the disastrous unscripted comments, the telling off-message remarks that the plan's iron discipline was supposed to suppress, [would] come not from a wayward backbencher, but from the Prime Minister himself." [26] Again, as in 2004 and 2006, it was Stephen Harper's comments that played an important role in preventing a possible Conservative majority government being elected. It was Stephen Harper himself who committed strategic errors in all three elections that knee-capped the Conservative campaigns.

The November 27, 2008, Economic and Fiscal Statement is perhaps Stephen Harper's most serious strategic error. The statement delivered by Finance Minister Flaherty would not have generated such political damage if it had not contained the '3 poison pills' Stephen Harper had decided to include at the last minute. Harper's modus operandi had been to impose a tight discipline over his cabinet and caucus. He controlled journalists' access to ministers and to government information. He made major decisions himself or with a very small circle of advisors. Perhaps if he had a larger circle of people to advise him and to act as a sounding board, his highly partisan instincts would have been tempered on this occasion. But he hasn't and he didn't. He acted. He didn't need to go for the opposition's jugular but Harper "saw a weakness, and he leaped – right into trouble." [27]

Again, as with the reoccurring strategic mistakes made in the election campaigns, Stephen Harper's intensely partisan nature sparked 'eight days of crisis on the Hill' and an extended time of uncertainty until another election is called. His strategic stumbling cost his party dearly on three separate occasions and plunged it and the country into a political crisis that could have been avoided.

While he deserves full credit for the successes he has had uniting the right and bringing it into power, he also deserves full condemnation for the failures he has directly contributed to. Stephen Harper *is* a 'master strategist' but he *is* also a 'master stumbler'. His 'stumbles' cost him, the Conservative Party and the country dearly.

When the opposition parties formed the coalition alternative government, Harper was forced to resort to arguments and language that sparked the 'political crisis', the 'constitutional crisis' and eventually the 'national unity crisis'.

Harper was able to hold onto the Prime Minister's job following the 'crisis on the Hill' and lived to present a new budget January 27, 2009. Facing the prospect of defeat if the budget didn't address the problem of an adequate stimulus, Harper reversed his earlier position and reluctantly accepted the need for a massive economic stimulus. And boy did he deliver one. The party and government that prided itself on balanced budgets vowing to never go into deficit financing, and, but two months earlier, had predicted budget surpluses, was now presenting a massive $83 billion spending package that would plunge Canada into deficits for the next five years.

A few days after the presentation of the budget, a public opinion poll indicated that "Canadians [believed that] Stephen Harper was motivated by political survival and would never have unveiled this week's multibillion-dollar stimulus budget were it not for opposition pressure. ... [It also found that] most Canadians continue to hold Harper responsible for the crisis atmosphere that prompted it and believe he hasn't fundamentally changed." [28] If Stephen Harper had gained a majority, would Canadians have seen another side to the man and his conservatism?

Conservative Party literature consistently refers to Stephen Harper as a 'real' leader – "Stephen Harper and the Conservative Party know exactly where they want to lead Canada, by standing up for change and standing up for Canada."; "You need to know what you believe in, what you want to do, and have a plan to do it."; "...you can't lead if you can't focus and determine what really matters." [29]

Canadians were getting a clearer picture of where Harper was leading them but still wouldn't know the full agenda until Harper and the Conservatives won a clear majority and could implement the policies that would transform society into a real conservative society.

Endnotes

1 Tom Flanagan commenting on Stephen Harper, CBC Interview, 2008 Election.

2 Conservative Party of Canada, campaign literature, <u>www.conservative.</u><u>ca</u>, 2006, 2008.

3 Stephen Harper, cited in William Johnson, "The Outsider", *Walrus*, March, 2009: 24.

4 William Johnson, *Stephen Harper and the future of Canada*, (Toronto: Stoddard, 2005) 360.

5 Johnson, 363.

6 Ipsos-Reid poll, *Globe and Mail*, 15 June, 2004, cited in Johnson, 365.

7 Johnson, 366.

8 Johnson, 368.

9 Johnson, 370.

10 Johnson, 370.

11 Johnson, *The Walrus*, 28.

12 Cited in Phil Hahn, "Conservatives campaign outpaced Liberals", CTV News, ctc.ca, 22 Jan., 2006.

13 Craig Oliver, cited in Peter Hahn, 22 Jan., 2006.

14 Oliver.

15 Oliver.

16 "Mr. Dithers", *The Economist*, 17 Feb., 2005.

17 Paul Wells, "Harper's Canadian Revolution", *Maclean's*, 29 Sept., 2008.

18 Tom Flanagan, cited in Kenneth Kidd, "How Harper let it slip away", *Toronto Star*, 18 Oct., 2006.

[19] Kidd.

[20] "Did a momentary blip cost Harper a majority?", *Canadian Press*, 15 Oct., 2008.

[21] Arron Wherry, "Welcome to Haprer's Bubble", *Maclean's*, 13 Oct., 2008: 30.

[22] Kidd.

[23] "Toronto gathering of top film and television performers", *Toronto Star*, 24 Sept., 2008.

[24] CBC Election website.

[25] Kidd.

[26] Jeffery Simpson, "After the storm", *Globe and Mail*, 6 Dec., 2008.

[27] "Budget fails to quell criticisms of PM", *Globe and Mail*, 31 Jan., 2009.

[28] Conservative Party of Canada, "Stand Up for Canada", Conservative Party 2006 election material.

Chapter 11
Where does all this leave us?

"What is there that you just don't get?"
Bob Rae responding to a CBC reporter's question, Dec. 4, 2008

The preoccupation of Canadians has moved on to the daily news of plant closures, corporate collapses, government bailouts, outrageous corporate bonus payments, and the spectre of losing one's own job. The tenuousness of the times and the prospect of this recession turning into a depression has become the primary concern in Canada and around the world.

In this environment, the events of last November-December have faded into memory just as episodes of yesterday's favourite television shows slip away from our consciousness. If asked today about that electrifying eight days of drama on the Hill, many would struggle to recall even a few of the events and exchanges that turned what should have been a straight-forward economic update statement into a political crisis, followed by a constitutional crisis, capped off by a national unity crisis.

But the 'crisis on the Hill' was an important time in Canadian politics. It capped a period of intense political confrontation between a party intent on dramatically changing how government operates in the country and its political opponent's intent on survival to fight another day. It revealed in stark form the lengths to which a leader, party and government would go to hold on to power. It exposed the prime minister's essential political character to intense public scrutiny. It exposed the fact that, when backed into a corner, even the strangest of dissidents would join together to face a common antagonist.

It also exposed the deep divisions that exist within the country, especially those along regional and ideological fault lines. This brief period of eight days provided Canadians a view of their politicians as few moments in their history has done in the past.

Stephen Harper chose to view the results of the October 14th election as a "strengthened mandate" in which he could govern without needing to consult and cooperate with the opposition. He had increased his party's number of seats in Parliament, had extended party support into new regions of the country, and, had made gains with women and new Canadians. His choice was also understandable given the divided nature of the opposition and the weakened condition of his main opponent, Stéphane Dion and the Liberal Party.

But there was more to this than what appeared on the surface. As witnessed in his first minority government, 2006-2008, Harper's personal and political nature was inclined towards a no-holds-barred, take-no-prisoners approach to governing. He repeatedly made normal legislative proposals confidence motions. He repeatedly defied parliamentary processes. He repeatedly changed his commitment or position whenever it was politically convenient. He repeatedly conducted negative personal attacks on his opponents that went well beyond normal partisan political exchanges. In short, Stephen Harper set the tone and tenor of political discourse in Parliament and the country. And it was not becoming.

On the economic front, the presentation of his government's economic and fiscal statement on November 27 should have been a straight forward affair even if it had contained little in the way of a stimulus package. But it wasn't because Harper succumbed to his partisan instincts and had Flaherty include three provisions designed to pull the financial rug out from under the opposition parties, undercut two groups Conservatives had little sympathy for, and, sell off unspecified government assets. Each of these provisions reflected conservative ideological goals. The opposition parties understood Harper's intent and they acted. They set in motion talks to bring about an alternative government, a coalition between the Liberals and the NDP with an agreement by the BQ to refrain from supporting any confidence motions for a minimum of 18 months.

Within hours, the battle lines were drawn. The fight for political survival began. The coalition was an unlikely amalgam of disparate personalities and parties but, at that moment, it shared a common purpose. The gauntlet had been thrown down by Harper and they had little choice but to respond.

Each new day brought news of both sides acting to neutralize the other or to label the other as a threat to democracy and/or the country. Exchanges in the House, especially on the government side, escalated into unfounded accusations of 'treason' and descriptions of events that were entirely false. Prime Minister Harper directly participated in these accusations and condoned those of his caucus members. For this he bears full responsibility. The opposition parties challenged the Prime Minister and his Conservative government to acknowledge their failure to place an adequate stimulus package before the House and to allow the House to perform its constitutional responsibilities through a confidence vote. Their exchanges avoided responding in kind to the hyperbole being thrown at them by the government side. The trust and civility that must exist between individual MPs, party leaders and parties was tested to the limits.

In the end, on the morning of Thursday December 4th, the toxic standoff between the government and the opposition ended with the Governor General agreeing to prorogue Parliament till January 26, 2009, at which time a new session of the 40th Parliament would convene with a new budget presented the following day. Whether the Harper Conservative government would survive beyond that date would have to be seen. It did but with provisions that it had to report back to Parliament on progress being made on the stimulus package.

The Conservative's presented a budget that would run a deficit of $85 billion over the next five years.[1] It was obvious that Stephen Harper and his party were uncomfortable with this massive economic intervention in the economy that the budget entailed. It went against their deeply held economic conservative values and principles. It was a budget composed and delivered with a gun at their head, the threat of defeat on a vote of confidence in the House. The Liberals reluctantly supported the new budget while the NDP and BQ voted against it. For the moment, Harper got to remain Prime Minister, the Conservative Party remained the government, and, the opposition Liberal party gained time to sort out its leadership and party problems. But how long could this state of affairs last? Speculation suggested not for long, perhaps until the fall.

The Conservative's Jan. 27th budget presented by Flaherty was diametrically the opposite of what had been claimed in the Nov. 27th statement. Rather than running surpluses for the next five years, there would be five years of massive deficits; rather than frugally managing government expenditures, the government would loosely oversee billion dollar infrastructure projects; and, rather than propose meaningful tax deductions to lower and middle income earners, the government would offer provisions that benefited most the top 8% of tax filers, those who earn more than $80,000/year, and who were largely male.[2] In order to save his job and his government, Harper was willing to abandon everything he believed in and preached. His credibility was in tatters.

As for economic leadership, Canadians learned that Stephen Harper was less than a stellar economist. His earlier policies were not prudent but highly political as the 2% cut to the GST attested. Virtually every economist in the country criticized them. Even the former Governor of the Bank of Canada criticized the cuts. In his view, they cut into federal revenue such that it left Ottawa with a structural deficit at the end of the 2007-2008 fiscal year. [3] With repeated claims that Canada was insulated from the turmoil south of the border, that our economy was not as vulnerable as the American and others were, and, that our recovery would be earlier and better than others, Harper repeatedly drew a rosy picture of the situation even though many others suggested otherwise. Repeated 'adjustments' to his deficit projections also raised questions about how well he had his finger on the economic pulse. His erratic economic claims and actions seriously undermined his economic stewardship and claim to leadership credibility. His claim to be the only leader and the Conservatives the only party capable of managing the economy and that the situation would be worse if the Liberals or the coalition were in power carried a hollow ring.[4]

On the political front, Canadians were given the opportunity to vividly see the true nature of the man. For all his and the party's efforts to 'soften' his image with the public, as witnessed in the 2008 election campaign with the baby blue sweater vests and family-friendly photo ops, the eight days of crisis on the Hill brought out his partisan and acrimonious nature. For his supporters and those who seek a conservative society, Harper fought a vigorous and successful battle. He out manoeuvred his opponents, portrayed the opposition leaders and parties as misguided and desperate power-seekers, and, retained power. He stood his ground. To his critics, he displayed an unbelievable degree of being out-of-touch with the real economic state of affairs, of being insensitive to the plight of Canadian workers and families, and, a willingness to put the wellbeing of the country in jeopardy in order to hold onto power. To his supporters, he was a strong leader. To his critics, he was dangerous.

Not many Canadians understand the real intent of Stephen Harper and the conservative revolution he is attempting to install on Canada. Various observers have noted how dramatic his 'vision' is for the country. And many have noted that he has not been shy to reveal the nature and scope of those changes to the public. Many Canadians seem to think that Harper and his Conservative party are just another version of the earlier 'progressive' Conservatives. Harper has worked long and hard to portray that image. He and the Conservative party are not 'just another version' of the conservatives Canadians have known in the past. They are committed to a more extreme right-wing conservatism that has not been seen in Canada.

Few Canadians have paid attention to Harper's speeches and interviews and to his writings. On public platforms, Harper works hard to convey a moderate conservatism and offer attractive policies, especially tax cuts and other financial benefits. When speaking to the party's supporters, a quite different and more extreme set of policies and proposals hark back to the days of Reform and to his economic and socially conservative beliefs. On those occasions, the real Stephen Harper comes to the fore.

At some point along the way though, if he and the Conservatives remain in power, Canadians will awake to a country that has been transformed and bears little resemblance to the one they have known. It will have happened incrementally. It will have happened through politically attractive policies that 'ride the waves' of passing public concerns. These 'goodies' will attract electoral support and like the pied piper, he will lead Canadians to his conservative promised land. It is in this conservative promised land that a new, dramatic and revolutionary change will become evident. Without going into details, it will be a social, economic and political environment that will look more like the 1920's than the 1960's. In another way, it will seek to recapture the Alberta of the 1950's and 60's under the Social Credit government of Ernest Manning. [5] And it will have a much stronger religious presence than modern society has experienced.

Now a conservative society is not necessarily bad. It is a view of society as old as society itself. It can be reasonably supported by historical and social evidence and by religious prescription. Its view of human nature and the kind of society that develops and is necessary is defensible. It's beliefs in the importance of traditions and the crucial role of social institutions (family, church, education, government and social class) as 'civilizing' forces can be reasonably argued. But like all ideologies, and it is an ideology regardless of Harper's claims otherwise,[6] it needs to be tempered by other views. No one ideology has a corner on the market of correct thought. In this context, arguing for a more conservative society is as appropriate as arguing for a more liberal or socialist society.

But Canadians should understand what the tenets of that ideology are and how they would affect their lives and reshape society.

On the constitutional front, Stephen Harper did an end run around the fundamental principle that he himself had enunciated, when it served his purpose prior to the 2004 election, that a government must be accountable to the people's representatives in Parliament. He put off the initial confidence vote on the economic statement and then prorogued Parliament to avoid facing an inevitable defeat by the coalition. By using such tactics, he successfully manoeuvred out of the tight spot his own actions had put him in and bought time for him to construct a new and improved budget statement. But he also became the first prime minister to use prorogation to run away from facing parliament.

By asking the Governor General to prorogue Parliament, Harper dragged the office of Governor General and the current occupant into the daily political fray. The Crown is intended to be above daily political give and take. This doesn't mean that there aren't times when the Crown must make controversial political decisions. The Crown is the political system's referee and the protector of the public's rights and freedoms. In this case, Harper was not hesitant to place the Governor General in a very difficult position, and, it would seem, quite ready to treat the office cavalierly.[7] In this way, Harper not only created the 'constitutional crisis' but took advantage of it to save his own skin.

As well, when John Baird proudly proclaimed on national television that the Conservatives would 'go over Parliament, over the head of the Governor General and appeal directly to the voters', he was advocating sedition and insurrection.[8] This might have been over exuberance on his part but it demonstrated a serious lack of self-restraint for a Minister of the Crown. His statements were never disavowed by Harper.

On the national unity front, Stephen Harper generated feelings among Canadians that pitted West against East, Alberta against Quebec, non-Francophone against Francophone, and Conservative supporters against Conservative critics. By accusing BQ MPs of being 'illegitimate' members of parliament and by branding Quebecers who supported the BQ as 'separatists', Harper offended all Quebecers.[9] In doing so, he resurrected ethnic tensions that had been dormant below the surface in the last few years.

Canada is a country in which regional and ethnic tensions are strong. They have long and tempestuous histories. These tensions do not need to be aroused.[10] But in order to fend off the opposition coalition, Harper was prepared and willing to engage in accusations by himself and his caucus that were inflammatory, inappropriate and slanderous. They were willing to arouse public outbursts of intolerance and bigotry in a campaign to turn public opinion to their side. Canadians were not well served by his efforts or that of the Conservative party.

Embedded in the regional and ethnic tensions that rose to the surface again, there was the additional division of Canadians ideologically between those that supported Harper and the Conservatives and those that lined up with the opposition. To some degree, the split coincided with existing regional and ethnic divisions. But for the most part, the split occurred at the individual level among family, friends and neighbours. Canadians were drawn into a political fight that had wider ideological undertones. The longer term consequences will only be evident in the future.

On the democratic deficit front, the Prime Minister actively contributed to the confusion over how the parliamentary political system operates. His claim that voters gave him a mandate to govern; that he could and would govern as if he had a majority; that it was undemocratic and illegitimate for the opposition parties to form a coalition and seek to replace the Conservatives; and, that only the voters in an election can determine which leader and party gets to govern, indicated either a serious lack of understanding of the parliamentary system or an outright deliberate intent to misrepresent the facts and mislead the public. In either case, Harper revealed himself to be a dangerous politician. Compounding these false claims was the deliberate misrepresentation of the role to be played by the BQ in the coalition; the repeated charge that the Canadian flag was removed from the coalition's press conference; and, that NDP and BQ MPs were 'tainted' as 'socialists' and 'separatists' and therefore less than equal members of the House. All of this did not speak well of Stephen Harper's character or political ethics. But it did speak volumes about his highly ideological and partisan approach to politics.

In addition, the wild claims of John Baird and the inappropriate accusations of 'treason' that emanated from the Conservative side of the House were never refuted by Harper suggesting that at least he was willing to condone these acts by his fellow party members. By failing to act, Stephen Harper demonstrated a failure of leadership.

The media presented a variety of viewpoints on the various events happening in the House and on the Hill. On closer examination, it becomes clear that there are identifiable political leanings that are reflected in the way stories are handled. While most media try to have some balance in their reporting, they usually stand to the left or right on the political spectrum. Only one newspaper of those followed openly endorsed the coalition. It was the *Toronto Star* which is noticeably progressive and left leaning. Its political commentators were generally critical of Harper and the Conservative's various statements and positions. On the other side of the political spectrum were the *National* **Post**, **Calgary** *Herald* and *Vancouver Sun* who criticized Harper and the Conservatives but were more critical of the coalition parties and leaders.

Reflecting their corporate owners and readership/viewers, various media take an over all 'left' or 'right' approach to the news. In Canada, the ideological/political right has gained a dominant position in the country's media. The dominant newspapers and television networks, other than the *Toronto Star* and the CBC, are owned and operated by conservative minded individuals and corporations. In this sense, there is an ideological tone that seeps into coverage of news generally and politics particularly. It could be said that one of the divisions or fault-lines that runs through Canadian society is the ideological split that divides families, communities and regions. Frequent media pundit's comments, that the left-right divide no longer applies, exposes their lack of understanding of what the left-right political spectrum is about and how to identify it when it is operating before their eyes.

With the election of the Conservatives in 2006, Canadians experienced the determined effort of a prime minister and political party to reverse the prevailing political ethos that has guided Western democracies since the 1930's. Progressive social and economic policies, supported by liberals, social democrats and 'progressive'/ 'Red Tory' conservatives, generally support the basic values of equality and social justice that gives meaning to the 'welfare state'. Stephen Harper and the Conservative party are intent upon limiting those gains and hopefully, incrementally, dismantling them. In their view, "[t]he language of participation and of rights, so typical of the 1960's, had drowned out reverence for more traditional values such as authority and obedience. In this view, what is needed is a return to the old patterns of relations between governors and governed, coupled with reduced expectations of what economic and other goods governments should provide." [11]

There should be no mistaking the intent of Stephen Harper, the Conservative party and all those economic conservatives, social conservatives, libertarians and religious conservatives who support them. Harper and the party he so tightly controls are not 'just another political party' like the ones we have had in the past. They are not the old progressive conservatives. They are on the far right and are intent on reversing the progressive economic and social policies introduced by liberal and social democratic governments over the past 60 years. They are intent on dramatically changing the federal-provincial relationship that emerged since the 1930's. They are intent on establishing political, economic and social systems that reverse the whole western movement towards a more just and equal society. The label that best suits this brand of conservatism would be 'regressive conservatism'.

On the question of Stephen Harper's leadership, Canadians have been repeatedly reminded that he has training in economics and that he has a plan for Canada. These are both true descriptions of the man and his politics. He has put a great deal of time and effort into studying and analyzing Canadian economic, social and political conditions. He has presented, in his various capacities, some challenging and thought-provoking assessments of persistent problems in Canadian society. He has been a significant practitioner of the art of politics and has helped shift Canadian society towards the economic, social and political values he believes in.

He has demonstrated on a number of occasions the ability to communicate his analysis of problems to audiences and gain their support. He has demonstrated an ability to learn from past mistakes and overcome difficult obstacles to success. In these ways, he has demonstrated leadership qualities that have enabled him to gain the leadership of the Canadian Alliance and Conservative parties, moderate party policies, broaden the party's support and manage the office of prime minister. On this record alone, Stephen Harper has been a successful political leader.

But there are other aspects of his leadership that raise doubts about his capacity to lead the party and the country. Recognizing that he does not connect well with voters, he has repeatedly tried to 'soften' his image. As the BBC noted in the 2004 election, "A key element of Mr. Harper's campaign was his transformation in the public eye from extreme US-style, right-wing politician with a hidden agenda, to a progressive conservative who had a clear vision for the country." [12] In the 2008 election campaign, he tried to project the image of a family-friendly guy who might live next door. The blue sweaters and contrived photo-ops undoubtedly influenced some voters but its stage-managed nature was evident to many. It was also evident that many voters continued to distrust him. As one journalist noted at the end of the 2008 campaign, "Stephen Harper has definitively emerged as the most polarizing figure Canada has seen in almost two decades, eliciting negative emotions of a visceral strength not registered on the federal political scale since Brian Mulroney." [13]

When Harper spoke to the Manning Institute for Democracy in mid-March, 2009, he raised questions among many observers whether the 'kinder, gentler version wrapped in a sweater' had been replaced by the more partisan and abrasive flipside of his personality. "His speech was highly partisan and littered with snide references to 'left-wing fringe groups' and the 'liberal left'." [14] He also took swipes at some of his other favourite targets such as the Senate, judiciary, CBC, and Parliament. All politicians and governments have their bogeymen that they try to play off of but Harper seems to relish voicing his dislike towards those he perceives as his political and ideological enemies. The nature of these attacks suggests a darker side to his personality and leadership that is neither personally becoming nor politically wise.

Stephen Harper's plan for Canada is to remake Canada as a conservative society. It is a vision that he has been successfully advancing ever so slowly and with little observance by Canadians for the past twenty-five years. But he has repeatedly hit potholes in the road that have delayed his plans or derailed them. The calamity that resulted from the botched November 27th economic statement forced him to present a budget January 27th that contained everything he has stood squarely against. As Andrew Coyne wrote in **Maclean's**, "We are on a course toward a massive and permanent increase in the size and scope of government: record spending, sky-high borrowing, and – ultimately, inevitably – higher taxes." [15] In his view, Harper's monumental reversal of everything he and the party believes in and stood for over the years represents the 'death of conservatism in Canada'.

Whether this budget and all that it represents will derail conservative's incremental progress towards winning a majority government and Harper's intent to establish the Conservative party as Canada's naturally governing party will have to await future events. It may be a death blow to Harper's leadership and to the current conservative movement. But then again, it is unlikely to kill conservatism because its philosophy is a fundamental one that has existed as long as humans have lived in groups. As well, there will always be a need for a right- of-centre voice that helps temper and restrain the left.

The 2009 stimulus budget was a difficult one for Harper, the Conservative party and their supporters across the country. Harper indicated that he was a reluctant participant. Observers acknowledged that he took these unprecedented moves because of the seriousness of the economic meltdown, the need to satisfy the coalition, particularly the Liberals, and the fact that other governments were taking similar actions. His economic and political being rebelled against such actions but in order to save himself and his government, he had little choice. If these measures prove helpful then his leadership and government will be able to claim credit for their actions. On the other hand, if they prove to be badly managed, do little to ease the pressures on businesses and the economy gets worse, then Harper and the Conservatives will bear the brunt of voter frustration.

In another way, Harper is in difficulty over the January 27th budget. He has deeply offended his conservative base by conceding ground to the opposition and turning his back on the principles he and they hold dear.[16] "There's a lot of feeling of betrayal",[17] says Tasha Kheiriddin, university professor and co-author of *Rescuing Canada's Right: Blueprint for a Conservative Reformation*. "It is extremely frustrating, as a small-c conservative, to look at this. ... It flies in the face of all the principles Mr. Harper personally held for a number of years, as well as what the movement was hoping this government would achieve." Other leading conservatives shared those feelings. Close friend and former top aide Tom Flanagan said "This is survival without any sense of direction." [18] Monte Solberg, former Reform and Canadian Alliance MP and Conservative cabinet minister, and Gerry Nicholls, former colleague at the NCC, lamented Harper's abandoning of the economic principles that the conservative movement fought for under the Reform and Canadian Alliance parties. [19] But no matter how much disappointment there is among the conservative faithful, in the end most will see Harper's budget as a necessary concession to the opposition and to the fact other governments were making major stimulus moves too.

Conservative supporters across the country must be wondering what has happened to the leader who repeatedly vowed that he would "never abandon our principles and policies".[20]

While Harper has publicly distanced himself from the Reform and Canadian Alliance parties and their strong right-wing policies, the question lingers as to whether he has truly moderated his views or whether he has moderated his views for purely political purposes. As opposition MPs asked in the House back in early December, 'how can Canadians trust this prime minister?' Does he still envision the kind of society that Reform and the Canadian Alliance offered Canadians? Has his 'moderation' been a calculated political front designed to advance his ideological political agenda? Is Stephen Harper Canada's new 'Machiavellian'?

At the Conservative Party's 2nd convention in Winnipeg November 15-16, 2008, Harper claimed the party's new willingness to intervene in the economy was "a solid marriage of fiscal necessity and Conservative principles." [21] Previous accusations that the Liberals and NDP were 'big spenders' must have seemed hypocritical given the massive spending spree the Conservative government was proposing. What happened to sound fiscal management and balanced budgets? Harper has always portrayed himself as a prudent guardian of the public purse even though he increased government program spending by 19% in his first two-and-a-half years in office.[22] Reformers must have been squirming at Harper's sleight of hand and wondering what had happened to other cherished policies such as democratic accountability, recalling parliamentarians, two-tiered medicine, referendums on abortion and capital punishment.

As a political activist, Stephen Harper demonstrated a recurrent behaviour that raises questions about his long term future. When he became dissatisfied with the Progressive Conservatives in the 1980's, he retreated back to Calgary. When he encountered difficulties with Manning and Reform in the 1990's, he withdrew to the National Citizens Coalition. When he considered the leadership of the Canadian Alliance, he said he was a reluctant candidate.[23] Shortly after winning the leadership, Harper withdrew from public appearances for the summer. Then again, when he failed to win the 2004 election, he withdrew for the summer to weigh his options. [24] Perhaps it was a 'strategic' absence but many wondered now that he has had to present a 'Liberal-Socialist' budget, will he retreat again? He has taken the conservative movement to the seat of power but may be stalled there with a minority at best. Given recent setbacks in Quebec [25] and the seeming return of a Liberal alternative,[26] will he decide that his chances of getting a majority government have evaporated? Some observers are predicting he will be leaving by the end of the year.[27]

Shortly after becoming Prime Minister in 2006, Harper set about to change the way he interacted with the Ottawa media. He felt journalists were biased towards his government. He stated that "the press gallery at the leadership level has taken an anti-Conservative view".[28] He wanted reporters to sign onto a list drawn up by a press secretary who would then decide which reporters could ask a question of the Prime Minister. Reporters in the press gallery voted unanimously to boycott the list fearing that it would be used, like the Bush White House, to shut out reporters considered unfriendly and reward reporters whose stories they liked. At the next press conference reporters refused to sign in so Harper left the room. His anger towards the press led him to boycott the annual press gallery dinner.

In another way, Stephen Harper has a problem with Ottawa. His intermittent tours of duty on the Hill, as legislative assistant to both a Progressive Conservative MP and a Reform MP and then as a Reform MP himself, left him frustrated and cynical. In each case, he left to pursue other interests either at university or with the NCC. As Reform's chief policy officer, he helped formulate and advocated for radical changes to the Senate, Supreme Court, representation in the House and changes to the electoral system. In the 2006 election campaign, he suggested that any fears voters might have that he or his party could make major changes were unfounded. He said that the Senate, Supreme Court and the public service were Liberal appointed and therefore would act as a check upon a Conservative government. These comments were meant to allay fears but instead may have served to remind voters that there may very well be something to be fearful about if he and his party were elected with a majority. He wasn't and many observers consider that remark as one of the factors that held the Conservatives to a minority.

When Harper returned to this theme that he had expressed before that there are institutions and forces in society that are holding up his conservative reforms, it has to be wondered what kind of 'world view' he holds. In his speech to the Manning Institute for Democracy in mid March, 2009, he again referred to 'left-wing fringe groups', the 'liberal left', the 'Senate, the judiciary and countless other federal institutions and agencies' that are filled with 'Liberal insiders and ideologues', the 'CBC', 'Parliament' where "I would never use Parliament and reality in the same sentence", and, finally the failure of the United Nations to take the principled positions his government was taking. He definitely harbours a world view that regards his conservative values and principles as under siege, as fighting to bring about the promised land of "freedom, family and faith".[29] It's almost a fight along biblical lines. [30] His references to "left-wing fringe groups" and the "liberal left" reflect a broader view among conservatives, neo-conservatives, libertarians, social conservatives and Christian fundamentalists that society has been subverted by the 'progressive, liberal-socialist left' policies that have guided western societies since the Depression. In their view, the social and sexual revolution that swept in with the hippy generation of the 1960's greatly compounded that sense of subversion.

Who are the groups he was referring to? They would include women's, worker's, Aboriginal, poverty, children's, legal aid, gays, tenant, and, prisoner rights groups and all the other various groups that have sought a more equal opportunity to participate in society. It would include all those who think that there are conditions operating within traditional social, economic, political and religious systems that need to be modified to give everyone a more equal and fairer chance to succeed. Because these 'progressive' forces in society look to individuals and the state to make changes and introduce government funded agencies to implement various programs, conservatives rebel and want to limit the government's responsibilities and funding ability.

They disagree with the whole 'progressive' approach and want to opt out. They want to return to a time where government was less intrusive in their lives and in society's affairs. They cling to the ideology that individuals should have maximum freedom/liberty, that traditional relationships within the family, workplace, church and society should prevail, and, that the free market should govern all. In short, they want to restore an earlier version of society that reflects the traditional conservative view of human nature, social organization, sources of morality and responsibility and that restricts change from below in favour of change from above, from the economic, political, social and religious elites.

While there are undoubtedly many 'progressive' changes that have not turned out well since the Depression and the hippy revolution of the 1960's, that have been disturbing to many non-conservatives as well as conservatives, a return to the 'true blue conservatism' of Harper and his Conservative party would represent a pendulum swing of major proportions. In the words of one political journalist, "the Civitas speech offers conclusive proof that Mr. Harper has a secret, hidden agenda to reverse the progressive social values that distinguishes Canadian society, replacing them with a bigoted and intolerant religiously driven alternative." [31] Returning to times past may be possible but is not probable. Modifying the present is the more likely course. A 'progressive' conservatism would not have the same difficulties that Harper and his Conservative Party are encountering. Stephen Harper and the conservative movement that he is promoting have limited prospects in Canada. The present minority status may be the best the party can hope to achieve. Certainly the collapse of Reagan's neo-conservative revolution in the United States in 2008 will impact on the conservative movement in Canada. Neo-conservatism, as advocated and practiced by various governments and economists, has become a discredited economic philosophy that will survive the current backlash but will not reappear again for some time.

This forebodes ill for Canadian politics because within Canadian society there are true believers, centred in the West and among fundamentalist religious movements that cannot and will not moderate their conservative and religious ideological beliefs. They will remain 'true believers' in the way Eric Hoffer described them in his book *The True Believers*. Just as the U.S. has become divided between the 'red' and 'blue' states, Canada may follow suit with its own deep divisions.

One final observation, Stephen Harper and the Conservative party had the good fortune to face a Liberal party weakened by scandal, extended years in office, internal leadership divisions and overall weak leadership. That has changed. Following prorogation of Parliament, Stéphane Dion resigned as leader and Michael Ignatieff was chosen by the caucus to be 'interim' leader. He has since restored Liberal credibility as an alternative to the Conservatives. The next federal election should be a more balanced contest between the two leaders and parties.

Stephen Harper's *"long term goal ... is to make Conservatives the natural governing party of the country. ... You do that in two ways. Two things you have to do. One thing you do is you have to pull conservatives, to pull the party, to the centre of the political spectrum. But what you also have to do, if you're really serious about making the transformation, is you have to pull the centre of the political spectrum toward conservatism. And whether it's an agenda that has a high emphasis on tax reduction as opposed to spending increases; an agenda that focuses on delivering benefits to people and families instead of creating bureaucracies; whether it's restoring pride in the country - not just in things like, you know, health care or various government programs, but pride in things like our institutions, our military, our history – I think we're also doing that. We're also building the country towards a definition of itself that is more in line with conservatism."* [32]

Did the '8 days of crisis on the Hill' and its aftermath help or hinder his long term goal? Were those events nothing more than political blips or were they the derailing of Harper's conservative revolution?

Or has there been a change of tsunami proportions as a result of those '8 days of crisis on the Hill'? Was the question Liberal MP Bob Rae asked the reporter who asked if Liberals could work with Harper and the Conservatives after all that had happened right on the button? "What is there that you just don't get?," he asked indicating that the fundamental trust and civility that enables parliamentarians to overcome their ideological and political differences had been destroyed. Stephen Harper's credibility was shattered.

The question now becomes whether Canadians "get it"?

Endnotes

Editorial, "Budget strikes the right balance", *Calgary Herald*, 28 Jan., 2009.

[2] Lisa Philipps, "Tax cuts: why the opposition should have insisted on changes", *Globe and Mail*, 30 Jan., 2009.

[3] David Dodge, "David Dodge criticism doesn't shake PM Harper's vision of economic recovery", *Globe and Mail*, 18 March, 2009.

[4] Stephen Harper, "Only conservatism can lead Canada forward", *Toronto Star*, 17 March, 2009.

[5] William Johnson, "Old blueprint for a new realignment", *Globe and Mail*, 14 March, 2002.

[6] Stephen Harper.

[7] By scheduling a political announcement and photo op for early in the afternoon, Harper was indicating that he expected the Governor General to have no concerns about his request for prorogation and to grant it forthwith. She had concerns and kept him for an unexpected long time forcing him to cancel his afternoon engagement.

[8] James Travers, "The quiet unravelling of Canadian democracy", *Toronto Star*, 4 April, 2009.

[9] Antonia Maioni, "The end of the affair", *Globe and Mail*, 4 Dec., 2008; Chantal Hebert, "Charest is in, Harper very much out in Quebec", *Toronto Star*, 8 Dec., 2008; Hebert, "Quebec offers latest proof of Liberal comeback", 30 Jan., 2009.

[10] Nancy Macdonald, "Will the West revolt?", Macleans.ca, 3 Dec, 2008; Nicholas Kohler, "A very different view from the West", Macleans.ca, 4 Dec., 2008.

[11] Philip Resnick, "The Ideology of Neo-Conservatism", in Warren Magnuson, et al., ed, *The New Reality*, (Vancouver: New Star Books, 1989) 133.

[12] Sarah Shenker, "Canada's right returns from wilderness", BBC NEWS website, 24 Jan., 2006.

[13] Chantal Hebert, "Harper still draws strong emotions", *Toronto Star*, 13 Oct., 2008.

[14] Editorial, "Is this the real Harper?", *Toronto Star*, 17 March, 2009.

[15] Andrew Coyne, "The Right in Full Retreat", *Maclean's*, 9 Feb., 2009.

[16] Gillian Steward, "Harper gurus feel betrayed by their star neo-con pupil", *Toronto Star*, 1 Feb., 2009; Thomas Walkon, "Bizarre actions show a leader losing his grip", *Globe and Mail*, 7 April, 2009.

[17] Brian Laghi and Stephen Chase, "Some of the budget's biggest critics: Tories", *Globe and Mail*, 29 Jan., 2009.

[18] Laghi and Chase.

[19] Laghi and Chase.

[20] Steward; Joe Paraskevas, "CA won't sell out to Tories: Harper", *Calgary Herald*, 7 April, 2002.

[21] James Travers, "Harper pulls shroud over Reform", *Toronto Star*, 15 Nov., 2008.

[22] Carol Goar, "PM needs a scalpel not a cudgel", *Toronto Star*, 5 Nov., 2008.

[23] Judy Monchuk, "Leadership run wasn't original plan, says Alliance candidate Stephen Harper", Canadian Press, 18 March, 2002.

[24] Rex Murphy, "You must not hide, Mr. Harper", *Globe and Mail*, 3 Aug., 2002; William Johnson, *Stephen Harper and the future of Canada*, (Toronto: McClelland and Stewart, 2005) 374.

[25] Daniel LeBlanc, "Tory support plummets in Quebec, poll finds", *Globe and Mail*, 9 March, 2009; Lysiane Gagnon, "Harper gets the cold shoulder", *Globe and Mail*, 16 March, 2009.

[26] John Ward, "Liberals, Tories neck and neck in poll", *Globe and Mail,* 13 March, 2009.

[27] Lawrence Martin, "The smart money says Harper exits this year", *Globe and Mail,* 1 Jan., 2009.

[28] Alexander Panetta, "Harper thumbs nose at national media", *Toronto Star,* 24 May, 2006. Also see Panetta, "Reporters walk out on prime minister; Press increasingly frustrated Harper won't answer their questions", *Halifax Chronicle Herald,* 24 May, 2006; Stephen Maher, "Harper will have things his way, but will we like it?, *Halifax Herald,* 20 May, 2006.

[29] Editorial, "Is this the real Harper?", *Toronto Star,* 17 March, 2009.

[30] Lloyd Mackey, *"The Pilgrimage of Stephen Harper,* (Toronto: EWC, 2005). The very title captures the religious nature of Harper's 'mission'.

[31] John Ibbitson, "How much social conservatism?", *Globe and Mail,* 12 June, 2004.

[32] Paul Wells, "Harper's Canadian Revolution", *Maclean's,* 29 Sept., 2008: 18.

Bibliography

1. Blair,R.S. and McLeod, J.T., 2nd ed., *The Canadian Political Tradition*, (Scarborough, ON: Nelson Canada, 1993).

2. Brodie, J., ed., *Critical Concepts, An Introduction to Politics*, (Scarborough, Ontario: Prentice-Hall Canada, 1999).

3. Brownsey, Keith, and Howlett, Michael, *The Provincial State, Politics in Canada's Provinces and Territories*, (Mississauga, ON: Copp Clark Pitman Ltd., 1992).

4. Cassidy, Carla, and Clarke, Phyllis, and Petrozzi, Wayne, editors, *Authority & Influence: Institutions, Issues and Concepts in Canadian Politics*, (Oakville: Mosaic Press, 1985).

5. Cohen, Andrew, *The Unfinished Canadian, The People We Are*, (Toronto: McClelland & Stewart, 2007).

6. Dobbin, Murray, *Preston manning and the Reform Party*, (Toronto: James Lorimer, 1991).

7. Flanagan, T., *Waiting For The Wave*, (Toronto: ON, Stoddart, 1995).

8. Fleras, Augie, and Elliott, Jean Leonard, *Multiculturalism in Canada, The Challenge of Diversity*, (Scarborough, ON: Nelson Canada, 1992).

9. Gibbons, Roger, *Conflict & Unity, An Introduction to Canadian Political Life*, (Scarborough, ON: Nelson Canada, 1994).

10. Gibbons, R., and Youngman, L., *Mindscapes: Political Ideologies Towards the 21st Century*, (Toronto: McGraw-Hill Ryerson, 1996)

11. Harper, S., "Rediscovering the right agenda", *Citizens Centre Report*, (Edmonton, AB: June 2003, Vol. 30, Iss. 10; 73).

12. Harper, S., "Rediscovering the right agenda", Civitas, Citizens Centre Report, Vol. 30,Issue 10, June 2003.

13.   Hiller, Harry H., *Canadian Society, A Sociological Analysis*, (Scarborough, ON: Prentice-Hall, 1976).

14. Hiller, Harry H., *Canadian Society, A Macro Analysis*, (Scarborough, ON: Prentice-Hall Canada, 1986, and 3rd Edition, 1996).

15.   Hyde, A., *Promises, Promises, Breaking Faith in Canadian Politics*, Toronto: ON, Viking, 1997).

16.   Hurtig, Mel, "Never Heard of Them...They Must Be Canadians", (Toronto: Books for Canadian Education, 1975).

17.   Jackson, Robert and Jackson, Doreen, *Politics Canada, Culture, Institutions, Behaviour and Public Policy*, 2nd edition, (Scarborough, ON: Prentice-Hall Canada, 1990).

18. Johnson, W., *Stephen Harper and the Future of Canada*, (Toronto, ON: McClelland & Stewart, 2005).

19.   Joseph, Thomas, *Essentials of Canadian Politics and Government*, (Toronto: Pearson Education Canada, 2001).

20.   Mackey, L., *The Pilgrimage of Stephen Harper*, (Toronto, ON: ECW Press, 2005).

21.   Manning, Preston, *The New Canada*, (Toronto: Macmillan, 1992).

22.   McInnis, Edgar, *Canada, A Political and Social History*, (Toronto: Holt, Rinehart and Winston of Canada, 1969).

23.   Pitt, Gordon, *Stampede!, The Rise of the West and Canada's New Power Elite*, (Toronto: Key Porter Books, 2008).

24.   Reform Party of Canada, Principle and Policies, *The Blue Book*, 1991.

25.   Resnick, Philip, "The Ideology of Neo-conservatism", in Warren Magnusson, et al., eds., *The New Reality*, (Vancouver: New Star Books, 1984).

26. Reesor, Bayard, *The Canadian Constitution in Historical Perspective*, (Scarborough, ON: Prentice-Hall Canada, 1992).

27. Robin, Martin, ed., *Canadian Provincial Politics, The Party Systems of the Ten Provinces*, (Scarborough, ON: Prentice-Hall Canada, 1972).

28. Johnson, W., "The Outsider", *Walrus*, March 2009.

29. Wells, Paul, "Harper's Canadian Revolution", *Maclean's*, 29, September, 2008.

Index